This Was Funnier in China

An American Comedian's Cross-Cultural Journey

Jesse Appell

AVID READER PRESS

New York Amsterdam/Antwerp London
Toronto Sydney/Melbourne New Delhi

AVID READER PRESS
An Imprint of Simon & Schuster, LLC
1230 Avenue of the Americas
New York, NY 10020

First Avid Reader Press hardcover edition February 2026

AVID READER PRESS and colophon are trademarks of Simon & Schuster, LLC

Simon & Schuster strongly believes in freedom of expression and stands against censorship in all its forms. For more information, visit BooksBelong.com.

For information about special discounts for bulk purchases, please contact Simon & Schuster Special Sales at 1-866-506-1949 or business@simonandschuster.com.

The Simon & Schuster Speakers Bureau can bring authors to your live event. For more information or to book an event contact the Simon & Schuster Speakers Bureau at 1-866-248-3049 or visit our website at www.simonspeakers.com.

Interior design by Carly Loman

Manufactured in the United States of America

1   3   5   7   9   10   8   6   4   2

Library of Congress Control Number: 2025947222

ISBN 978-1-6680-8756-5
ISBN 978-1-6680-8758-9 (ebook)

Let's stay in touch! Scan here to get book recommendations, exclusive offers, and more delivered to your inbox.

For my teachers

The past is a foreign country; they do things differently there.

L. P. Hartley

Author's Note

At the end of some of the chapters in this book, you'll find scannable QR codes that will bring you to photos and other media related to the content you just read. I hope you enjoy!

Prologue

I sat in the dark at a long desk with four Chinese comedians. Our outfits were all absurd.

I wore a suit jacket made of about fifteen different colors and materials. When the head of the costume department showed it to me for the first time, I thought it was something an Italian Renaissance explorer would wear if they time-traveled into a Japanese game show.

Astonishingly, mine wasn't even the weirdest outfit. That honor went to Wang Jianguo, the comedian beside me, who had a fake bird perched on his shoulder. Its glass eyes stared out unblinkingly, offset at just a tiny angle, amplifying the derp factor by at least three times.

Apparently, these outfits were parodies of the ones worn on an old Taiwanese talk show. I had to take the other comedians' word for it, since, unlike them, I hadn't grown up watching the show we were about to parody.

And yet, whether I got the jokes or not, the lights were about to go up. And when they did, I would see three hundred rabid fans, seven cameras, and a crew of interns crouched at the edge of the stage holding cue cards with our lines written on them, scrawled in handwritten characters.

"Wu . . . si . . . san . . . er . . . yi!"

The lights went up. The audience cheered.

Nobody said it out loud—mainly for legal reasons—but we all were thinking the same thing:

Live, from Shanghai, it's Saturday Night!

Funny, You Don't Look Chinese

When I tell people back home in America that I am a Chinese comedian, the first response I get is usually, "Funny, you don't look Chinese."

Badum tish. Thank you. I'll be here all week. Try the veal.

The second question is: "Why Chinese comedy?"

That part is harder to explain, so I'll start there.

"Why China?"

The truth is, I really struggle to answer this question.

Seeing as I spent my first nine years out of college in China, I feel like I should have a better answer as to why I'm here. But I don't. There's always the "LinkedIn bio" version of things: I love the culture, the challenge of the language, the novelty of forging a career in a context nobody has ever walked before.

But that's really just the application of hindsight to the blur of what really happened. It would be lying to say it's wrong, and lying to say it's even close to the real answer.

"Why China?"

Sometimes I answer by expressing a feeling: that living in China at this period of history is like being perched atop a high mountain peak at the head of a fast-flowing river. Growing up in the United States, a country that felt like its course was firmly set, it never felt like I could be a part of anything big. But in China, at this specific moment, my own tiny contribution might infinitesimally influence its trajectory. A small thing—a joke, an internet video, a deep conversation in a dark bar—might alter the course of this river by just an inch, a fraction of an inch . . . but the flow of the future being what it is, moving the river an inch at the source might mean huge changes years in the future, hundreds of miles away.

"Why China?"

Because from my first day here, I've always woken up excited for the next day.

The first day I arrived in China, I signed a contract promising to speak no English for six months. The contract was in Chinese. I couldn't read it. That was sort of the point.

I'd arrived in Beijing for six months of intensive Chinese classes. I'd always wanted to live abroad and learn a new language. Meeting new people and cultivating meaningful relationships with them because you learned their classified code? Knowing another secret word for every word you know in English? It seemed like a superpower: almost impossible. But cool, too.

So, instead of spending the summer and fall of my junior year at Brandeis University, I found myself in Beijing. I chose China because I'd studied a bit of Chinese and a bit of Spanish, and it seemed way more interesting to go to China than to Spain.

Every day I had to memorize a hundred new Chinese characters. Every day there was a test on twenty of those new characters, followed by five hours of classes.

On my second night in Beijing, my pen ran out of ink. I regarded the cheap pen and its empty barrel with blank, unfocused eyes. I don't think I'd ever completely used up a pen before without losing it first. I put it aside.

By the end of the semester, I had a whole box of empty pens. It was my little trophy case. Each was a cheap plastic testament to a diligence I hadn't known I was capable of.

Beijing Language and Culture University was so large, it almost felt like a village. There were multiple food halls, restaurants, soccer fields, and basketball courts. The print shop would make copies of any textbook you needed without question, copyright be damned; the avenues between buildings were a slow-moving chaos of bicycles and pedestrians.

As a school specifically focusing on the study of language, the campus was packed with international students, mostly from other developing countries like Thailand, Nigeria, and Kazakhstan. While I lived in a tiny—but private—single room, these students lived in dorms of four or eight, eager to get their undergraduate degrees from a better school than they could attend at home, while still being one they could actually afford.

No matter where you came from, Chinese was hard for everyone. Yet, the moment you left the school gates and stepped out into the city, language was the crucial skill required to overcome the fear of Beijing's buzzing madness.

Beijing is a hot, delicious, absurdist puzzle box of a city. Everything is simultaneously new and old, fast and slow, loud and unspoken. It was, and still is, an object of my perpetual fascination.

I couldn't read the signs or understand what people were saying; Chinese pop music crooned out of every store; vehicles weaved in and out of the street in every direction; traffic lights appeared to be more suggestions than anything else.

As a foreigner I was sometimes the most interesting person in the room, sometimes completely ignored. I was always fully engaged, never fully comfortable.

Nothing was easy, nothing was boring. I loved it.

My second day, I visited the Forbidden City, the eight-hundred-year-old imperial palatial complex of otherworldly scale located in the exact geographic center of the city. Mile upon mile of flowing, golden-glazed ceramic roof tiles; nine thousand, nine-hundred, ninety-nine rooms built down the north–south central axis of the city. A remnant of a dynastic age. A center of power.

There was also a Starbucks in there, which was good, because I needed to use the bathroom and it was the only non-squat toilet around for a mile.

Beijing was winding alleyways of brick laid down by Mongols that led to the doors of garish dystopian pyramidal glass shopping malls built by nouveau-riche tycoons.

Beijing was fashionable women holding loud phone conversations on the street directly next to a table of shirtless old men squatting on tiny stools, drinking giant bottles of beer.

Beijing was a bowl of cheap noodles in the morning and sumptuous Peking duck at night. It had a Great Wall and a tech hub, a Tibetan Lama temple across the street from a KFC.

Living amongst these buildings that dated anywhere from two thousand years to two weeks ago, I met the most eclectic collection of people imaginable, some of whom seemed to be the product of traits spit out of a video game's random character generator.

I met a man on the street with a long beard and a giant plastic sack full of raw meat. He told me he had brought it back from Kashgar, out on the old Silk Road, and Beijing marked the end destination of a three-month motorcycle trip he'd taken with friends. He'd kept the meat on ice in a Styrofoam container affixed to the back of his Harley with pink plastic ribbons.

I met a woman at a bar who sold medicinal dog water. The water was infused with trace minerals normally used in (human) hospitals as an intravenous infusion for (human) patients with anemia. Her company was, she said both proudly and anxiously, the only one in the world selling such a product to dogs. I think her pride came from being out on the forefront of a new market, and the anxiety from the fact it was clearly doomed to failure.

I recommended, as a joke, that they hire a famous celebrity's dog to serve as a spokesdog. She told me they'd already tried, but the dog's appearance fee was too high.

"It's not easy selling dog water," she sighed. "Maybe I should go back to grad school."

Beijing was real-life TikTok: a new scene every seven seconds. It was a blaring loudspeaker announcement. It was a tender, quiet conversation. It was a twenty-cent ice pop and a ten-dollar coffee. It was sound and fury. It was lights, camera, and action.

And every day, I stared down one hundred new characters in my textbook. Every day, another test. Every day, no English allowed.

A new part of my mind opened. Speaking a new language didn't split me into English Jesse and Chinese Jesse. Instead, I felt myself dilating, like a droplet of water expanding over a new surface.

As I learned the language, a veil lifted off of the face of the city. It felt like passing through a waterfall and discovering a hidden world that had existed all this time—and finally, I could access it.

Learning the language and the culture unlocked stories and dramas playing out in plain sight. Every day, I would get a milk tea from a hole-in-the-wall street stall on my way back from class. The first time, I pointed at the pictures because I couldn't read the menu.

By the time I left, I could read the menu, and I could also talk to the tea vendor. She told me that this stall was part of a chain that a man from her village had started ten years ago. She and all her coworkers were from that same village and slept in bunks in the back of the shop; actually, the more than one hundred branches of the original tea shop were staffed entirely by young people from that village looking for their first foothold in the big city.

"Do you like it here?" I asked.

"No. I want to go home. But then I'd just be bored and want to come back."

I could also read the "Now Hiring!" sign on the side of the shop and its shameless promise of a $200-a-month salary in a city where my rent alone was $800. I assumed the low wages were not offset by stock options.

I thought I had gone to China to learn Chinese. In the end, I learned some Chinese and ten thousand other things.

And for every new thing I learned, I actually learned two things. The first was how they did it here, in China. The second was how we did it back home, in America. Sometimes things were the same. Sometimes they were different. Both seemed significant.

Everything—from how the milk is packaged (in China, it comes in bags) to whether people wait for others to exit the subway car before cramming in themselves (they don't) to how long you need to know someone before you could ask them to help you move (not long at all, and they will jump at the chance if they like you and want to build a friendship, as it indebts you to them)—seemed to contain a hidden question: Why do you do things the way you do back in the States?

Did you even know you did things differently?

What does it mean that you've never thought about this before?

How many other things have you taken for granted, that this is just "how things are"?

I also learned one other thing I didn't expect, though in hindsight it seems obvious: They had comedy. And even ten thousand miles away from home, comedy was my thing.

"Why comedy?"

That's much easier to answer.

When you tell jokes and get laughs, you get a high. It feels fantastic. It's instant gratification. My earliest comedy memories are of entertaining friends at playdates. Then came school talent shows, where once I socked away a cool fifty bucks by singing "The Elements Song" by Tom Lehrer.

In eighth grade, for reasons that probably made sense at the time, I made a whole rap album entirely in the voice of the illustrious chef and media trailblazer Julia Child.* Amongst the twelve tracks of pure fire were classics like "How I Killed Emeril" and "99 Heart Problems." I recorded the songs, printed out covers, burned CDs and slipped them into jewel cases, and sold *Julia Raps* albums for five dollars apiece.

I hustled the album hard and made about two hundred bucks. Kids bought the album because they thought it was funny. Adults bought

---

* Julia Child also spent time in China as a spy for the United States Navy. Look it up.

the album because when a prepubescent boy shows you his Julia Child rap CD and asks for five dollars, you fork the money over immediately, because otherwise nobody will believe you. I used the money to buy Magic cards.

Julia Raps was a breakthrough for me. I had initiated an absurd project that had started with something funny to me, pushed through challenges to arrive at a final form, and managed to get someone else to pay for it.

Basically, that's still my job.*

I tried out for the improv comedy troupe at Newton North High School, in the suburbs of Boston. The moment I did my first improv show, I knew it was My New Thing. I was fourteen, afflicted with/ blessed by ADHD, and my thoughts banged nonstop against the still-elongating walls of my skull. On the improv stage, I could make jokes, play funny characters, and be a general lunatic—and my class-mates would come and watch, laugh, and cheer. It was the best.

It was also hard work. We practiced five days a week, three hours a day. The dozen other troupe members were the first humans I'd ever spent so much time with in a creative space, and we developed a close-ness that can only come through the shared experience of risk and performance. I almost feel like the rest of my life has been a quixotic journey to regain that feeling.

We would lock ourselves into the band room, turn off the lights, and in the pitch black improvise "voices-only" scenes like old-timey radio plays. We would sing absurd musicals about mangoes. Once, during a scene, my fellow troupe members picked me up and used me as a trowel.

---

* What do you think you're reading?

Improv also served as a tonic for my anxiety. I have always been an overthinker and over-worrier. In improv, there is no time to worry. There is only time to listen and respond. Success and failure are difficult—or often meaningless—to define. The lesson I needed to learn was that the cost of failure is not as high as my mind makes it out to be, and in this, improv was my first teacher.

I became known as the kid from the improv troupe. Comedy, both the show onstage and the community backstage, became who I was. It was where the stuff that made me special—the excess energy, the loose mental filter, the bizarre irreverence—was praised. It was my ticket to the middle class of our high school social hierarchy. Throughout high school, and then through college, I was always doing improv.

"Why comedy?"

Because, sometimes, when you're onstage and working the crowd just right, you lose yourself in the show. You enter a flow state. You see yourself from above. The air opens up. The present is huge.

And in that endless series of brief, interlocking moments, it feels like you can see the future. The faces of the audience swirl in a pool of light and color and you think to yourself, *I know what I am about to say, and I know you will laugh, and I know this before any of you know it.* And when you hit the punch line and the audience roars, you get a rush. You feel like a god, like you called down lightning and lightning struck.

And if you do that in another country, in another language, for people who might only think of America as a place on a map or a sound bite from a social media video, you know that there are only a few human beings in the world who can do such a thing, and you are one of them.

Perhaps the whole reason I moved to China and spent over a decade doing comedy is really just because of a two-minute comedy scene that happened in a dark bar in Beijing.

It was the last week of study abroad. I was in a grimy, soulful bar called the Hot Cat Club, where Beijing Improv held a weekly bilingual improv workshop.

I was watching two Chinese comedians do a scene. I was mesmerized.

The scene began as a woman came onstage and held her hands up, fingers curling into elegant shapes. These gestures told me she was a Buddhist bodhisattva, an immortal guide to mortal souls on Earth.

The second person came onstage and asked for life advice. And they got terrible life advice. Every bad piece of advice—Sell your house! Buy a goat! Become a master hairstylist!—got laughs. I had never seen Chinese people performing comedy. Yet somehow it was giving me a flashback.

I'd seen this scene. I'd *done* this scene.

In high school, I'd done a scene where I played the God of the Old Testament, reclining across a school desk with one finger outstretched to Adam, who asked for—and received—similarly bad advice.

We were dealing with different languages, cultures, religions. Everything that at a glance makes countries countries, and people people, was different. But everything about why the scene was funny was the same.

What was comedy like here?

How did it work?

Can humor be translated?

I started to dig for answers.

I learned there was a traditional form of Chinese comedy called xiangsheng. The two characters that made up the name literally translated to "face and voice" but everyone called it "crosstalk." It was all over TV and social media, and it burst out of the speakers of ten thousand taxis all over Beijing.

Two people onstage—a joker and a straight man—and over a hundred years of comedic works going back to the Qing dynasty behind them. A whole comedy ethos I had never heard anything about.

I had a thousand questions. I needed to find someone with a thousand answers.

Face and Voice

The first thing you notice about Master Ding is his voice.

"来了来了!"

I'm here!

The voice sounds like something out of an old movie, or a Broadway show, or a vaudeville stage. It tricks the ear into thinking that no matter where it came from, that spot is now the center of the room. It's the voice of a man who performed for thousands before there were microphones. It's stage technique, brought through the fourth wall and into real life.

A dozen heads, attached to people from half a dozen countries and aged anywhere from seven to seventy, swivel to face the door.

"Traffic's crazy today!" he barks, laughing. The voice and the laugh mix together, so everything he says sounds funny. It's a depth, or a subtle change in inflection, that somehow carries an extra frequency of data hidden inside the transmission.

Some people can say one word and conjure entire experiences and emotions. George Carlin spits out the word *religion*; the audience erupts. Nothing is said and everything is said. That voice is both setup and punch line.

But at the same time, Master Ding's voice is something wholly unlike those voices. Even now, I don't pretend to understand it. If I knew how to do it, I'd be a lot better comedian than I am now. All I know about his voice is this: It just works.

The Master has arrived.

On the day I first met Master Ding, he did something I had never seen another comedian do before.

It was a Saturday afternoon in late August, a year before I formally began my study with Master Ding, and I was on my way to watch him and his disciples rehearse. I was very nervous—not from preshow jitters, but because I would be flying back to Boston the following day to complete my senior year of college, and I had only this one chance to meet the Master and convince him to take me on as a student.

My return to China hinged on this man, and the art form he had spent his life honing. I had decided that applying for a Fulbright fellowship to research Chinese comedy was going to be my way back to Beijing. However, since this topic couldn't be taught at a university, and Master Ding was the only xiangsheng master in the whole country who took foreign disciples, his letter of recommendation to the Fulbright Commission stating his commitment to teaching me was essential.

When I arrived at room 204 of Beijing University of Chemical Technology, I found that the rehearsal had begun ahead of schedule. Kicking myself for showing up on time and not earlier, and not wanting my first interaction with the Master to involve me distracting everyone, I snuck in unaddressed and unintroduced and sat in the far back row to watch.

Master Ding was overseeing a scene between two of his disciples, who I later learned were from Canada and Japan. They were trying to get the timing down on an opening bit.

"Let me introduce myself! I'm a xiangsheng performer, An Renliang," said the Canadian, on the left, in impeccable Mandarin.

His partner, the Japanese student on the right, smiled, but when An Renliang said nothing more, he quietly asked, in equally good Mandarin, "Are you finished?"

An Renliang smiled, and said, "Yes."

The Japanese disciple looked embarrassed, and said again, a little bit louder, "How come you didn't introduce me?"

"Stop, stop, stop!" Master Ding said, running out onto the stage. It seemed urgent that the unfunny be addressed immediately. Both disciples broke character and listened alertly. "Was that funny?" Master Ding asked us.

The people in the audience muttered. No, not really.

"Not funny," Master Ding said. "Xitian Cong, you're the straight man in this bit. This timing relies on you."

I leaned forward eagerly. I hoped a demonstration was coming. I wanted to see Master Ding in action.

"An Renliang, take a seat."

The Canadian stepped off the small dais at the front of the classroom, and Master Ding stepped up to replace him. I was confused—wasn't he giving notes to the Japanese disciple?—but had no time to think. Master Ding bowed to the audience, prompting Xitian Cong to immediately bow in turn. The show had begun again.

"Let me introduce myself, I am a xiangsheng performer, Ding Guangquan." He hit the audience with a massive, heartfelt grin.

After a pause, Xitian Cong looked embarrassed, just as the last time. "Are you finished?"

Master Ding swung his grin around to look at Xitian Cong, said nothing, gave a microscopic nod, and returned to mugging for the audience.

This time, the energy was totally different. That tiny nod was such a small thing, but I could imagine being up onstage like Xitian Cong and feeling completely hung out to dry. It would be infuriating. And so this time, instead of meekly asking for an introduction, he did something else.

He shoved Master Ding on the shoulder.

The shove wasn't super hard—but it was hard enough to make the Master stagger.

Everyone laughed and gasped in shock. "Why didn't you introduce me?" Xitian Cong asked, miffed, and this time, the line hit: a second laugh.

"What???" Master Ding asked, his grin dropping completely.

"Introduce me!"

"Fine, fine!" The grin snapped back into place like a deadbolt lock. "Let me introduce myself. I'm a xiangsheng performer, Ding Guang-quan, and this is my partner."

A short pause, then Master Ding looked back over with another infuriating small grin, as if to say, "Are you satisfied?"

Xitian Cong was clearly not. His facial reaction alone—"'This is my partner?' That's all?"—got another laugh.

"What's my name?" Xitian Cong asked.

"You don't know your own name?" Master Ding asked him.

The audience was dying now, and Master Ding nodded to Xitian Cong and stepped off the stage. "Much better!" he said. "See, it's working now. You need to care. If you care, the audience cares. OK, An Renliang, back onstage."

The Canadian ambled back onstage and the rehearsal continued, but I was still stuck on what had just happened. I'd been in drama classes, and even comedy-specific performance classes. I've seen teachers give notes, but almost always they did this by tapping out the performer, showing them how they should perform, and then asking them to try again.

Master Ding had done the opposite. He wanted to teach Xitian

Cong, so he tapped out An Renliang. Through carefully controlling his own delivery of the exact same lines, Master Ding had inspired a radically different reaction from Xitian Cong—the reaction needed to make the bit work.

Comedy isn't easily taught. Like swimming, technique is one thing, but no amount of study on dry land will prepare you for that first cold shock of the water, how it crushes your lungs, the fear as your head goes under.

Something about Master Ding's stance, his wide grin, the edge-of-the-knife precision on how much he could "disrespect" Xitian Cong without being called out on it, said he had thrown Xitian Cong into the deep end. And when Xitian Cong's reaction was a shove, he played it off as if he knew it was coming the whole time.

To make an actor give the performance you want by showing him how to do it was hard. To *induce* the performance you want, without even changing the script, was something I had never seen.

But beyond that, to be a mentor, a teacher, and a master, and a sixty-something-year-old man, and still be the type of person your students felt comfortable hitting unexpectedly if it was needed for the bit?

And to have your first reaction be the exact type of funny that works? I had never seen this in a comedy teacher. Forget comedy teacher, I'm not sure I'd ever seen *any* teacher do something like that.

I forgot all about the Fulbright application. I wanted to study with him, period. I didn't care if I needed to get a day job to make it work. I wanted to get back into this nondescript classroom, be part of this bizarre group of foreigners with top-level Chinese, and learn how to pull bits off from a master.

All that said . . . it would make my life a lot easier to get that letter of recommendation.

"Master Ding!" I said, as everyone prepared to leave at the end of the rehearsal. Now was my moment. I felt light-headed as I crossed the room to shake his hand. "I am Jesse Appell—Ai Jie Xi. Professor David Moser gave me the info about today's rehearsal."

"Oh, yes! Professor Moser said you would be here. What did you think of xiangsheng? Is this your first time watching it?"

"Yes, yes, it is . . . and I . . . I really loved it!" I stammered. "I . . . I really want to study with you, and I have this application, and it's for this grant . . ."

I started babbling semi-coherently in circles, bumbling toward the ask. I knew it was wholly inappropriate in Chinese culture to meet a master and ask for a favor before they even know you. The whole thing felt doomed.

"And so, if you . . . I mean if a master teacher . . . I mean you . . . could write me a letter of recommendation, I think it would do a lot for my application."

"Sure," he said.

What?

"Sure?"

"Sure. Let me know what you need. I hope you can come and join our Happy Classroom."

That's it?

"You'll help?" I asked, still shocked.

He laughed, slung his small side-pouch bag over his shoulder, and left the room.

Fulbright: Weirdos of the Best Sort

The day before the rehearsal, I had arranged to meet Professor David Moser in a Starbucks near the campus of Beijing Capital Normal University.

Professor Moser was a lifelong *laowai*, a foreigner who lived in China. An Oklahoman by birth, he had moved to China to study abroad in the 1980s, making him one of the first students from America to study in the country since the fall of the Qing dynasty in 1911, and never left. In those thirty-plus years he had lived many lives: xiangsheng performer, radio host, jazz musician, and now scholar and director of the study-abroad program I had attended last year.

"How was your first summer by yourself in Beijing, free from the burden of homework?" he asked me.

"It was a lot of fun. I interned at the Nature Conservancy."

My work at the conservancy mostly consisted of translating English to English. They had commissioned some reports on the status of pollution in China's main river systems, but the reports' English was so bad, they needed someone to go back to the original reports in Chinese to see what the author actually meant in the first place. I could read Chinese and had no other useful skills, so that became my job. But when I came back to China, I wanted to do comedy.

"I tried Chinese comedy when I was younger. Sometimes the jokes even landed," Professor Moser told me. "One day, when I was a student at Beijing University, our teacher came in and asked if any of the foreign students wanted to be part of a comedy show. It turns out the comedy show was a xiangsheng routine for the Beijing University New Year's Gala."

"The one aired to the whole country on Chinese New Year?"

"Yes, that one. Xiangsheng is traditional Chinese comedy. There's a straight man and a joker, and they go back and forth and do a dialogue. Someone thought it would be funny to see foreigners trying to do this traditional comedy. Back then, there were so few foreigners in China, and so to see a non-Chinese person speak Mandarin was already good TV by itself."

"How did you learn the routines?"

"The top xiangsheng comedian of the time, Great-Master Hou Baolin, had a disciple called Ding Guangquan. Master Ding took to foreigners performing xiangsheng and helped us adapt old routines to make sense with non-Chinese comedians. That was the beginning of years of shows. A lot of traditional xiangsheng had gotten stale by that time. We were something new."

Traveling around the country, doing TV shows in Chinese, riding the pioneering wave of how Americans were seen in China—the man sitting across from me in this Starbucks had lived his own version of my wildest dreams. "Was it fun?" I asked.

"It was very fun. We would do shows and then head back to Master Ding's place, and he would cook for us. He's an excellent cook. He's a Hui Muslim, so we never had any pork, but everything else was to die for. I did the xiangsheng circuit for a few years with him and even wrote my master's thesis on xiangsheng."

I explained how I wanted to pursue something similar with the Fulbright program, a State Department–run academic exchange program where American scholars go to other countries and other countries send scholars to America. Every job in China required me to either teach English or be twenty-five years old to get a visa. With the Fulbright, I could pick a topic, any topic, and if I could explain in my application essay why my research was important to US–China understanding, they would give me a year to do independent research.

"And why do you want to study comedy?" Prof. Moser asked.

I paused.

"Every Wednesday night, there's this group of Chinese and Westerners that do bilingual improv—I've been to every one of them, even gotten onstage myself. It's so fascinating to see how humor changes, how it doesn't, what makes people laugh. I also think it's really important. I mean, we have so many Americans who can do business with China, but almost none who know how to make Chinese people laugh. It seems crazy that the two biggest, strongest countries in the world have such a gap. What if trade goes bad? What if we need to talk about difficult things, if we need something to break tension? . . . What do you think? How should I pitch this in my application?"

Professor Moser sized me up and took a sip of his coffee. Mandopop music played softly overhead. "Don't apply to research Chinese comedy," he said.

I was crushed. "You don't think they'll take it seriously?"

"Well, these Chinese improv shows, this stuff isn't really traditional. And comedy as a topic is too broad. So, don't apply to research 'Chinese comedy.' Apply to learn xiangsheng. Xiangsheng is a traditional art form. It has an established history, a deep background, and other than my master's thesis, there probably aren't more than a dozen articles written in English about it. As far as the outside world is concerned, it almost doesn't exist at all."

"But it does exist! Every cab driver in the city listens to nothing but xiangsheng."

"Exactly," he said, his eyes glittering. "And Master Ding is still teaching disciples. Secure a letter of recommendation from him, promising to teach you, and I think you'll have a unique application."

"Apparently, the assistant secretary of state is going to be the keynote speaker."

"Is he pro-China or anti-China? I guess it doesn't matter; they can't rescind the grant now, anyway."

It was 8 a.m.—far too early, in my opinion, to talk about anything important—and I was trying to eye up which of the pastries on the breakfast table seemed the least day-old. Milling around the room in the Washington, DC, hotel breakout room, discussing various East Asia–themed political issues, were sixty or so scholars: my Fulbright cohort, here for orientation.*

Some scholars were in their sixties, and I was only a month out of college, so while everyone was warm and inviting, I gravitated toward a table with a few people my own age.

---

* In the first draft of this book, I wrote about four pages on my senior year of college, my hours grinding away at essays for my application to Fulbright, and my general state of anxiety that all my backup plans to get a job in China failed. In the end I cut all that, since being publicly anxious is how I progress my standup career and I think it will be more profitable putting my stress onstage than putting it here.

"Nice to meet you, nice to meet you," we all repeated before immediately diving into the easiest topic to break the ice: "What is your research topic?"

"I'm Meghan, I'll be researching adolescent autism in Xi'an."

"I'm Sophie, I'm doing oil rights claims and maritime sovereignty in the South China Sea."

"I'm Annie, I'm actually an alumni from last year—I'm doing a PhD in shadow puppetry."

"Doctor of Shadow Puppetry!?" I immediately had so many questions. "How do they make the puppets? Did you learn to make them? Did you learn how to sing the operas?"

It only took a few minutes for me to realize I had found my tribe. Everyone at the table was, like me, super eager to spend a year of their life tilting at their own esoteric windmill. And it was a testament to our shared flavor of curiosity that my questions launched a series of fascinating back-and-forths instead of earning me strange looks.

Every project was fascinating and—most interestingly to me—had no clear definition of success. The people were from all sorts of backgrounds, and while Ivy League schools had more than their fair share of representatives, many smaller universities and state schools had scholars there as well.

As we would soon learn during the orientation, this eclectic mix of topics and people was intentional. The Fulbright Program was founded after the Second World War by Senator William Fulbright, who hoped to build something that had the intercultural social glue aspect of the Rhodes Scholarship with less of an Old Boys' Club approach.

Since it was run by the State Department and its Chinese equivalent, this made us all semiofficial cultural ambassadors, so it was in the best interest of America to send representatives of as many parts of America as possible. I had a feeling that my interest in comedy had been to my benefit, as nobody in the history of the program had ever applied to study xiangsheng.

Even by Fulbright standards, the China cohort was unusually all over the place. Whereas some countries who exchanged Fulbright scholars have been open to the West for centuries, China had virtually no visa categories for curious foreigners, preferring to grant access mostly to businesspeople, English teachers, and the occasional spouse of a Chinese national. Going to China as a Fulbright scholar was one of the few legal and sanctioned ways Americans could chase the unknown in China, and that attracted a certain type of person willing to live on the edge between worlds.

Take Jonathan Kaufman as an example. We first met at the sterile hotel ballroom in DC; five months later, he was showing me around ancient Silk Road mosques in Gansu Province.

"It's beautiful here," I said, as we walked through sun-drenched courtyards. The architecture seemed like it was born directly of the mixed DNA of China and the Middle East—marble spires with bulbous green crowns shot up into the bright blue sky, while the inner sanctums with covered outdoor corridors would not be out of place in a Buddhist temple.

"It is amazing here. They have been so nice and open to me. The imam is going to come to drink tea with us. Just don't tell anyone that you're Jewish. It's easier that way."

"Roger."

"Don't tell them I'm Jewish, either."

"They don't know? What did you tell them?"

Jonathan, a dark-skinned, Middle Eastern–looking man, shrugged and smiled. "I didn't tell them anything; they didn't ask. I know a lot about Islam, since that's what I study. They probably just assume I'm Muslim. My Arabic is better than most of theirs, and we all speak Chinese together anyway. It doesn't come up. So just don't mention it."

We sat beneath flowering trees and drank hot tea with the imam, who had an awesome beard.* The imam chatted and laughed with these funny Chinese-speaking Americans for half an hour. We really clicked, discussing the crossover of Middle Eastern and Chinese food while sipping from cups so thin, the tea burned my fingers through the plastic membrane.

Eventually, he sighed. "You are both so nice. It's a shame America and Islam are enemies. It's not your fault George Bush crashed planes into the twin towers to start a global war against Islam."

I opened my mouth and Jonathan shot me with the most amazing stare I'd ever seen. *Not now. Not here. This isn't a Facebook post. You won't win this fight.* I sipped my tea and admired the wooden engravings on the walls.

We were a cohort of offbeat, knock-off Indiana Joneses: daring, unstable, and bookish (though not all archaeologists). Over the course of a few days, we shared knowledge about all the things one needs to know to be a visiting researcher, with a focus on brass tacks: how to rent an apartment, how to build relationships with other scholars and their departments, how to find the nearest international hospital.

Advice like this from previous scholars was useful, but it was the stories of their research that stuck with me. Every one of them had gone into the geographical and intellectual unknown and come back with tales. Some were funny, some were inspiring, some were upsetting. None were boring.

---

* In my experience, old Chinese men seem to only have two types of beards: awesome beards and sad beards, and there's almost nothing in between.

The story that rested deepest in my heart came from a scholar named Kuoray Mao, who lived for a year in a drought-afflicted village—also in Gansu Province, part of China's rapidly desertifying West.

Kuoray was an environmental researcher, and he had planned to research Qing dynasty water usage records to see if the region had previously been wetter than it was now. Maybe comparing the past to the present could give insight into how to restore the region. Is this area supported by outside water? Or did it used to be self-sufficient, its current arid reality possibly caused by climate change?

When he arrived, he found the village on the cusp of collapse. What's more, he discovered that the village police chief was not at all interested in him poking around, tracking down old documents. In a place where survival was a day-to-day struggle, Kuoray was essentially conscripted as a field hand for eight months, working the land to help the village stay alive.

The night before he had to leave, as he was packing his suitcase and mentally chalking up the year as a massive failure, he got a call from the village police chief. A half hour later, he was sipping tea with the chief and a young woman from the village who knew something about "old papers" that might interest him.

The woman said their family used to live in a nearby town, one now abandoned to the ever-expanding sands of the desert. But her grandmother had lived in that village, and once had mentioned to her that, back in the 1970s, officials had come to enforce the special madness of the Cultural Revolution: out with the old, in with the new. Anything from "Old China"—the thousands of years of dynastic history—should be turned over.

Grandma was illiterate, but she knew somewhere in their house were those old papers, the ones with the fancy seals, written in traditional characters and, even in the '70s, already faded yellow and brittle.

She didn't know what they were; she just thought they shouldn't be destroyed. She wrapped them in an old bedsheet, and while the Red Guards searched the living room, she threw her treasure down a dry well behind their home.

A few years later, the whole village had been abandoned.

The papers were probably still there.

Kuoray hopped in a car and drove into the night. Soon, he was shining his iPhone flashlight down every dry well in an abandoned village that hours ago he didn't know existed. At the bottom of one, he hooked something on the end of his makeshift fishing rod and drew up, perfectly preserved, the original Qing dynasty records for the county's water usage from the 1870s through the 1890s.

He carried it home clutched in both arms. It was his baby. He spent the next seven hours standing in the town's only print shop, sweating bullets and photocopying every page twice. The originals he returned to the granddaughter. Kuoray pulled up ten years' worth of work from that well—enough undiscovered data for his doctorate thesis and perhaps two books.

My fellow Fulbright scholars sat in rapt silence throughout the whole story. Their eyes were shining, hungry. They were strange people who lived in strange places and conducted strange research—and they wanted their own well baby, more than anything else in the world. I discovered, to my surprise and delight, that I fit in perfectly.

We were all weirdos of the best sort, a breed of people tumbling down their own personal rabbit holes, deeper and deeper into some exceedingly narrow part of human knowledge. I hadn't known to look for these people, but I had found them nonetheless, brought together by chance and the United States government.

It was as if I had graduated college with plans of interviewing for a marketing position at a faceless corporation—because isn't that what you do as an American college grad who speaks Chinese?—and had mistakenly wandered into the circus instead, only to find that they needed a Chinese comedian, and would I join?

I ran away with them, all the way across the Pacific to Beijing.

When—if?—I came back, it would be as a different person.

Interlude: Today, We Will Be Performing Xiangsheng

A: Welcome, dear reader, to the traditional Chinese art of xiangsheng "crosstalk" comedy!

B: Welcome!

A: We should introduce ourselves, I suppose.

B: That's how it usually starts.

A: I'm the Joker. I stand on the audience's left. Of the two people, I'm the funnier, smarter, wittier—

B: Humbler . . .

A: The most humble of the two! For the last hundred-plus years, the best comedians in China have been crosstalk Jokers! And now you know me!

B: Fabulous.

A: Now, xiangsheng is a Chinese linguistic performance art, hailing back to the Qing dynasty—

B: Whoa, whoa, whoa. Aren't you going to introduce me?

A: Oh! Sorry. Almost forgot. This man, standing beside me, is the Straight Man! (*Pause.*) Where were we? Oh, yes! Xiangsheng is a Chinese linguistic performance art, hailing back to—

B: Wait!

A: What now?

B: That's it?

A: That's what?

B: I'm just "the Straight Man"?

A: You're not straight?

B: That's—you should introduce me!

A: I did introduce you.

B: What'd you say?

A: You're the Straight Man!

B: That's all?

A: Well, you're not that important.

B: I'm very important! You need to tell them what the Straight Man does! I'm half the show! Introduce me like you introduced yourself!

A: Like I introduced myself?

B: To the word!

A: That's gonna be really awkward . . .

B: Just do it!

A: Fine . . . Hello, dear audience! I'm the Joker, the funniest, cleverest, wittiest, and humblest of the two. And this is the Straight Man: the funniest, cleverest, wittiest—see, this is awkward, nobody believes this!

B: What kind of intro is that?

A: You said "to the word"!

B: I can't believe this! Xiangsheng has been around for over a hundred years! And you know the old phrase: three parts Joker, seven parts Straight Man. The Straight Man's the harder role!

A: I don't believe you.

B: The Jokers never do. The audience usually doesn't, either. But you can act as nuts as you want, it doesn't change the universal truth of comedy: The funny is in the silence.

A:

B: You OK?

A: No funny in that silence.

B: Gah! Whatever! Keep telling them about xiangsheng.

A: Crosstalk.

B: Whatever! Same thing!

A: In the late Qing dynasty—

B: They don't know when that is!

A: Late 1800s!

B: Don't act all cultured and leave them behind.

A: I got this! Late 1800s. One of the Qing Emperors goes kaput.

B: "Kaput?" Was he a Yiddish emperor?

A: Maybe.

B: The Qianlong Emperor was definitely not a Yiddish emperor!

A: But he did die. We can agree on that?

B: He did die.

A: Kaput! He died. Great sadness and sorrow across the land! Beijing, the northern capital, is plunged into deepest mourning!

B: Well, the court was. Everyone else was probably just trying to get through their day.

A: But you know the way of the world! When the powerful are sad, the meek must be sorrowful, too!

B: It's only appropriate.

A: And so there was a new decree: No more Beijing opera!

B: A temporary ban on entertainment.

A: Back then, Beijing opera was like Oakland on 4/20: hella dope.

B: That is an awful metaphor and outdated. Please take that back.

A: Everyone in the city was upset at the loss of their favorite shows! And the actors had no work! And don't forget, these people went through Jackie Chan–type training. The trainers would be like, "Do a split! A full split!" And the actors in training would be saying, "I'm four!"

B: Rough—only a toddler and already unemployed. But forget the children. If the adult actors couldn't perform, what did they do?

A: They began to sell themselves on the streets.

B: Ugh, really?!

A: What?

B: They sold themselves on the streets?

A: They sold their skills on the streets.

B: That is not what you said!

A: Every Beijing opera performer had to come up with their own way to make money. The singers sung. The acrobats acrobatted. And the clowns started telling jokes!

B: I've heard of this! They call it "The Flowering of the Hundred Minor Arts." Some of the most popular ones are still done today. Clapper boards, some singing styles, shadow puppetry . . .

A: Exactly! And amongst these out-of-work actors, there was one man . . . a former opera clown whose mix of ugly facial features and self-deprecating hilarity started a comedic revolution!

B: What was his name?

A: I Do Not Fear Poverty!

B: OK? What does that have to do with anything?

A: That was his name. His stage name, Qiong Bupa—"I Do Not Fear Poverty."

B: That's a weird stage name.

A: It sounds better in Chinese.

B: I trust you.

A: This guy was hiiiiilarious. The dude was so funny, when he told jokes, people would form a circle around him and give him money. Like a pole dancer at a strip club, but instead of a pole, he had jokes, and instead of a strip club, he was on the street.

B: So not similar at all, then.

A: The guy was so funny that the Empress Dowager Cixi heard about him.

B: I know her! She's the one with the long, golden fingernail things in those old photographs.

A: Hey! She was basically empress of China and you want to talk fashion accessories? You, sir, are an awful feminist.

B: I'm . . . that's not the point! I'm just trying to paint a picture!

A: Now, the empress dowager heard about this funny man and went, "Hee hee hee . . ."

B: Oh, now she's a witch? Very feminist.

A: "This man . . . I've heard he is super funny. *Bring him to me! Hahaha!*" Lightning! Thunder!

B: She's literally a witch.

A: OK, no lightning, no thunder. It's a beautiful summer's day, and they bring I Do Not Fear Poverty to the Summer Palace.

B: The man has to change his name.

A: "Make me laugh, peasant!"

B: Not a good thing for a comedian to hear.

A: But that's what he was dealing with: the empress, the court, the whole shebang. In the Summer Palace, there's this opulent five-square-mile garden with painted corridors and dragons covered in gold everywhere. Now, we both do comedy; we'll tell the audience straight up: This is not a funny room.

B: So, what'd he do?

A: He told a story about a very poor, starving man.

B: What was his name?

A: Does it matter? Let's just call him Bill.

B: He was 100 percent not called Bill.

A: So? The guy's name's not important. If the joke works with the Chinese name, it should work with Bill.

B: Not if there's a pun on his name!

A: Let's not get into translating comedy! We have a whole chapter on that later. Anyway, so Bill's not doing so hot. He's poor. He's starving. One day he collapses on the door of a monastery. He's found by a monk. "Well, I can't just leave him here . . ." So the monk drags him inside. "I don't even have any food for myself . . . well, let's make do with what we have." The monk's got to improvise. He slops together some dirty water, trash, rotting vegetables . . . classic Taco Bell.

"Drink this!" he says.

Bill's like, "What is it?"

"It's . . . the house special. We call it white jade pearl soup."

B: Tasty.

A: By the way, I could totally see one of those clickbait cooking videos done on this. One quart of dirty water, three spoons of gutter oil . . .

B: The joke, man! There are people reading this book right now!

A: I don't think anyone's reading this book—

B: *The joke!*

A: OK! Right. So, Bill's starving, and he drinks the mess. But he so trusted the monk, and the monk sold it so well, he doesn't know he's basically chugging biohazard material. Down the hatch it goes! He thinks he's eating real good food, and so he miraculously recovers and pledges to better himself.

B: That's not funny.

A: This is the setup, man! Setup . . . punch line. There's an order! That's true everywhere.

B: OK, OK, go.

A: Years later, Bill's rockin' it. He's gotten off the street, and has even bested the test to become a high court official. One day, the emperor, intrigued by his new official, asks him how he came to court. He tells the truth—started from the bottom, white jade pearl soup, now we're here.

The emperor's totally into this. He's like, "We should hold a feast, invite the monk, and serve the white jade pearl soup as the main course." Bill's all for that. Good karma, he thinks, coming to this monk who saved him.

"Good news, man! You're gonna be serving that special soup to—no, wait for it—the emperor!"

"Dude, the white jade pearl soup is actually mostly shit!"

Now they realize they're both in deep. They can't come clean, because that would be a nightmare. They can't lie and make a new soup, because the emperor's expecting something magic and if they get caught, they could be in bigger trouble. And the emperor wants his magic soup!

B: Oh, damn.

A: So, they have the feast. Bill tries to dissuade the emperor, but he's ordered to make the same dish he gave to Bill all those years ago. Nothing for it. The bowls of rotted veggies in dirty water are served to the Emperor, to Bill, to the whole court. The emperor takes a whiff . . .

"Ah, I can smell the fragrance!"

"Yes, yes, it is very fragrant!" Meanwhile, Bill and the monk are freaking out, but holding it in.

He takes a sip . . . "I love it!"

Then the whole court—sycophants all, of course—comes in. "It's fantastic!" "It's amazing!" "You can taste the flavors!"

And they get away with it!

B: Ha! That's great!

A: But here's the thing—this wasn't being performed on the street corner. It's being performed in the Summer Palace. For the empress dowager. The poor dude from the street just came to the empress's home and told a story of a poor dude from the street coming into the emperor's home and feeding him rotting garbage—and the emperor is like, "Gimme more! Gimme more!"

B: That . . . is a risky joke.

A: Yeah, I'm sure he was thinking, *If I pick this routine and it goes wrong, I'll be stuck in the dungeons going, "You can't say anything with this goddamn PC culture anymore!" every time they come to torture me.*

B: So, the empress? What did she do?

A: She slapped her knee and shouted, *"Bie ai ma le!"*

B: What the hell does that mean?

A: Basically "OH NO YOU DI'INT!" in Manchurian.

B: She loved it!

A: She loved it, which means her court got to love it, too. They were all instant fans. And so xiangsheng evolved to be this art that was of the streets, from the streets, but also patronized at a high level and seen as real culture. It jumped into teahouses and was performed there—still is, actually, if you go to a teahouse in Beijing.

B: So the street jokers mingled a bit with the literati.

A: Yeah, and so even nowadays you have this split in the xiangsheng community. Some people see their art as high culture, and dignified—others are just like, "Can't I do a fart joke? This is funny!"

B: What happened to I Do Not Fear Poverty?

A: So, he started taking students. To teach them how to perform, he performed alongside them, two people side by side. Once that happened, they realized, "Hey, we're twice as loud, we're twice as funny, and we can do bits together."

B: That's how you get the two-person style.

A: Yeah, and people have been doing it ever since. But the cool thing is, since we know the first performer, and his first student, and the student that student took, the xiangsheng community has tracked master to student, master to student ever since that day. So, if you want to study xiangsheng for real, you've got to apprentice with a master who's in the family tree. There are even routines that have been passed down over a hundred years, and you've got to learn them as part of the study.

B: Wow, so people have made their living off of doing xiangsheng for a long, long time.

A: Yes! Though it's really hard to make a living off of xiangsheng alone.

B: Well, we're making a go at it.

A: We are?

B: We're making a living performing xiangsheng right now!

A: Oh, we're not getting paid for this show. I told you that, right?

B: *Son of a—*

(B smashes A over and over again with his fists, chasing him off the stage.)

END. Please slam your book cover open and closed at this page to simulate applause.

Teahouse Crosstalk

Come with me to my first xiangsheng show in Beijing.

No, really, it'll be fun. Don't worry if you can't understand it. It's 2012, and I don't get much more than every third sentence myself. I'm seeing everything for the first time, too.

Besides, everyone should go to at least one comedy show in a language they don't understand. It's an experience in straining your mind, looking for patterns you're only half-certain exist, and coming away surprised at how much you got. Worse comes to worst, you're out two hours and ten bucks.

We enter the theater through big, red wooden doors with giant gold handles. You hand over the ticket and walk through a doorway into a performance space with a high ceiling. Your eyes settle on a large stage flanked by four giant pillars of painted wood, golden calligraphy cascading inside framed rectangles embossed on the face of each pillar.

On the dais there is a low, flat table covered by a decorated silk-stitched cloth that overhangs the edge. On the table there is a folded fan and a small block of wood inlaid with silver. The show hasn't started yet, and the room is at a low thrum, with the occasional punctuating shout. The overall atmosphere is one of relaxation. It's a Friday. Everyone has worked hard today. They've been looking forward to going to the show since lunchtime.

Below the stage, there are rows upon rows of square wooden tables surrounded by straight-backed wooden chairs. We get ushered into the correctly priced section and are left to find our own seats.

A small tray of snacks are on the table—sunflower seeds, peanut crunchy things, an individually wrapped dried plum with the pit still inside. These are all free. A woman comes by with a pot of chrysanthemum tea, plops it on the table unceremoniously, and throws in a small plate of sugar—big crystals that look like rock candy. The tea costs three bucks.

The lights go down. Two men walk onstage in freshly pressed flowing robes, one bloodred, one pastel blue. They look like something out of an old-timey black-and-white movie about a bygone age, but the colors here are bright and there are top-of-the-line Sennheiser speakers in the ceiling that blast sound down onto the audience.

They bow. The audience applauds. The air shifts—something about moving from the space of "waiting for the funny" to "the funny is beginning" feels primal and timeless. You get the feeling this has happened ten thousand times, at places all around the country, for years and years and years.

One of the men takes the wooden block and *smacks* the table, and the sharp sound sets an opening tone. The show has begun.

Then the patter begins. Classic xiangsheng is a two-man routine, and the magic of the art is in the back-and-forth. The performers quickly get into a comfortable rhythm. They let the laughs breathe.

A guy in the audience sneezes. They stop, point him out, and roast him for a few minutes. The guy starts out apologetic, then gains confidence and tries to bandy with the performers. He gets shut down again and again. The performers are too quick. The audience loves it. The guy's friends love it. He loves it.

Then the show continues. "Where were we?" The patter resumes.

The dude behind us laughs loud. Like, way too loud. It's more like an air horn than a laugh, and it comes in one staccato burst: *HAAAAAAAAAAAAAAAAAA.*

A quick check over the shoulder reveals some slim dude of about fifty in a tan polo shirt. His janky, yellowed teeth are on prominent display because he's laughing so much. Eyes locked onstage, he absent-mindedly brings a sunflower seed to his face, working it around his mouth area like he's forgotten where the hole is. He breaks the shell with his teeth, and spits it on the ground.

Looking down, there's a carpet of seed shells on the ground now, like a snowfall, but covered in spit.

I personally don't mind this at all. This is why I wear shoes. And the dude is having a good time. I'm having a good time. I almost feel like I'm having a *special* good time, a good time of a type that most people from the hemisphere I was born in have never experienced. It's only a silly comedy show . . . but it's more than that. If not for xiangsheng, I never would have met Mr. Jankytooth, and while I don't know what that is worth, I do know that nobody else I know can claim it.

The opening duo does fifteen minutes, then is replaced by a second duo that does a half hour. Then, the headliners, who are apparently quite famous, come on, take their bow, *smack* the piece of wood, and go nonstop for two more hours, bit after bit, culminating in a long monologue that receives thunderous applause. Happy and exhausted from laughing, the audience is very mellow.

At the end of this show, I am a little less comfortable than most. This is because I didn't understand a goddamn thing. My Chinese training up until this point has been mainly in conversational Chinese, with specialties in ordering food and finding an apartment to rent. This has allowed me to make friends, order food, and rent an apartment where the electricity only intermittently cuts off. Apparently, I have not been trained to understand traditional Chinese comedy.

I understood some of it. Snippets, sentences. I gathered that the main theme of one of the pieces involved a guy trying out for a singing competition and being god-awful at singing. But did I "get it"?

No. Not tonight.

I feel a brief hiccup of anxiety. I've moved halfway across the world to do this comedy. I need to go from not getting it to performing it.

This first encounter with classic Chinese crosstalk has prompted me to realize that to perform xiangsheng means knowing jokes within jokes, plays within plays. It means knowing history, and loving history, and being with other people who know and love history. It means inserting myself into that history, going onto that stage in a robe and *smack*ing the wooden block and having my own reason to be in this space as a rando white dude from Boston.

It means doing jokes that make fifty-year-old men in tan polo shirts with bad teeth whom I've never met laugh.

I'm not sure I can do it.

I *think* I can.

Luckily, I get to study with the Master.

Fame and Foreigners

Master Ding is name-drop famous in China. I know this because the Chinese police knocked on my door once in the middle of the night.

Not long after arriving, I was the subject of a visa shakedown. The public security bureau sent three officers to my apartment, asking to see my passport, visa, and residence permit. I stood there in my underwear, the door half-open, unsure if it would be more respectful to leave and put more clothes on or simply stand and answer their questions.

"你在中国干什么？"

What do you do here? one of them asked me, squinting down at my passport.

I had hoped to have more time in China before needing to have such an important conversation in Mandarin. I hoped he didn't misinterpret my nervousness as suspicious. "I am a student of Master Ding Guangquan. I am researching xiangsheng."

The man's eyes jerked up. His face was split in a massive grin. "You do xiangsheng?" he asked. "I love xiangsheng!" He turned and shouted over his shoulders at the two officers hanging back in the hallway. "*Hey!* He does xiangsheng! He's one of Ding Guangquan's students!"

Looking more closely, I noticed the officer was about my age, and one of those classic comedian types—jokey, warm, fast-talking. We chatted about comedy for five more minutes.

I wrote down the names of a few xiangsheng artists he liked that I hadn't heard of before ("Watch Guo Degang's older stuff—it's the best"), then the three men politely apologized for the inconvenience and bade me goodnight.

In 1989, a Canadian man named Mark Rowswell performed xiangsheng alongside Master Jiang Kun at one of the major Chinese New Year's galas. These galas are four-hour-long variety act TV shows that air on the first night of Chinese New Year. Hundreds of millions of people tune in. It's like the Super Bowl halftime show, if the halftime show also had to feature nationalist messaging in between songs and jokes.*

Most Chinese had never seen a white person speak Chinese fluently, not to mention pull off xiangsheng jokes that required precise language and comedic timing. Mark became known overnight by hundreds of millions of people by his Chinese name of "Big Mountain": Dashan. He has more fans than there are Americans. Probably twice as many.

Shortly after that first show, Master Ding met Dashan and they began a fruitful collaboration. Master Ding taught and mentored Dashan in the art form of xiangsheng and helped him turn what were previously sporadic xiangsheng appearances into a professional-level touring career. The two toured all over the country—and later the world—telling jokes to audiences of hundreds and thousands.

In being the first photogenic, funny foreigner known broadly

---

* To be more precise, it is as if the Super Bowl had to incorporate additional nationalist messaging above and beyond the enormous American flag on the field and uniformed soldiers saluting as jets fly over the arena.

across the land, Dashan also became the yardstick by which all other Chinese-speaking foreigners are measured. Even today, when I open my mouth and speak Chinese, people will say, "Wow, you're as good as Dashan!"*

Or they'll say, "Your Chinese is great! But it's not as good as Dashan's."

That gala show, along with years of working with Dashan, started a thirty-year odyssey for Master Ding. He continued to teach his Chinese disciples, but he brought Dashan on board, becoming the first master to mentor foreign pupils. A few other masters tried to ride the fad and find foreign faces to teach, but they couldn't make it work. Master Ding, as I would learn, was a fabulous intercultural communicator at a time when that phrase did not exist.

He spent three decades doing xiangsheng with foreigners better than everyone else because he did the big things right: he opened up his home and heart to his students; he treated them like people and not props or "dancing monkeys"; and he gave all of himself to his new mission: bringing China and the world closer through xiangsheng.

At the time Master Ding and Dashan began their tours, China was just coming into the global sphere, emerging from a closed-off mentality where foreigners were rarely seen. Chinese didn't know much about them, and they assumed foreigners knew even less about China. To see young, energetic foreigners perform xiangsheng meant the world was taking an interest in a part of China that touched people personally. However well or poorly they performed, they were treating the Chinese people on their own terms.

---

* I've gotten to know Mark over the years; once, he confided to me that even he sometimes can't live up to his own myth. "When I meet people, half the time my Chinese is as good as Dashan's and half the time it isn't." One day, he'll write a book and you should buy it.

Master Ding claimed to have taught over two hundred students from eighty countries. Some stayed for months, some for years, some for decades.

If you count anyone who took a single class with Master Ding, that number would surely be higher. Many students came to a few classes and left, because it turns out doing xiangsheng is really, really hard.

Happy Classroom: The Funny UN

"你先给大家介绍一下！" Master Ding said to me. *Introduce yourself to everyone!*

The first moment of the first class, and I was being asked to speak?

Master Ding took a half step to the right and dipped a shoulder. *The stage is yours.*

I honestly don't remember what I said, probably something about performing improv and stand-up in college. It doesn't matter. What mattered is that I looked out over the room at Master Ding's disciples and thought to myself, *God, I've found the funny UN.*

They all came and went, but they stopped in on Saturdays when they were in town or between shows. This weekly convocation to learn, rehearse, perform, and share news was called the Happy Classroom.

In time I would come to know some of these people quite well. Pouya Azadeh from Iran weighed at least three hundred pounds and sometimes nodded off in the middle of classes. Seeing a skinny Jewish guy and a giant Iranian man perform Chinese comedy together felt like the physical manifestation of the setup to a bad knock-knock joke.

Of course, it only felt like that to me. The Chinese audience, unfamiliar with those stereotypes and unaware of what a knock-knock joke even was, just treated us as two foreigners. Compared to them, we surely must be more similar to each other than we were to the Chinese.

The whole cultural stew of the Jewish–American–Iranian–Muslim con-
flicts in the world were irrelevant to the audience. We were just jokers;
the audience, the straight men.

There was Jie Gai (Francis Tchiégué), from Cameroon, an eru-
dite talk show host who spoke six languages. He sings Beijing opera
like a Beijing grandpa on the bus with a radio, learning long pieces
largely thanks to his incredible ear. When he first moved to China,
he spoke almost no Chinese but became enamored with xiangsheng
and discovered Master Ding. But he couldn't speak the language, so
Master Ding sought to put him off studying comedy by requiring him
to memorize a whole routine. The next week, he came in and nailed
every single line.

"Master Ding laughed," Jie Gai told me. "Then he asked, 'Do you
know what that all meant?' I told him, 'Not a word.' He laughed again,
and he let me keep studying."

Satoshi Nikida was a Japanese exchange student who did Japanese
comedy in Osaka and found a home with our squad in Beijing. Charles
Cziya was a Rwandan PhD student who never stopped smiling and
kept trying to work singing into his routines, even though it had never
worked, even once. Thiên Tú, a tiny firecracker of a girl from Vietnam,
was so natural and fluid onstage, Chinese people couldn't believe she
wasn't Chinese.

The common language of our multicultural clique was Chinese. I've
gone to many Chinese classes, and the Happy Classroom was probably
the only learning environment where it felt perfectly natural to speak
Chinese to non-Chinese people. Even today, I know most of the other
disciples only by their Chinese names—I had to look up half of their
"real" names just to write this section.

Outside of Master Ding's Happy Classroom, we didn't see too much
of each other. Everyone had his or her own work, life, studies. We were

all very different people, brought together by a common interest and diverse circumstances.

But we also shared an inherent familial love that didn't need to be explicitly addressed. In order to survive in a new culture, we had all dulled our edges, flattened our curves, to fit into boxes that were close to, but not quite, the real shape of ourselves. As we assimilated, we chafed. We wanted to break out of that box, sharpen ourselves again, and re-become the version of ourselves we were back home.

You know. Make jokes. Be funny. Like real people.

But we also knew something deeper. We all knew we were very far from home, and we were all odd ducks. In a country that was new and challenging, we didn't want to just survive, we wanted to laugh. We wanted to thrive. If we didn't treat each other as family, then we had no one for miles and miles who would.

We were a family—and Master Ding was our father.

Teacher, Father

The word for "master" in Chinese, 师父 (*shifu*) is made up of the characters for teacher (师) and father (父). It is different from the word used to describe a slave owner, or even an expert at their craft. It is a powerful word that is used very sparingly. To become a disciple to a master is to join their family.

Master Ding's master was a man named Hou Baolin, who is probably the most famous Chinese comedian of the last hundred years. Known as "the Chinese Charlie Chaplin," Great-Master Hou was a xiangsheng heavyweight and the star of China's first-ever comedy movie. He has a wax statue in the Beijing Madame Tussauds. When Mao Zedong wanted to laugh, he called Great-Master Hou to his private quarters to perform xiangsheng over and over again. Master Ding went with him.

Great-Master Hou's master was a man named Zhu Kuoquan, who went by the stage name Big Bread. And *his* master . . . the family tree goes on and on, all the way back to Qiong Bupa from the Qing dynasty.

When I first arrived, I was a "student" to Master Ding, but not a formal disciple. Almost three years later, I kowtowed before him at a ceremony and accepted his gift of a fan. Unfurled, the front sheaves of the fan showed Master Ding's own calligraphy, reading, "弄月嘲风": "Joke the moon and satirize the wind."

The moon references the heavens—the eternal firmament; the celestial, expansive canopy that envelops us all. The wind recalls the ever-changing vagaries of fashion and convention; here one moment and blown away the next, sometimes never to return, sometimes ebbing and swirling, always moving.

The message was about the nature of being a true comedian, that one can—and should—be brave and artful enough to make comedy about anything. The space between tradition and change—between the moon and the wind—encompasses all.

This gift, and the ceremony, made me a true disciple, and a member of our little family forever.

Like a father, the master is an educator, adviser, confidant, friend, and mentor. In the comedy world, they also serve as an acting coach, editor, writing partner, booking agent, PR front-runner, and spokesperson. I don't know any better way of describing the relationship, other than to say that if I were stuck in jail and only got one phone call, I'd call Master Ding, because I know he would move heaven and earth to get his son out.

First Lesson, Little Children

Master Ding's students, Chinese and Other alike, all have the same first assignment.

"This is a monologue called 'Little Children.' I want you to learn it." He handed me a script—a dense, block-shaped monologue of about a hundred Chinese characters. At a glance, I noticed that I knew probably about 60 percent of them. That seemed pretty good at the time.

"Mo Kai, come over here and perform 'Little Children' for him."

Mo Kai was an American named Canaan Morse. Canaan was born in Maine and had lived in China five years already, four of which he had spent studying under Master Ding. A Chinese poetry fanatic who ran a literary magazine in Beijing, he was a little taller than me and much, much better at Chinese. I was a bit in awe of him, like I was looking at a version of myself that I could attain, if I worked hard enough.

He opened his mouth, and sound blasted forth with precision and pitch:

"在相当出, 大宋朝文彦博幼儿倒有罐穴浮球之知," said the Mainer.

In ancient times, Wen Yanbo of the Great Song dynasty possessed the knowledge to float a ball up from a hole by pouring in water.

It went on like that, full bore, nonstop, literary reference after literary reference, for a full minute.

And I knew 60 percent. Of the characters. Ha. Ha. Ha. Not even close to useful.

I'll always remember this, though: Even though I had no clue what was being said, it sounded awesome. Xiangsheng performers are taught to speak with such energy, intensity, and purpose that they can draw the audience into the performance with just their technique. It had a pace and a pulse to it that drove through the air. It was great to listen to.

That being said . . .

What the hell was all that just now? Wen Yanbo? Song dynasty? Something about a ball?

"These are stories," Master Ding told me and the rest of the Happy Classroom. "Wen Yanbo was a child who lost his ball down a hole. But, very cleverly, he realized that he could pour water down the hole and get his ball back."

I realized that each sentence was a different historical reference to a child who, despite their age, either attained high social status through merit or came up with clever solutions to problems that even adults couldn't figure out.

I wasn't immediately sure how this related to comedy. The piece wasn't particularly funny. Unless I was missing something?

Which was possible. If I missed the joke, I wouldn't notice.

It didn't matter, in any case. I had to learn to do this bit. The first challenge had been set.

It seems really stupid, but the first problem I had in learning "Little Children" was how to breathe.

When I did my first at-home read-through, I found myself getting tongue-tied and short of breath. It wasn't a language problem—though

I had plenty of those. It was that the length of the sentences dictated a breathing pattern that needed to be followed precisely or else the whole piece unraveled.

"These monologues are an important part of the core skill set of becoming a xiangsheng performer," Master Ding told me. "It's about *how* you get the words out. Bring the audience into the show with your language. Show off your skill. First, make them like you."

In improv comedy, there are literally an infinite number of "right" ways of moving a scene forward. In stand-up, I have the freedom to write my own jokes, which means that for better or worse, the way I breathe is totally up to me while I'm performing.

But "Little Children" was part of a group of pieces called *Traditional Works*, which have been passed down from master to disciple for the last hundred years. Since every artist is different, there were still many ways to do the pieces correctly. But all of those many ways involve getting through the routine without becoming out of breath or tongue-tied, and the works were written with specific places to take breaths.

I sat on my ratty black couch in my Beijing studio apartment, read the piece fifty times aloud to myself, and slowly learned how to breathe again.

Wrong Tones

At Beijing University of Chemical Technology, there is a massive statue of Mao Zedong made out of some kind of pinkish rock. He is raising his hand in greeting and is so tall his sightline stares over the entry gate, straight at a highway overpass across the road.

Every Saturday, I ride past Mao (hi, Mao!), air-high-five his massive, outturned hand, park my e-bike, go up a flight of stairs, take a right, and find myself at room 214: Master Ding's Happy Classroom.

Why is comedy taught at Beijing University of Chemical Technology?

Because the guy who runs the key room is a fan of Master Ding, that's why.

Welcome to entertainment, where things happen for every reason but making sense!

"'In ancient times, Wen Yanbo of the Great Song dynasty realized he possessed the knowledge to float a ball up from a hole by pouring in water.'"

I managed to get through the whole piece, only peeking at my script twice. It felt pretty good. Everyone clapped. That felt good, too. My spirits lifted. Back at home on my ratty couch,* it seemed silly to spend

---

* This couch was really gross. When I rented the furnished room, there was a nice-looking blanket on the couch. But after signing the contract, I removed the blanket and found the

hours to memorize a one-minute monologue. Now it seemed totally worth it.

This was one of my first introductions to the bipolar mood swings of being a comedian. When you do well, the world seems amazing, and your life is not just meaningful, but blissful and somehow sacred. When you bomb, you suck, your life sucks, and what the hell are you doing with yourself, you waste of space?

"Not bad!" Master Ding said, then turned and addressed the others in the room. "Did anyone understand what he said?"

Silence. Some shaking heads. Very quickly, I was a waste of space.

Master Ding saw my reaction and grinned at me. "It's not that bad. But you've got a tone problem."

I should explain: Mandarin Chinese is a tonal language, which means that the pitch at which one says a word is an inseparable part of the meaning of that word. If the pitch is off, the word doesn't make sense—or, more likely, you've just said something completely different than you intended to.

In Mandarin, there are four tones: first tone, high and flat; second tone, rising pitch; third tone, low dip; and fourth tone, sharp fall. This seems hard. In Cantonese, there are *nine* tones. I cannot speak Cantonese, and honestly don't know how anyone does.

In Mandarin, there's also a fifth, neutral, tone. When speaking this tone, you need to be purposefully blank.

---

faux leather was so rotten it literally just started shedding everywhere. For a long time, I would often accidently rub against the couch and it would just come off on me, leaving flakes all over my clothes for me to shed the rest of the day, like dark dandruff. Of course, I was too cheap to buy another couch in a rented apartment. I am using this footnote as a sort of exorcism— perhaps, by making you all think about the couch, I will finally be able to leave it behind and never think about it again. Then, its torment of me will be finished, transferred to you.

As you can imagine, this means that misunderstandings accumulate quickly. I often show my friends a meme online to explain how far things can go because of a missed tone. The meme shows a language teacher introducing a simple sentence:

"Miss, how much for a bowl of dumplings?"

"小姐，水饺一碗多少钱？"

Xiao(2)Jie(3), Shui(3)Jiao(3)Yi(1)Wan(3)Duo(1)Shao(3)Qian(2)?

With two tonal mistakes, this becomes "Miss, how much to sleep with you for a night?"*

"小姐，睡觉一晚多少钱？"

Xiao(2)Jie(3), Shui(4)Jiao(4)Yi(1)Wan(3)Duo(1)Shao(3)Qian(2)?

Perhaps you are beginning to see the outside edges of how screwed I am. How do you tell jokes in a language where one mistake in tone can completely change the meaning of the words?

Speakers of tonal languages like Chinese can learn nontonal languages without major readjustment to their concept of spoken language.

The "Chinese accent" in English usually swings between two challenges: Speakers may remove all affect altogether, rattling off words flat and like a machine gun:

"WhereAreWeGoingTonight?"

Or, they wind up adding tones to words that have none:

"Where are WE goING toNIGHT?"

These language snags are real, but it's a whole different ball game to go from nontonal to tonal languages. For nontonal speakers to learn tonal languages, the whole concept of what a word is has to shift. It requires changing who you are as a human being. That process has several stages.

---

* Also, the Chinese word for *Miss*, which is an innocuous enough word in English, can also be slang for *prostitute*. Hooray context!

I will take you through the emotional phases of recognizing tone challenges, one by one. Imagine you are arriving in China for the first time.

Stage One: Denial

You have just arrived at the airport in Beijing for the first time. You've been here three minutes.

But hey! Already you've seen a poorly translated sign, dodged a sketchy man trying to get you into a black cab, and almost been run over by a bus. You also got a glimpse of someone wearing a shirt saying, "Y'all Need Jesus," and you are 95 percent sure they don't know what that means. You feel excited. You're in China!

You know that Chinese is hard and that the language is tonal, so some miscommunication will be unavoidable. But it can't be that bad, right? Is it really possible that a minor change in the tone of a word can change a dumpling order into a proposition? A pig into a spider? Shoes into diarrhea?* Surely there must be something, you know, evolutionarily impossible about that. Yeah. Darwin's got you covered.

It's time to get into the cab. You're heading to a hotel, and you've got the address written out in English letters. It now strikes you that perhaps the cab driver will not be able to read English letters. Maybe you should have copied and pasted those Chinese characters from the website. But the characters showed up in Microsoft Word as just a weird series of boxes, and at the time you felt prepared due to the mere fact

---

* Both real examples. You think I'm joking but I'm not; I got hundreds of these.

you'd printed things out ahead of time on actual pieces of paper and put them in a folder labeled "China."

At the time, you felt like this meant you were really on top of your shit. Now, this seems like a capital-O Oversight.

But no problem! You can read him the address in English letters and he'll probably get it.

It doesn't work.

You try again.

It doesn't work.

You enter stage two.

Stage Two: Anger

Really, what is this guy's problem?

You're speaking slowly enough and clearly enough. It's almost like he doesn't want to hear you. It can't possibly be this difficult.

Also, isn't this a tourist place? Don't they expect English speakers around here? Wasn't the whole point of those two hundred years of colonialism and global dominion by those people from that island that speak the same language as you so that you can personally benefit by saving a few seconds of time communicating with underpaid, overworked cab drivers?

Really, it's quite rude at this point. You. Are. Speaking. Clearly.

Why. Will. He. Not. Understand.

Jing. Cheng. Da. Sha. That's what it says on the paper.

Sounded right to me!

Jing. Cheng—no! Don't look at your phone, listen! *Why aren't you listening closely?!?!*

You enter stage three.

Stage Three: Bargaining

OK, OK. Calm down. We can find a way to make this work. Let's forget that literally thirty seconds ago I was yelling at you as if you were a slow child. We can deal with this like adults.

Maybe if I give you the paper to hold, things will change. Yes! Take it. See? Maybe you can understand it. I know it doesn't have any of those tone markers on it, but between the two of us we can probably ferret it out. It's near a place called San Li Tun. Wait, why did you make a motion like drinking a beer? Are you trying to take me to a bar?

Hmm. OK. A bar isn't bad. I could get a drink. Maybe there is someone at the bar that can speak English. I can drag the checked bag and put it under a table, relax a bit, get a little sloshed. That will probably even help out with the all-consuming waves of anxiety pulsing through the left side of my brain right now.

See, we're moving! We're getting somewhere!

It's not the plan I came with, but it's the new plan! It's a good plan! We came up with it together! I am still in control!

You enter stage four.

Stage Four: Depression

Where are we going?

When will we get there?

I have lost control of my life.

Why am I in a place where I cannot communicate with anyone.

Am I really going to live here.

How will I eat.

How will I get coffee.

Do they have coffee?

Oh my god. They might not have coffee.

I didn't think of that.

How will I know which bottle is shampoo and which is conditioner? They're going to look exactly the same.

Conditioner is usually in the skinnier bottle. Right?

Let me think back about all the conditioner I've ever used. Is there a pattern?

This is unproductive.

My hair is going to be a mess.

I want to ignore the fact that China exists and go back home where things make sense.

Hmm. Ignoring the country with the biggest population and the largest economy in the world because it makes me uncomfortable and I don't know how I fit into this new world does not seem like a good idea.

Damn.

You enter stage five.

Stage Five: Acceptance

You know what? This is OK.

No, not in that "I'll convince myself it's OK but it's actually giving me an ulcer" way. It's actually OK.

It's the first great story of your adventures in China. It makes sense that things are hard. You've flown halfway across the world. And you know what? I bet those tones get easier the longer you stay here. It will start with learning the address of the hotel, but eventually you'll be able to talk with all sorts of people about all sorts of things.

It might take longer to get there than expected. But that's OK. It's not like you're in a rush anyway. The cabs are cheap, the world's an adventure, and it's only going to get better from here.

And maybe one day, the tones will stop sounding like tones. Your brain will fail to distinguish pitch independent of meaning. Then, you'll be left with a ghost in your brain, a memory imprinted from the beforetime when you heard the world differently and, perhaps without meaning to, judged the people with the singsongy, silly-sounding language.

But now your ears and brain have developed new wiring, and in what seemed before like noise, you can now hear the fever of life. You realize that language divides us like a sharp, straight-line shadow cast by the overhang of a cliff. Despite the sunlight ending suddenly in what appears to be a black pit, in reality the ground continues, solid and the same as the step before, just lit differently. The boundary between here and there—between us and them—does not exist. The boundary is an illusion.

And if one boundary is illusory, how many more are just like that?

You've just arrived in Beijing for the first time. You've been here five minutes.

Family Guy, the Song Dynasty, and Translating Comedy

My first attempt to solve my tone problem was through brute force.

I took a pen and marked out the tone of every character I'd misspoken at the last Happy Classroom meeting—which was most of them. I sat on the couch and repeated them over and over.

The next week, I stood on the small stage at the Happy Classroom and tried it again. This time, I had the tones down perfectly—in the way a robot speaks "perfectly."

The tones were right; the language was awful. This is a hurdle that many Chinese learners come to. In trying to conquer the challenge of Chinese that is unique to English speakers—the tones—they forget the flow.

I was a choppy mess, speaking! Every! Word! Perfectly! No linguistic flow, definitely no comedic flow. It was probably worse than last week's effort.

At the end, there was a pause.

"Did anyone understand him?" Master Ding asked.

A couple of raised hands tentatively bubbled up in the classroom.

"Did anyone enjoy themselves?"

Laughter. Nope! My. Performance. Was. Not. Fun. At. All.

"Jesse, do you know what you're doing here?"

"Learning xiangsheng?"

"Telling stories. Tell the story."

This time, I set about researching the stories in the piece.

Wen Yanbo of the Great Song dynasty knew the trick to pouring water down a hole to float a ball.

Master Ding had told me that one. What's the next one?

Sima Wengong had the idea to break the cistern to save the child.

In this story, a baby had fallen into a big clay jug of water, one with a mouth too small to reach into. As the adults freaked out, Sima Wengong, a child himself, smashed the pot with a stick, and saved the baby.

Cool. Next?

Han Kongrong knew at four years of age the correct way to gift pears.

What is this stuff?

Part of me—the part of me possessed of a masochistic curiosity—was fascinated by these stories. They were a glimpse into the seemingly bottomless well that is Chinese culture. But another part of me kept saying, *These stories have nothing to do with you. You are possibly the only American comedian in the country. Doesn't comedy come from life? You need to do stuff that has to do with you and your life—stuff that works for you.*

What future was there in doing comedy concerned with ancient history? This piece was a hundred years old—even contemporary Chinese people nowadays wouldn't find this funny.

Zhou Yu from the Wu kingdom was appointed admiral of the navy at the age of thirteen, gathered great armies from six provinces and eighty-one states, tricked others by harming himself to create a false sense of weakness, engaged many ploys designed to fool his enemies, caught the eastern wind,

burned many enemy boats, causing Cao Cao to turn and flee, almost result-
ing in him losing his life south of the Yangtze . . .

I'm missing all the references.

Is this how Chinese people feel when watching American shows?

I watched a lot of comedy shows when I was growing up. I really liked *Family Guy*, specifically because of its insistence on making purposefully obscure or obtuse references. Like in one episode, where Peter Griffin says, "I've screwed up worse than Disney did when they cast Michael J. Fox in that *Zorro* remake." Then, the scene cuts to two Mexicans:

"Who was that masked man that saved us?"

"I don't know, but he left his insignia!"

The camera then pans to a wall incised with a bunch of illegible scribbles with the vaguest likeness of a Z.

If you don't know Michael J. Fox or Zorro, it makes as little sense as Wen Yanbo and his ball.*

We have our celebrities, stories, people, names, places. They have theirs. Our comedy is ours because we reference what is ours—our lives, our people, our places. Theirs is theirs because they reference theirs.

But who are "we" and who are "they"? Sure, Americans won't get a Zhou Yu reference, but they would get Jackie Chan. Chinese wouldn't get Zorro, but they would get Michael Jordan. The reference divide is real. But it's not total. We do have middle ground.

If I'm going to do comedy in another country, for another culture, I need to know what they know. If I reference something, will they get it? If they don't get it, can I explain it?

How can I explain it, if I don't know their references?

---

* L. P. Hartley wrote that "The past is a foreign country; they do things differently there." Our own country is its own foreign country—I bet all the younger people that follow me on TikTok or Instagram might not get the reference to Michael J. Fox or Zorro, either.

I needed to learn to know what they know.

It kind of felt like a Venn diagram: There were things I knew, things they knew, and right in the middle, that's where I would find my best LOLs.

I realized what Master Ding was doing by giving me these old, seemingly irrelevant xiangsheng routines. He was keying me in to what the audience knows, the deep-background culture that created the world we live in today.

The modern references in our jokes—our movies, our online hot takes, our fashion sensibilities—are like trees in a forest: some big, some small, expanding outward and upward to near infinity, groves upon groves to the end of our vision. How to count them all? How to know them all? Impossible.

But the deep-background culture references in traditional xiangsheng are not really like a tree. Maybe they were at one point, but they have long since fallen, decomposed, and turned into mulch. Now, they are the soil the new trees grow in.

Master Ding knew I wanted to get laughs, as soon as possible. But rather than picking one tree in the forest, and making me practice one joke, he instructed me to reach into the dirt, spread my fingers, and feel what holds the forest together.

I *could* talk about my life, my experiences, my point of view. But if I wanted them to laugh, too, I could only do that within the framework of what they know about me already.

This idea—start with what they know—became the basis for how I later began writing my own Chinese stand-up. When I found a topic I cared about, and that the audience could reference their own context, I tried to develop it. If I thought it was funny, but it turned out there needed to be too much cultural translation in order to get the audience there, I put it aside.

For instance, I do a joke about being a Bostonian in Beijing:

"We've got our own accent in Boston. We drop the *R*'s from everything. Instead of 'I park my car in Harvard Yard,' we say, 'I pahk my cah in Hahvahd Yahd.'"

That already gets a laugh here—apparently the Boston accent sounds funny even to people who don't understand it.

"So, when I got to Beijing, I discovered something: All those *R*'s we left off of our words . . . they're all here in Beijing!"

Another laugh from the Chinese audience, because this is playing into their knowledge pool. They know that Beijingers have a special accent where they love to add *R*'s onto the end of words.

All that's left now is to do an act-out: accenting all the *-er*'s:

"My Beijinger friend called me on the phone, like '*Gemer! Yaobu qu dongwuyuanr pangbianr de fanguanr chi yidiar!*'"

In English, this sentence isn't funny—"Hey Bro, let's go to a restaurant near the zoo and get a bite to eat!"—but in Mandarin it sounds like a bunch of dogs yapping at each other. The audience gave me a big, start-and-stop-and-start-again laugh.

What do *I* know? What do *they* know? What do *we* know?

The moment I realized that it was *their* references I should look for, and not my own, things clarified. I began hitting more jokes in my open mics; I found that starting with references they knew meant I had a shot at connecting my own experiences in a way they found funny and original.

For instance, when I do jokes about going to the gym in China, there are some that aren't China-specific:

"I hate working out, because while I am working out, I only have one thought, and that's, 'Damn, I hate working out.'"

But for the Chinese audience, there are specific gym-related references that only work there:

"You know those guys that stand outside the gyms, giving out discount fliers, who attack you on the street going, 'Wanna work out? Wanna work out?'"

In Beijing, that's usually good for a laugh already, since yes, everyone knows those people, and everyone has thrown a few dozen of those fliers in the trash can, probably while still in view of the guy who handed it to them.*

However, I told a story of a time I actually was looking for a gym, and, to the guy's shocked delight, gave him my email and phone number in exchange for a week's free access to the gym. The true price? A deluge of spam phone calls every day about buying a membership, which no phone-number-blocking technology could stop.

"You give them one bit of personal information and they'll never give up until you join the gym. I think their talents are wasted on gyms. They should send these guys to catch terrorists.

"'This terrorist killed sixty civilians in Syria. He's a bad man.'

"'I don't care how bad he is! All I care is: Does he wanna work out???'

"'Yes! Yes! He *does* want to work out. And! He wants to buy a membership. But first you have to find him.'

"'I'm on it!'"

Big laughs.

Once I started thinking about comedy references through the lens of "What we know" vs. "What they know," it was a quick leap to the next question: Who are "we"? Who are "they"?

Does this have everything to do with me being American, and them Chinese?

---

* "Wanna work out?" was such a known catchphrase that a friend of mine named their improv troupe, "We Don't Work Out."

Or, does it have nothing to do with that?

I did find that jokes comparing Americans and Chinese worked—but so did other ways of dividing people into groups.

It could be gym people vs. non–gym people, gamers vs. non-gamers, people who use selfie sticks vs. tolerable, respectable human beings, etc.

I found I could also pit myself against myself: the part of myself that wants to be in good shape vs. the part of myself that wants to eat a whole basket of fries right now. In that joke, we are all "us," and we are all "them."

In the end, I started to think of the whole difference between "Chinese" comedy and "American" comedy as simply the graph of how these two circles overlap, or don't. But knowing what country someone was from was really less useful than knowing things about how they lived. Do they live in a city or the countryside? Do they take transit or have a chauffeur? Did they go to college? How much money is a lot of money to them?

These questions have something to do with nationality, but not as much as you might think. The line between what "they" know and what "we" know is very blurry. So, I tried to stop thinking of things in terms of nationality, or race, and instead in terms of life experience, where nationality and race only came into play if it meant those things were core to the topic of the joke.

To do comedy for people who are different from me, I found I needed to stand in their shoes. But I don't need to stand in their passports. And I definitely don't need to stand in their 23andMe results.

So, if nationality isn't the most important thing, or race, or ethnicity, then what does that leave us with?

It leaves us with stories.

All humans tell stories, and the broad strokes of those stories are more similar than we think.

Storytelling through comedy is both delicate and strong; the delicacy comes from how easy it is for a joke to die—one reference to an unknown part of the story can kill the funny. But the opposite is also true: If we see ourselves in another person's stories, it can connect us in a way that seems deeper than culture itself.

We tell stories every day, not realizing that our stories are built on stories, our references built on older references, our worldview shaped by what our parents thought to teach us, and what they learned from their parents. We are all trees, our roots dug deep in our native soil.

Can you get by, day to day, without knowing about Wen Yanbo of the Song dynasty and his cleverness? Definitely.

Can you do comedy in another country, and culture, without knowing their history, their stories, their references?

I wasn't sure, but I knew what Master Ding thought.

How to Be a Good Disciple

In the Happy Classroom, almost all the learning was taught implicitly. I just had to keep my eyes and ears open and absorb a hundred-plus years of best practices in comedy.

I also learned how to be a good disciple. Here are some tips.

Take the Master's Bag

Whenever Master Ding enters a room, there is an instant shuffling of chairs. People from all spots in the room rush over at a pace somewhere between a jog and a dash. It's a bit like the giddy-up half step that people do when crossing a street and they see a car coming, so they can show the other person they are hurrying without breaking into a run.

Their job is to take Master Ding's bags, coat, water bottle—whatever he might be holding. His job is to refuse this small nicety, twisting this way and that, and then "give in" and allow his disciples to carry the bag the fifteen feet or so to his seat.

At first, I saw this and I thought it was a bit silly. All these people from all these countries—why are they participating in this charade? But after studying with Master Ding for years, I noticed other, seemingly unrelated small acts that reminded me of the entire Happy Classroom darting for his bag.

For example: Once, during a visit to his home, I spotted on his computer five different versions of meticulously maintained Word documents introducing me and my other disciples. These were promo materials primed to be sent to the various TV stations, newspapers, and other parties that would contact him about our shows.

Or once, during a TV shoot, he wandered back around to me and whispered in my ear, "That woman over there is the booker. I told her you do stand-up, too. Reach out to her again and you can try to get on the show again in a few months."

Master Ding did all sorts of things for us without our asking. Carrying his coat, refilling his hot water bottle—these were little things we could do without his asking.

And since we knew Master Ding was a man who would never ask for help—not even, as I would later find out, when in deathly peril—we knew the value of these little tasks, to make sure he knew we were here for him, just as he was here for us.

Once I figured that out, I began to rush over and take his bags, too.

Fold the Master's Robe

The traditional Chinese robe worn during xiangsheng is called a *da gua*, which means . . . "robe."*

Back in the late Qing dynasty, it was something a normal person on the street—or a street performer telling jokes—might wear. Back then,

---

* See, I bet you thought it was something strange and mystical. That's called Orientalism and most Chinese people hate it, because it means Westerners might see them as a nation of Crouching Tigers and Hidden Dragons and not real people who wear jeans and just got scratches on the screen of their brand-new phone, for the third time.

It's a robe. Just a robe.

it served a practical use, too. Performers would roll up the tops of the sleeves but not the bottoms, because that way they could take coins from passersby, tuck them inside, and continue gesticulating without delay.

Nowadays, performers still perform with the tops of the sleeves rolled up, but the robe itself has become a cultural prop of sorts. It is synonymous with xiangsheng itself, so much so that I incorporated it into one of our logo designs for my US–China Comedy Center.

It's also extremely comfortable.

Shortly after I arrived in Beijing, Master Ding brought me to get fitted for a robe. Along with us came Lao Cui, a sixty-year-old Chinese disciple of Master Ding who was himself a high-level xiangsheng performer.

"This woman makes the best robes in the city," Master Ding told me. "All the best performers get them from her."

Her "shop" turned out to be in a basement apartment in a rundown Soviet-era residential block in poorer south Beijing. Walking down to the second basement level, the lights in the ceiling overhead were coated in an eternal layer of dust and turned on only when triggered by an ancient motion detector, meaning that every half-flight of stairs we had to smash our feet against the concrete to keep the staircase lit.

A nondescript door led to a scene that seemed straight out of a low-budget fairy tale. In a room with the grim ambiance of a dungeon, tall bolts of dyed cloth leaned against all four walls of gray concrete. A single, sepia-colored light bulb hung from a greasy, knobbly wire, its light confusing the eye, shifting the colors of the cloth. The entirety of the tiny space was occupied by massive machinery—strange clothes-making devices with spindly metal arms and sewing machines that looked straight out of a 1950s Soviet version of the Sears catalog.

The woman, whom Master Ding and Lao Cui referred to simply as "Auntie," measured me up and down ten different ways. Her hands flew around my body with unconscious competence. "Where's this one from?"

"America," they answered for me.

"America." She repeated back, bored. There was not much chatting.

We spent less than ten minutes in the cloth-ringed room. Two weeks later, I went down the creepy staircase again to retrieve my robe. It was a creamy vanilla color with Chinese-style knot buttons that fit through loops attached to the sides of the garment. It even had a pocket sewn into the lining by the chest just the right size for a smartphone.

Once, Master Ding and I performed at a retirement center for old Communist Party cadres. About fifteen minutes before our show, we changed into our robes. I put mine on and he practically hissed.

"Look at these creases! Stand up straight."

He tugged at the cloth near my shoulder. There was a deep furrow that connected the right overlapping flap to below the left shoulder. I stood there feeling like a five-foot, ten-inch toddler who tried his very best to get dressed but apparently couldn't manage it.

"Take it off and lay it on the table," Master Ding ordered, his eyes scanning the room. As I laid the robe out, Master Ding found what he wanted: a bottle of Nongfu Spring water.

He took a quick sip and then spat all over my robe in a fine mist. "*Pull!*" he ordered. We grabbed opposite sides of the robe near the crease. Master Ding put the bottle to his mouth again and atomized another small sip of water. The crease disappeared almost entirely.

He looked down with satisfaction. "Nobody spits like that anymore," he told me, completely unironically.

Nope! They don't!

We performed fifteen minutes of a traditional piece entitled "Matching New Year's Scrolls," a good fit for an older, more conservative audience. Afterward, we stayed for a swift lunch at a big, round table, and then packed up our outfits to head back into the city.

Master Ding saw me folding my robe and sighed. "Let me show you how to do that." He grabbed it from my hands and deftly folded the long, awkward garment so fast, it looked like a magic trick. I had to ask him to slow down again so I could see his hands extend the sleeves, pinch the nape of the neckpiece, and hook his elbow underneath to fold the robe in half.

"There was a time when new disciples would spend their first two years doing nothing but folding the master's robe," he said. "I don't ask that of my students. I want you to learn quicker. But you should know how to do this. The robe is the first thing the audience sees onstage. Try to make it look good."

After this day, whenever we finished shows and took off our robes, I would hurry over at the classic little skip-jog pace, and relieve Master Ding of his robe and fold it. I am glad to say he never had to spit all over my clothing ever again.

Always Be Available

I got a text message. "What are you doing on Thursday night?" Master Ding asked.

That means, "Make yourself free on Thursday night."

When I first arrived to study xiangsheng, I didn't know what that would actually look like. My Fulbright essay about how I would spend seven days a week studying comedy was pretty vague, with a lot of "reading scripts" and "going to shows" as research.

It turned out that Saturdays were spent in the Happy Classroom, and other than that we self-studied—except for shows we performed at, which we needed to be able to slot into our schedules on short notice.

The Master's job includes that of a show booker. People with theaters, TV stations, and companies that need entertainers know Master Ding and his disciples. This meant he was always getting shows for us—and turning down shows that he felt used his disciples as puppets and tools.

A comedian needs to be funny, but a disciple is useless if they're not able to drop whatever they're doing to do some shows. I learned to keep a few days free before a show, too. We would use that time to practice our routines over and over again wherever we could—anywhere from an extra room at a college where Master Ding had connections to the lobby of Master Ding's building, or even in his apartment.

This "always on the clock" mentality was encouraged, but not compulsory. Obviously, if there is a real excuse—illness, school finals, taking family around China—you can turn down a gig and say you have something to do on Thursday night. But all things being equal—you should free yourself up Thursday night.

That's what a good disciple would do.

Listen to What They Say. But Actually.

Here's a challenge: Shut up.

I found it really, really hard at the beginning of my study with Master Ding to say *nothing*. Saying *something* felt like an innate human reaction for me. After all, Americans, especially artists, are brought up to believe that the soul of being an individual is to have an opinion. This is doubly true of artists, and three times as true for comedians. And what is the point of having an opinion if you don't IMMEDIATELY TELL EVERYONE???

In the beginning of learning with Master Ding, after he gave me notes to improve my performance, I asked questions. I probed. I thought it was my job to make sure that his advice took into account what I felt were my own thoughts and experiences.

When I did this, things dragged. It took a lot longer to get through feedback. Some of the older disciples squirmed uncomfortably. *Just take the note.*

Eventually, I decided to try something new. What would happen if I just shut up? After all, Master Ding had done comedy for over fifty years. Maybe he knew what he was talking about.

Of course, we always "listen."* Some of us learn to "take the note" and disagree silently. These are both things that mentors and students do outside of a master/disciple system.

The hard part was taking this to the next level: listening, and regardless of what you think, integrating what the Master says as true.

This is easy when the Master's advice is obviously correct.

"Jesse, you have a tendency to shuffle your weight from foot to foot, and it makes the audience dizzy. Stop doing that."

"Jesse, you are staring over the heads of the audience. Stop doing that. Make eye contact."

"Jesse, you talk too fast."

"Jesse, you talk too slow."

"Jesse, stop trying to steal the stage."

It is harder when the advice is not as obviously correct.

"Jesse, you need to stop making blatantly political jokes."

Master Ding gave me that advice after I showed him a copy of a comedy music video I had made, called "Reimburse That $hit." In it, I play a lowly office worker at a Chinese company who is at the bottom

---

* My work as an improv performer and teacher has taught me that no, we don't actually listen that well at all. But that's another topic for another time.

of the totem pole at work—but lives the luxury life of a rap god because he can reimburse everything with company money.

The piece was a satire of a real phenomenon that takes place in Chinese companies all the time—everyone knows if the paperwork is real, it doesn't matter whether what the papers say happened actually happened. I sing the song along with the music video in my live shows and it kills: *This kind of help only comes from heavenly assistance / Giving us capitalism with reimbursable characteristics.*

But Master Ding was upset. "You want the audience to like you. All of the audience," he said, stressing the *all*. Meaning, there are many audiences in China, and some of them are not to be messed with. "I know you want to do these jokes. But don't. Just don't."

I normally found little to argue with in Master Ding's advice, so my doubt stuck out like a thorn in my mind. I thought I knew the note's psychological roots: Master Ding had survived a lot of turbulence. For ten years during the Cultural Revolution, he had performed for coal miners in rural Shanxi Province, doing "reformed" crosstalk shows, hundreds of shows a year. He'd lived through bad times, and seen some bad things.

But on this point I felt like I was right—everything I knew about comedy told me that there needs to be a certain edge, or else it feels flat. I felt I was doing the right thing for the piece by giving it that edge. And if I can't express myself, what's the point of doing comedy?

A few months later, I overheard Master Ding backstage.

We were at a random show—I forget where and when. Just a standard variety show, where we performed a twenty-five-minute piece as one of five or six acts. Sometimes at these shows, we bump into other members of the old-school xiangsheng circle, and Master Ding will have long discussions with the other masters about who's doing good xiangsheng (almost nobody), who's doing bad xiangsheng (pretty much everybody), and how their masters were better than anyone around now.

"Great-Master Liu Baorui, for example," Master Ding said in conversation with another septuagenarian xiangsheng artist. "That guy was so good. He could go on for hours and everyone would love it. He had great timing and rhythm. You could know every word of his routine and it would still be funny. Then there was the Cultural Revolution."

There was a pause in the conversation. A pull like a rubber band stretching. A black hole four seconds deep.

China is full of these silences. It is a country where sometimes, for cultural or political reasons, there are no words to say. They show up everywhere—in discussions about sex, or pollution, or criminal justice, or corruption. Words are a butcher's cleaver hacking through the silken spider's web of propriety; silence is a porcelain scalpel that slices the web with a whisper.

Oftentimes, the right thing to say is nothing. For many Chinese, those extra, engorged, untimely lulls are louder than shouted expletives.

Except that Master Ding is old, and apparently doesn't give a shit anymore, because after a few beats of silence he completed the sentence.

"Such a great xiangsheng performer, and nobody knows where he's buried."

I felt a stone drop into the pit of my stomach. I entertained the idea that my Chinese was lousy and I'd misheard. Even years later, I wondered if I had let my anxiety get the better of me and, in reality, Liu Baorui's grave is a celebrated cultural landmark. But I don't think it is.*

---

* When I wrote this chapter I decided it was time to see if this story was true or if I had misheard. The following is from Baidu Encyclopedia's entry on Liu Baorui: "During the cultural revolution, Liu Baorui suffered severe persecution and was sent to the Beijing suburb of Fangshan for reeducation through labor. On August 6th, 1968, while laboring, he suffered a public denouncement and was killed at the age of 53. His body was hastily buried and subsequent searches have not yielded any results. His cenotaph is interred at Chaoyang Cemetery."

I wanted to keep my comedy "edgy" because my focus was on my one piece, my one joke. For one piece, and one joke, I might have been correct. Master Ding was looking out for all my jokes, for my career. I was correct; he was *right*.

We are a long way from the Cultural Revolution. The times we live in are far from the most open period in Chinese comedy, but comedians today are not disappeared and killed.*

But Master Ding's point to me was greater than that. *Look at the comedians who succeed in China. The shows that air, that get large audiences, that are renewed season after season, whose performers are respected, successful, and happy.*

Are they doing overtly political comedy?

No, they aren't.

In China, you can have an opinion. You can share that opinion anytime you'd like with your friends. Usually, you can also share it at small live shows, and sometimes you can even share it with millions. Even if it's unpopular, or political, you won't get deported, or fined, or dragged to the Public Security Bureau. And even though I have seen friends get in trouble over the years, it almost never has to do with the joke—the joke is merely the excuse to justify action.

But even if the stakes are not quite life and death, if your comedic mindset doesn't fit with the long-term strategy of the development of the nation, you won't win in the long term, either.

"You want the audience to like you."

Tell the jokes you can so you can keep telling them.

That was Master Ding's advice.

---

* Comedians that run afoul of things today are essentially just blacklisted and never get to perform again. This has, unfortunately, happened to a couple friends of mine over the years. But all of them are alive and contactable.

Master Ding is human. Despite his wisdom, he isn't some fairy-tale fortune teller who dispenses ancient knowledge in the form of riddles. By the time I met him, he was old, conservative, and stubborn in his worldview, even though that world was changing very quickly. Sometimes that led me to question him. The thorns would once again sprout.

But he is one of the best teachers I've ever had, and I'm not from this country.

I ignore him at my own peril.

Speak, Imitate, Joke, Sing

Master Ding's hand swirled across the blackboard, leaving in its wake four characters on the blackboard in red chalk. The characters flowed together elegantly; he had developed some type of calligraphy that meant he never needed to lift his hand. The chalk did not squeak, though the resulting characters were (to my eye) nearly illegible.

说学逗唱

Speak, imitate, joke, sing.

"These are the four fundamental skills of xiangsheng," Master Ding told the Happy Classroom. "Everything we do comes back to these four skills. There are many types of comedy in the world. Xiangsheng is specific because the audience wants to see you speak, imitate, joke, and sing."

Master Ding handed me a script. This one was not a short *guankou* monologue, heavy on culture and light on humor. It was twenty pages long. There were jokes, physical bits, singing, even a pratfall. It was my first real xiangsheng piece.

The cover read, "Singing the Three Kingdoms." It became the focus of my life for the next three months.

In the xiangsheng routine, I play an American who has started a Beijing opera troupe in America. Master Ding plays a Beijing opera lover. When we discover our common hobby, we agree to perform a piece of opera together, a show within a show.

But our opera is a train wreck from the start. Master Ding keeps singing about the three kingdoms of Wei, Shu, and Wu; I keep singing about the "new" three kingdoms of America, Mexico, and Canada. We disagree heartily on the correct lyrics, roles, and story lines. The whole piece involves hopping in and out of character, in and out of opera, and across cultural boundaries.

I had first seen the script one day at Master Ding's apartment. He wore an old, loose Boston College T-shirt and sat in a rolling office chair, pushing himself around his study with his feet.

"Come to the computer. Let me show you the script."

He brought up the file on his PC; I noticed the file was one of many with almost the same name, but with different versions, marked "American version," "Cameroon version," "Romanian version." Each version of the main script had different jokes based on the nationality of the foreigner he would be performing with that day.

Except for . . .

"'Pig version'?"

"Oh, that's for Julien Gaudfroy. His name in Chinese is Zhu Li An. His last name, Zhu . . . that sounds like 'pig,' *zhu*—get it?"

The file name was a pun. Love it.

"This piece, we call it 'Singing the Three Kingdoms.' But it is actually based on a traditional piece of xiangsheng called 'Huang He Lou'—'Tower of the Yellow Crane.'"

"What have you done to change it?"

"I've adapted it for each of my foreign disciples. You will do the jokes differently than Julien, correct? So, I need to change the script to fit you. You're American, so . . ."

The script played into the Chinese audience's knowledge of *The Romance of the Three Kingdoms*, a classic so pervasive in Chinese culture that everyone knows it even if they haven't read it.[*]

It's clearly their story, but I'm a part of it—exactly the type of thing I'd been looking to perform. I actually thought the schtick worked even better with a foreigner as the funny man, since "mistakes" I made about the plot of the *Three Kingdoms* were more justified than in the original.

But could I pull it off? Twenty minutes of traditional Chinese comedy. Speak, imitate, joke, sing.

Speak

It's practice day at the Happy Classroom. I'm the Joker, on the audience's left. Master Ding is at my side, on the audience's right.

DING: Jesse! I haven't seen you in ages! Where have you been?

JESSE: I've been back in the States.

DING: Back home! What have you been up to?

JESSE: I started up a Beijing opera troupe in America.

DING: What? That's amazing? Do . . . Do Americans even like Beijing opera?

JESSE: They do. It's actually easier doing it there than here.

DING: Really?

---

[*] It's kind of like how even though I'm Jewish, I still know what happened in the Bible. No spoilers here—go home and read it yourself, or watch one of the movie remakes.

JESSE: Yeah, because in America, nobody knows if we're singing right or not.

DING: Yo!

The back-and-forth feels good, but afterward Master Ding is displeased. "I feel some of that improv comedy leaking into your performance," he said.

Improv had been my entry point to comedy: four years in high school and four in college, playing in troupes called Spontaneous Generation and False Advertising. I'm used to coming onstage, making up a character, letting the dialogue roll with the flow.

When it came to xiangsheng, my improv training is a double-edged sword. The upside is I'm comfortable onstage and not worried about forgetting my lines. I've been onstage without a script before; I've even done it in Chinese, with my Chinese improv troupe.

But the downside is that improv made me into a lazy scripted-comedy performer. I didn't memorize my lines tightly; I usually just tried to get the gist of them, which meant the dialogue was loose. In my non-native language, these problems got worse.

In stand-up, I found I could get away with some of the material being loose if the important parts were tight. But xiangsheng is a linguistic art form, and the audience comes to the show expecting to see verbal fireworks. Every word is like a motion in a great two-man tai chi interaction—sometimes slow, sometimes fast, but never sloppy.

So, each week I would rehearse, come to the Happy Classroom, and perform the routine up to the point I had memorized. The first few minutes slowly got tighter, and I found myself able to devote more energy to switching up the inflection, the pace. As the words became burned into my brain, I slowly recovered the smart-assitude that helps me come alive onstage.

Certain parts of the routine were particularly linguistically challenging, as in two short, dense monologues where I reveal to the audience my knowledge of the particular piece of Beijing opera we are doing:

DING: Let's do some *Three Kingdoms* opera for everyone!

JESSE: The whole thing? Way too long.

DING: Don't worry, we'll cut some stuff out.

JESSE: Clever, we'll skip the best part.

DING: No, we'll do the best part!

JESSE: The best being . . .

DING: Here, let's sing the part where Zhang Fei crosses the river. He bursts into Zhuge Liang's pavilion. We'll end there.

JESSE: Oh, I know this part! Liu Bei goes to Eastern Wu to see about a marriage of alliance. Or that's what he pretends! He actually goes for a secret meeting with their head of state, in order to create a united front!

DING: That's . . . actually correct!

JESSE: *But!* Zhang Fei hears this and isn't having any of it! He bursts into Zhuge Liang's pavilion to demand the truth, to insist that his undercover terrorist operation be curtailed immediately, that his best Bro Liu Bei not be turned into a suicide bomber!*

DING: What the—

JESSE: I told you! I got it! Let's do it!

---

* Part of the joke is that my description of the scene is barely—barely, barely, barely—accurate to the actual story. Another part of the joke is the use of modern terminology like "suicide bomber" to describe a scene based in the Warring States period, more than 2,000 years ago. It'd be like using the phrase "surface-to-air-missile" in an episode of *Game of Thrones*.

This is a delicate part of the script and needs to be executed perfectly. We need to set up something very specific so the punch lines will hit. The audience sees a white performer onstage, about to perform Beijing opera. It's going to go badly; they just don't know how. I need to clue them in to the disaster that will follow, but not reveal the whole picture.

In this piece, I screw up the Beijing opera not specifically because I'm a foreigner and "don't get it." I mess it up because I get the ancient Chinese geopolitical intrigues and modern Western geopolitical intrigues mixed up. And to make sure the audience is clear that this is the "game" of the scene we're playing, I need to:

Display a decent knowledge of the *Three Kingdoms* piece—by getting the story's Chinese geopolitical intrigues (mostly) correct.

Twist that knowledge in a very specific way—by mixing in Western geopolitical intrigues.

After each such twist, bring it all back around. Master Ding is doing the Old Three Kingdoms, and I'm doing the New Three Kingdoms.

Comedy is all about specificity, finding an original thought that people know but haven't realized they know. It's about sharing that thought clearly, concisely, and cleanly. Then, you can riff off of the same premise again and again.

The more I learned about xiangsheng, and Chinese comedy in general, I found that comedy theory transcends cultures, how much of the machinery works the same way. So, if your tongue is sloppy, if you stutter, or speak choppily, or without the correct affect—basically, if you don't tell the joke well—the audience doesn't laugh. This is true everywhere.*

---

* Unless, of course, the joke is that you speak badly. But, if that's the joke, you need to speak badly *correctly*—meaning in a specific way that clues the audience into the fact your character blew it but the scriptwriter knows what they're doing.

But if you're a non-Chinese comedian in China, messing up this way—just once—means you've blown the whole routine. This is because, if you mess up the language, the audience in China changes its mind about the nature of the show. The show is no longer a "real" comedy show, where the audience engages with the content; the show becomes a novelty act, where the foreigner *tries! so! hard!* to do this comedy.

Isn't that cute? they think. *He came all the way here to try and make us laugh. We should support him!* And then the audience's role turns from audience to host, and they clap at things not because they think they're funny, but to fill the space where there should be laughter.

All comedians know it's better to bomb than to get applause you don't deserve. Comedians are like Michelin chefs, but we care about attention, not food. We can even distinguish between many distinct subtypes of attention. A belly laugh. A groan laugh. A "Wait, what did he mean?—Oh!!!" laugh.

And when we get applause when we know we should've bombed, it's like salt in the wound. It's offensive to the effort we put into being funny, and devalues the laughter we so crave.

My whole career as a Chinese comedian was spent trying to prevent the audience from making this mental shift, because while it is very polite, it is the death of real comedy. The moment the audience thinks it's responsible for helping the performer out of a bombing set, the last real laugh has already happened.

This is why *speak* is the first skill for a xiangsheng performer to learn. Language is your greatest tool. It binds the audience to you, your character, your thought process. If you're from another country, it's the thing that allows you to bridge the cultural gap and change people's minds about what it means to come from your part of the world.

So, I needed to have the lines down cold. I needed to deliver them with perfect timing and the authenticity that comes from playing the character in an immersive way. I needed to nail every single tone and accent.

Some days, I feel like rebelling against xiangsheng's high standards, because I know that, as a foreigner, the fact I speak Chinese fluently enough to do comedy is so overwhelming that a portion of the audience will never be able to see past that fact. They hear me speak Chinese, but no matter how funny I am, the essence of the humor won't reach them.

But most days, I thank xiangsheng for its history and fan base that produced such a high standard, because if I meet that standard, it means doing something that few people—Chinese or foreign—can do. It's a true accomplishment, one that has a real merit.

In the end, either you can speak, or you can't. The audience will tell you.

Imitate

Master Ding and I are rehearsing the middle part of "Singing the Three Kingdoms." Behind us are three characters, written in simple, flowing lines of chalk:

听,学,演。

Listen, imitate, perform.

In "Singing the Three Kingdoms," the emperor, Liu Bei, greets the warrior-poet Zhuge Liang, who aims to construct a secret alliance.

I play Zhuge Liang, and Master Ding plays Liu Bei.

We mess up the greeting.

DING (*as Liu Bei*): Ah, sir!
JESSE (*as Zhuge Liang*): Ah, Mr. Liu!

DING (*breaks character*): Wh-what? Mr. Liu? You can't call me Mr. Liu!

JESSE (*also breaks character*): What's your name?

DING: Liu Bei.

JESSE: See? Liu Bei. Mr. Liu. What's the matter?

DING: I'm the *emperor*! You need to refer to me as *Your Majesty*.

JESSE: Oh, emperor. That's like the president in our New Three Kingdoms.

DING: Exactly. Try it again. (*As Liu Bei.*) Ah, sir!

JESSE (*as Zhuge Liang*): Ah, Mr. President! Wait—I mean—Mr. Emperor!

DING (*to audience*): I guess I'm Mr. Emperor now.

Part of the challenge of "Singing the Three Kingdoms" is playing a character within a character.

For most of the bit, I play Jesse, but an exaggerated Beijing opera dilettante version of myself. That's my first character. But then, partway through, I start to play Zhuge Liang. That's my second character.

How do you play a character within a character?

Becoming another person onstage, and copying their physicality, mannerisms, accent, and temperament—this all falls under the second skill: *imitate*.

It was refreshing to see this similarity between stand-up and xiangsheng. In stand-up, I also play a version of myself, and sometimes I embody the other people I interact with. I share stories about meeting crazy cab drivers or explaining to my mom I have no idea what I'm doing with my life. When I do it, it's not a verbal ramble:

"And then I called my mom. And then my mom said, 'When are you moving home?' And then I said, 'Mom, I can't see the future. It's China, I can't even see across the street some days.'"

You bring in some physicality (press a phone to your ear), change the voice (Mom's Bronx accent), and eliminate all excess words:

"Hey Mom."

"WHEN ARE YOU MOVING HOIME?"

"I don't know! I can't see the future! It's China, I can't see across the street some days!"

In xiangsheng, becoming other people by "studying" accents and mannerisms is a key part of enlivening the show. You study the world, how people talk, walk, and think, and bring that knowledge with you onstage in order to transport the audience.

And China has no lack of characters to imitate. In the first five minutes of my Chinese stand-up set, I play a street food vendor, cab driver, airport security personnel, child on a cruise ship, old lady on a cruise ship, a Uighur and a US Border Security officer. If I do it right, just hopping in and out of the characters and accents is funny in and of itself.

Imitating voices correctly is important because there is no "Chinese" language. Mandarin, the most common language, is spoken by just about everyone in China, but it's virtually nobody's "native" language. Everyone grows up in a city, town, or village with its own distinctive dialectal markers. If you're not a news broadcaster, your Mandarin has some sort of twinge, and that twinge is the first thing Chinese people use when they have to puzzle out which one of 1.4 billion people you are.

Urban or rural? Rich or poor? Educated or illiterate? Ostentatious or down-to-earth? A whole cast of prefabricated characters can be accessed by the right accent, by dropping a sound, by bending a tone. When I get these right as an American, people lose their shit. It's like a Chinese person moving to Tennessee and talkin' 'bout sweet tea.

They even have associated stereotypes to go with people from each province.* Which of the following best describes you?

Northeastern accent? You've probably got a nickname like "Iron Egg" or "Stupid Doggy," wear gold chains and fur coats, drink until it comes to blows, and maybe have connections to some sort of mafia. Also, you probably steal shit.

Shanxi accent? You're either a coal baron or a coal miner, so you might be rich or poor, but either way you've got no class and smoke lots of cigarettes. Also, you probably steal shit.

Henan accent? You're a cheat and a scoundrel, probably making your money by coming to the city and stealing heavy iron sewer covers to sell for scrap metal. You *confirmed* steal shit.

Shanghai accent? You're probably a pompous faker who thinks they're better than everyone else and tries to slip English into random conversations to show off your worldliness. If you're a girl, you also have impossibly high standards and nobody is good enough to marry you. You won't steal shit, but you probably will make people sign some sort of complicated contract and threaten to sue them.

Tianjin accent? You've got the funniest accent, everyone agrees, and an inherent sense of humor. Everything you do is probably funny! Everyone loves you! If you're into xiangsheng, though, you're probably a comedy snob, since the Tianjiners think their xiangsheng is the best in the country and won't laugh at mediocre jokes.

Beijing accent? You're probably loud, proud, and think you're the center of Chinese culture. You have lots of Old Beijing friends with

---

* Of course, these are Han Chinese stereotypes, toward themselves and others. When you think of "Chinese" people, you're thinking of Han Chinese—the most common ethnic group that makes up 92 percent of the population and almost 100 percent of the top positions of authority. Theirs are the stereotypes that "count" if you're pitching a comedy show.

whom you sip tea and shoot the shit in the shade, content in making lots of money on the land you've rented/sold to out-of-towners.

Xinjiang accent? You're probably a Uighur Muslim, speak heavily accented Mandarin, sell lamb kebabs on the street, as well as "big cake," a type of table-sized cake sold on carts by men with large knives. Also, if you happen to be a brown-eyed, brown-haired, Chinese-speaking Jewish American comedian, you might find that people mistake you for being Uighur and apply these stereotypes to you.

Until recently there was very little American-style PC culture that discouraged stereotypical humor in China. But while in recent years there has been a bit of a backlash against making fun of the poor and disabled, regional stereotypes are all pretty much fair game.

As an American who is super sensitive to race in comedy, doing political jokes in China feels like doing race jokes to an American audience. Audiences want to hear about it, but they're super sensitive to doing it "right," and to get airtime on mass media, you need to address it in a very specific way. But in China, you *can* play big, bold, stereotypical characters with accents and not worry about being thrown out of the theater. Improv here was my trial by fire for learning how to pull this off—join me onstage and see how.

It's a small show at a bar with cheap drinks. Forty in attendance, five performers, nothing fancy, nothing complicated. We're asking for audience suggestions: What film or TV style do you want to see in this next scene?

The audience shouts out: "Horror!"

"Action!"

"Kung fu!"

But we're in China, so we also get:

"Rural love story!"

"Palace intrigue drama!"

"Korean drama!"

Tonight, the host picks the last one. I'm the only foreigner in the room, and the only one who's never watched any Korean dramas. But that's no reason to avoid the scene!

The next two minutes are a high-speed, high-intensity education as I strain to process the Chinese perception of a genre well enough to join in myself. Apparently, if you're going to do a Chinese parody of a K-drama, you must shoehorn the word *oppa* (big brother) in front of every sentence. Extra points if one character speaks with the bombastic tone and fake intensity of that North Korean newslady, and they finish each sentence with the phrase *si-mi-da.**

Congrats! In two minutes, we've both learned how to imitate a hackneyed Chinese rendition of a Korean drama!

Beyond accents, short-form improv often comes down to imitating and melding different acting archetypes. What does a doctor sound like in Chinese? How does he stand? What special words does he use? You can't say, "I'll tell your family," if you're a doctor in America; you have to say, "I will notify your next of kin." In Chinese, surely there are similar differences?

Then, once you've learned those intricacies, improv challenges us to add levels. What about a sci-fi Chinese doctor? What about a Bollywood Chinese doctor? What about a Cultural Revolution-era propagandistic Beijing opera Chinese doctor?

For me, there was yet another level of difficulty: What about a white, American, Chinese-speaking doctor in a Cultural Revolution-era Red Beijing opera?

---

* This is kind of like how in middle school Spanish class we made up a stereotyped "Spanish" that adds "-o" to the end-o of every wordo.

Imitate that. Don't think twice!

Being a Chinese comedian forced me to imitate, because it was all I could do at any moment to try and keep up. But all that imitation eventually meant I had some technique under my belt when I tried to make new things.

Master Ding summed up his whole theory on how to go from xiangsheng novice to professional in three words, which he scrawled on the blackboard in his flowing chalk script:

听,学,演。

Listen, imitate, perform.

"First, listen. You can't speak if you don't listen, because you won't be able to hear yourself to see if it's good. Then, imitate others who are already capable. They will show you one way to do the show, and you will know enough to get onstage. Only when you've imitated can you then create. Go up there, make the words your own, and add your own special talent."

Joke

I never felt fully prepared for the Happy Classroom because rehearsing at home, with no partner and no audience, felt flat. I tried to project, to joke, but it just gave me muscle memory, and no confidence.

Joking with nobody around felt like being asked to cook a meal for someone in your mind. How would you know what it tasted like?

For whatever reason, I found that there was often no better place to rehearse than on my electric scooter, weaving in and out of Beijing traffic. I spent so much time on the back of that vehicle that I didn't need my brain to navigate. My body would balance me automatically as I weaved through Guozijian Hutong, past the Confucius Temple, taking a left at the Yonghegong Lama Temple, under Beixinqiao Bridge, and keeping the Temple of Earth on my left as I shot toward the third ring road and Beijing University of Chemical Technology.

All throughout my ride, the upcoming show played in real time in my mind's eye—the stage, the audience demographics, the timing of Master Ding's parts of the script. These merged with my own lines, which I shouted for real out into the traffic, trusting they would be blown away by the combination of horns and engines until they were swept off in the Mongolian winds that flowed through Beijing.

The Happy Classroom was hot. The August heat beat down upon Beijing from a bright, cloudless sky, and the AC on the second floor was not quite strong enough to make things comfortable. This was definitely a rehearsal for shorts and T-shirts, not long, flowing robes.

"Enough, enough!" Master Ding shouted, and I recoiled as I stood next to him. The dozen or so disciples in the audience laughed at my overreaction.

We were ten minutes into our first full run-through of "Singing the Three Kingdoms." Master Ding's character was getting more and more frustrated at my character's distractions and tangents.

I was playing a troll. At this point, the audience knew that. But what they did not know was, did I *actually* know Beijing opera? After all, I was not Chinese. Can I actually sing, or is the whole show just one big bit, teasing them over and over again?

My goal was to make Master Ding pitch a fit trying to find out.

DING: It's your turn to sing!
JESSE: OK! But first—my lines. You know them?
DING: Yes, of course.

JESSE: Well, say them and I'll see if you're right or not.

DING: Your first line is—wait, do you know them or not?

JESSE: Psh, I know all the lines! I can sing six kingdoms! (*Extends hand outward to audience, with the hand signal for "six."*)

DING (*slaps down Jesse's hand*): Cut it out with the "six kingdoms" stuff!

After we had finished, Master Ding clapped me on the back and turned to the crowd.

"Well? What do we think?"

Master Ding's take on giving notes was the direct opposite of every other Chinese teacher that I had studied with before. He began by asking the newest, lowest-skilled people in the room for their thoughts. New students who might have thought they could treat the Happy Classroom as a free Chinese lesson, chilling in the back and getting free entertainment, always found themselves dragged into comedy analysis from day one.

I absolutely loved what this did to the classroom vibes. It meant we were all responsible for each others' improvement, and the downside— that we might get bad notes—was always balanced by the fact that advice of the more experienced disciples came later and drowned out the less informed notes.

At the end of the disciples' comments, Master Ding himself mixed critique with encouragement. He would use his fifty years of comedy insight to blast the smallest mistakes in your performance in front of all the disciples. This sucked, mostly because he was almost always right.

But then he would also use that approach to complement what was working. This was awesome, mostly because he was almost always right.

Master Ding's compliments were not just high-school-theater "all choices are valid" different. Their rarity and truthfulness meant they were hard-earned and kept you grinding. They made me feel like a di-

amond miner in a deep shaft, willing to hack through as much rock as
needed to find another gleaming bright spot. This time, I got rewarded
for my efforts.

"That 'six kingdoms' joke was well done, Jesse!" he said, beaming.
"You laid down the sheet perfectly."

"I—I what?"

"Laid down the sheet. Then I opened it up!"

"You—you what?"

"You know, laying the sheet, and opening it up," Master Ding said,
and opened his arms wide, before suddenly *whooshing* his arms forward
and out and up, into a "ta-da!" motion. "Laying the sheet" apparently
meant "setup." "Opening it up" meant a punch line.

Studying xiangsheng has helped me realize that, technique-wise, almost everything in the comedian's tool kit that makes things funny in
America works in China, too. The rule of three applies (though sometimes in xiangsheng, it's the rule of four), absurdism works, sarcasm
works, irreverence works, slipping on banana peels works, fart jokes
work, puns work.[*]

But one thing that is different is the terminology. We use words like
setup and *punch line*, but these words clearly don't translate. Yet, come-
dically, setups and punch lines work in Chinese. I had all my old tools,
but I didn't know what to call them.

"What sheet is this?" I asked. "'Laying down a sheet?'"

"It's like, think back to when xiangsheng was street performance.

---

[*] While both Chinese and American comedians use puns, the audiences might disagree
on how many puns are too many puns, which honestly is the sort of cultural conflict I am
totally OK with. Generally speaking, there are more puns in Chinese, but they have to be
tighter, since the language is tonal and things that sound "close enough" to a nonspeaker are
not "close enough" to them.

You're on the street, and you're telling jokes," he explained. "You lay down a sheet in front of everyone, and start putting stuff in the sheet. That stuff is what you're saying—the clues in the joke. A character here, a detail there. Then, when everything's all in there, you grab the whole sheet, turn it upside down, and all the things fall out at once! That's when people see how everything fit together, and that's when they laugh."

It turns out the audience only cares about how funny the joke is, but if you want to make a living in China as a comedy writer, you need to know the lingo.

I learned this by nearly derailing a big opportunity for me and a comedy-writing buddy of mine, Eric Zhang. Eric, a Beijing filmmaker, and I had managed to get a pitch meeting to sell a sketch comedy show to Sohu, a platform that was (at the time) a big streaming network in China.

"Chinese comedy shows always have a 'host,' but if the host is funny, why not start the show with them doing a sketch, instead of introducing the show?" I asked the directors at Sohu, getting a few nods.

"So, we want to go directly into the sketch, a cold open,"* I said.

Now, no nods. Frosty energy.

Eric jumped in. "Not a cold open!" he said. "We want to *kai men jin*—'Open the door and walk through immediately.'"

Suddenly: "Oh!!!" Agreement from around the room.

Afterward, in our cab on the way back to the North Second Ring Road, I got a chance to ask for clarification.

---

* In sketch comedy, *cold open* is just the term for when the lights come up on the show and the show has begun—no host, no nothing, just directly into the show.

"You said '*leng kai tou*'—or 'cold opening,'" Eric explained. "Now, I know what you meant, but in China, 'cold' jokes mean understated, more cerebral jokes. The type of jokes you have to think about for a few seconds before you get them."

"Oh, that's not at all what I meant!" I said, shocked.

"I know! That's why I chose the Chinese lingo that fit. We're already fighting uphill to get this show on the air. We don't want any miscommunication."*

The term in xiangsheng for comedy lingo is *hang hua*—"industry speak." My time in the Happy Classroom slowly taught me some of the terminology I needed to be a Chinese comedian.

Master Ding had created an environment where we could learn such things without pretense, since he knew that each country had its own way of speaking comedy, and he never looked down on anyone for using their own terminology, even if he didn't always understand it.

Of course, in the rest of reality, there are always more comedians than opportunities. I found that if I didn't know "how to say things the right way," people in decision-making positions would instantly rethink whether I had any right to be in the room at all. So I took it upon myself to learn as much *hang hua* as possible, since it did some very heavy lifting for making Chinese industry people think I knew what I was talking about, even when I didn't.

In America, we call dirty jokes "blue comedy." I looked on Wikipedia and couldn't find out why it's called "blue," so that probably means

---

* The show actually did get made, though it was a dumpster fire, and to tell the story properly would involve defaming a CEO and a celebrity, so it's probably a story for a comedy club with no phones rolling and not a published book from a respectable publisher like you are reading now. In the end, I half-got-fired, half-resigned, and full-did-not-get-paid, but I learned a lot in a short amount of time.

nobody knows. In China, instead of "blue," they call dirty comedy "yellow." So, if a comedian does dirty comedy, an audience might say, "He's telling a lot of yellow jokes."

Yellow applies to anything dirty or sexual, not just jokes. Xiangsheng performer Guo Degang, arguably the most famous xiangsheng performer in China, had a joke that went viral on the internet from one of his specials. The video shows him onstage with his partner, Yu Qian, at Guo's fabulous De Yun She teahouse.

"Women are like eggs. On the outside they look white and pure, but on the inside they're actually yellow." Guo intones. The audience laughs. "Men are like mangoes," he continues, "yellow on the outside, even more yellow on the inside."

The xiangsheng term *floor after floor* referred to what stand-ups call *tags*—little one-line jokes that can be added onto the end of another working joke to get a second, third, or fourth quick laugh. The image was that the first joke was the ground floor of a building, and then you would add floor after floor of jokes about it.

Laugh point describes an audience's standing on the low comedy/sophisticated comedy gradient. People with "low" laugh points would laugh at anything—poop jokes, bad puns, you name it. People with "high" laugh points liked sophisticated comedy, the sort of jokes that take a moment to click, and then hit all at once.*

---

* I personally found the "high laugh point" people to be annoying comedy snobs. I roasted these people in one of my standup jokes:

"Sometimes we get audiences that just *insist* on not laughing. 'I have a high laugh point.' I don't get these people. What do they do after the show?

'Honey, how was the show?'

'Excellent. I didn't laugh once.'"

But since I also am an annoying comedy snob myself, I can't really say much more.

Some shorthands just had to be memorized. Music videos were called *MV's*. Song-and-dance-and-comedy revues were called *zong yi*—mixed arts. *Qingjing ju*—"emotional scene dramas"—were sitcoms.

Sketch comedy was called *xiaopin*, "little works," but only if you were at a state-owned TV station. If you were at an internet station, you would call sketch comedy *sketch*, in English, to signal your contempt for the boring, interminable state-owned stations' sketches.*

Some phrases had less history but were just as useful as writer's room lingo. I found that *inappropriate* and *excessive*† meant two different things. *Inappropriate* meant specifically politically inappropriate, whereas *excessive* meant "the audience won't go there."

Years later, as I moved out of the underground scene, where you could basically do anything, to the professional scene, where TV show scripts would be reviewed by the relevant authorities before being approved, knowing the difference between "inappropriate" and "excessive" became crucial, since the type of change you make to a joke so that it can reach air was different depending on where the problem was coming from.

For example, I once wrote a sketch with a friend, Jiabao, where I played an actor who got increasingly upset that my scene partner seemed to be going off script to get free English lessons. Even while dying in the scene, he kept asking me English questions.

---

* The word *xiaopin* only refers to stage sketches. If you do video sketch, you call it a "VCR." I have no idea where this term came from, especially because at the time VCRs were in use in America, people were too poor to buy them in China and now most people have still never seen a VCR. They just skipped that technology. I can only guess that the original, earliest video sketches on TV were brought into studios on VHS tapes, played on VCRs, and that name somehow stuck to the piece of entertainment itself.

† The difference between 不合适 and 过分.

JIABAO (*dying*): Tell my wife I love her.

JESSE: I will, buddy! I will!

JIABAO: How do you say, "I love you," in English?

JESSE: "I lo—*hey!* (*Shakes dying war buddy by the jacket.*) STAY ON SCRIPT!"

When we got notes back from the show producers, they said the joke was "perhaps inappropriate." We interpreted this note as two notes. The first was unspoken: my reaction, shaking my war buddy by the jacket, was "excessive." They just worried the audience wouldn't find it funny, and wanted us to make the bit even better.

The second was that shaking the jacket was also "inappropriate"—it was just not a good look, politically, to have an American soldier shaking a Chinese soldier, though this is not something most audiences would have thought of.

This difference was important, since we could have toned down the shaking of the jacket, which would fix the "excessive" part of the issue, but not the "inappropriate" one. Too many mistakes like this—of not correctly interpreting purposefully hazy political notes from people not in charge of the actual decision-making and just looking to avoid conflict with the authorities when it came time to submit the scripts for real—and you find the show producers stop calling to check in.

To fix the issue, we changed my reaction to getting upset and calling offscreen for the director, to ask him to double-check the script. I still got to blow up—just not at someone in uniform.

I found professional comedy writers in China incredibly skilled in this very specific technique—maintaining an open, funny, joking environment where everything could be said, but then turning a second lens onto a finished work and shaving the edges of the script to try and make things work.

The easy shorthand phrase to say, "We're going to take this as far as we can without crossing either limit" was *line ball.** Just as a tennis shot is counted as in if it's on the line, comedians in China, like anywhere, will try to push that line as far as possible without going over. Hitting the line itself—having a "line ball" joke, is a sign of great skill.

But no matter how you talked about jokes, the fact remained: A good joke was one that made the audience laugh.

So, how do you make the audience laugh?

I tried everything I could to practice, so that when the moment came, I got the laughs.

Stage time was best, but if we didn't have a show, I could only rehearse. Obviously, I tried to practice with Master Ding and other teachers, like Lao Cui. I also would try to practice with my Japanese brother Xitian Cong, or some of the other Happy Classroom crowd, though they often had work or school.

So, oftentimes, I had to practice by myself.

How do you learn a two-man routine with no partner?

I had to improvise, which led me to my bathroom mirror.

In my tiny studio apartment, I had a bathroom about half the size of a car. There was a toilet, a showerhead crusted with calcium deposits so thick only five or six holes let water out, a circular grate in the ground for water to drain out, and a small mirror at about head level.

---

*   擦边球.

I discovered that if I stood in the bathroom sideways, I could twist my head and it looked like I was talking to someone else—or rather, to someone standing where a xiangsheng partner would be.

This meant I could deliver the Joker's line, jump and twist 180 degrees in midair, land, and deliver the Straight Man's line.

ME (Straight Man): Is your New Three Kingdoms even real Beijing opera?

(*Jump. Twist.*)

ME (Joker): It is! But we don't use erhu and cymbals.

(*Jump. Twist.*)

ME (Straight Man): What do you use?

(*Jump. Twist.*)

ME (Joker): EDM rave hardcore.

(*Jump. Twist.*)

ME (Straight Man): What is—?

(*Jump. Twist.*)

ME (Joker): *Brwoowwhhhh . . . (beatbox) wub wub wub.*

Once, when I jumped and banged my knee on the toilet, I collapsed onto the ground and things got real quiet real fast.

As I lay on the ground clutching my knee, I thought back to how I had arrived here. My fellow graduates from school had real jobs. My fellow study-abroad cohort was scattered all around China, working in all sorts of industries, taking part in China's rise.

I was using my time as a scholarly researcher to spin in circles in my bathroom, telling jokes to nobody.

I thought to myself, *Someone who tells jokes to an audience is a comedian. Someone who tells jokes to no one is crazy.*

It occurred to me I was probably crazy—and that was probably fine.

Sing

In the Beijing suburb of Fengtai, the massive shopping malls of the Beijing city center give way to smaller shopping malls. The roads shrink from four lanes to two; the apartment buildings from twenty stories to ten. Traffic rules are somewhat more relaxed; farmers pile watermelons onto rickety motorized rickshaws and putter around in the bike lanes, happy to go against traffic if it means not having to cross the street.

Off of a main street shoots a smaller road shaded by willow trees; on the north side is a traditional-style teahouse: Fengtai Cultural Arts Center.

Inside is the classic xiangsheng milieu, the whole nine yards. There's the stage with its cloth-covered table, the big lights and nice speakers, the square tables with chairs on three sides, the audience, sipping chrysanthemum tea with sugar, the sunflower seed husks piling up on the ground.

Onstage there are two performers. One is an old Chinese man dressed in a tan robe with a wide smile and a powerful voice. The other is me, in my cream-colored robe from the Soviet-era steampunk basement. I've learned to speak, to imitate, to joke, and now it is time to sing.

DING: Enough of this! It's your turn to sing! (*Imitating opera instruments.*) *Canglang qilai-zhe canglang qilai-zhe cang!*

JESSE (*singing*): 主公上马心不爽! (*His Majesty travels, his heart deeply troubled.*)

DING: *Cang!*

JESSE (*singing*): 山人八卦袖内藏! (*Zhuge Liang has all the tricks up his sleeve.*)

DING: *Cang!*

JESSE (*singing*): 将身且坐中军帐！(*The general enters the main military pavilion!*)

DING: Breathe! *Cang!*

JESSE (*singing*): 等候涿州翼德张。(*And awaits the great Zhang from Zhou.*)

DING (*to the audience*): Hey, he actually did it!

(*The audience roars.*)

The Beijing opera piece took a short time to learn and a long time to do well.

If you've never heard Beijing opera before, it's one of those classic "not for everyone" art forms. The singing is high and screechy, often in falsetto, with notes stretched and held in vibrato so that they seem to break upon the audience in frenetic waves. The music is cobbled together from a bunch of instruments that I probably wouldn't want to hear individually—tiny, high-pitched two-string erhu violins with drums made of snakeskin, and cymbals of all sorts, the smallest of which are the size of a silver-dollar pancake and are worn around the thumb and forefinger. One squeeze and *clang! clang! clang!*

When I was in China for the first time during study abroad in college, our school took us to see a Beijing opera show. I bought a bottle of warm Coke ("We don't have cold ones," the attendant told me. "Drinking cold liquids is bad for you.") and a tube of braised pork–flavored Pringles and sat down to enjoy the spectacle.

The costumes were extravagant: mountains of gold and dyed cloth, decorated armor, and giant feathers ticking the air. The actors each wore intricate face paints that denoted their role in the play—the hero, the villain, the clown. They were all trained dually as vocalists and as martial artists, so their singing was punctuated by tumbling, kicking, and sword-fighting.

It was a visual marvel; the cymbals *clanged*, the erhus whined, and Sun Wukong, the Monkey King, fought off eight enemies with his twirling staff, ducking and weaving and flipping in a ball of cloth and fur, stopping only to stoop, stretch, and groom himself.

It was pretty cool. Fast-forward to my Fulbright research, and learning to sing a bit of Beijing opera myself had emerged at the top of my "I've lived in Beijing" bucket list. Occasionally in improv musicals with my Chinese troupe, we'd get "Beijing opera" as a suggestion, and flail our arms while screeching in falsetto voices. But I had always wanted to be taught the opera for real.

Luckily, I had the perfect teacher. Master Ding had learned directly from Great-Master Hou Baolin, whose masterwork "Operas and Dialects" was one of the greatest xiangsheng pieces of all time. I'd seen Master Ding sing opera pieces at a dozen shows; the older audience lost their minds. Even the younger audience members—who had never lived in a China without Pizza Huts and foreign Top 40 music—enjoyed themselves.

While I wasn't much of a singer, I was a comedian, which meant I also desperately craved the sort of rapt attention the audience gave Master Ding whenever he sang opera. I looked forward to advancing in the script to the parts where my character would sing.

However, on the day in the Happy Classroom when we reached this section of the script, he didn't give me any opera instruction at all. When we got to the section where I was supposed to sing, I stopped, not knowing what to do.

"Haven't memorized the opera yet?" he asked in front of all the disciples.

"Uhh . . . no. I don't know how to sing it."

"OK, OK! I'll teach you after the class."

I waited in anticipation, and as everyone else filed out of the classroom . . . Master Ding left as well.

"Master!" I called to him, chasing him into the hallway.

"Jesse!" he answered, then said nothing.

"You said you would teach me the opera?"

"Oh, yes! It goes like this: '主公上马—'"

"Wait, wait, wait!" I scrambled to get my phone out and record the video.

In the echoey, dark hallway at Beijing University of Chemical Technology, Master Ding sang all my lines, each musical phrase ending in complicated runs of "ah-ah-ahhhhhhhh!!!!" Despite no percussion to help keep time, the runs seemed to be of precise length, stopping perfectly based on some sort of internal clock.

As he sang, he swung his arms around in a series of motions that looked formal and codified. Sometimes he would extend one arm, his hand between his face and mine, his two smallest fingers curled in and tilted forty-five degrees to make an accusatory three-finger pointing motion; other times, both arms would swing in a sort of counterpoint, with the left arm gathering the audience's attention as the right circled at his hip, as if caught in an eddy.

Together, it formed a complicated motion, like a diver practicing a run-up and leap on the diving board, only to land back on the board, spring up, and perform a series of precise twists before disappearing into the water like a splash.

"OK! Got it?" Master Ding asked.

"That's it?"

"Those are the Joker's lines. The Straight Man has more."

"But, how do I do that? What do the arm movements mean? Do the lines have to be that exact length? How do I—"

"Imitate. Study. Have it memorized by next week."

Rote memorization in a foreign language is hard, but I found learning songs was easier. It wasn't tough to get eight lines of music down. But then, when I sang them next week, Master Ding's response was to turn to the Chinese disciples in the class and ask, "Does he sound like he's from Beijing?"

The consensus was no. No, I didn't sound like I was from Beijing.

The feedback was immediate and unrelenting. Some of my runs had been too long. Some had been too short. I started the whole piece a few notes too low.

It turns out it's easier to learn music by rote than to learn lines by rote, but much harder to unlearn and relearn music. I had done comedy all throughout my life, but never taken a single singing lesson. Despite the less-than-stellar reaction, I was happy to finally hit the last of the four skills and round off my core skill set of speaking, imitating, joking, and singing.

"What? No, no, no, this isn't singing!" Master Ding said.

"No?"

"No! This is opera. We're not opera performers. We're imitating opera performers. This still counts as 'imitation.'"

Apparently in the Chinese mindset, since the Beijing opera performers practice years and years to do their jobs well, to start singing a few notes and call oneself a singer would be presumptuous. Much in the same way xiangsheng performers might scoff if two people threw on robes, stood next to each other, made some jokes, and called it xiangsheng.

"Well, if the opera isn't the singing, then what *is* the singing?"

"*Taiping geci*. 'Peaceful lyrics.'"

"What is that?"

Master Ding reached into his bag and grasped two bamboo staves.

He clacked them against each other to create a simple beat, then sang a warbling melody, sixteen bars long, repeating over and over. The lyrics of the song rang out: a simple story about how the construction of the character for the word tolerance—容—could be understood:

小小的笔管空有空
Little writing brush, just an empty tube.
能工巧匠把它造成
Created by a skillful artisan.
先写一撇不算字
First I draw one stroke, which doesn't yet make a character.
后写一捺念成"人"
Then I draw another stroke and it becomes "人"—people.
"人"字添两个点念个"火"
Add two more strokes and it looks like "火"—fire.
为人最怕火烧身
Just what people *fear most: their bodies being burned by* fire.
"火"字头上添宝盖念个"灾"字
On top of that character, I add a cap and I get "灾"—disaster.
灾祸临头罪不轻
When disaster looms over your head, the suffering is not slight.
"灾"字底下添个口念"容"字
If beneath "灾" (disaster) I add a "口" (mouth), it reads "容"
    (tolerate).
我劝诸位得容人处且把人容。
I urge everyone, if they can, to tolerate people.

"Do you understand what this is?" Master Ding asked. "In the old days, back when the first xiangsheng performers were out-of-work Beijing opera performers, there were no stages to perform on. They would go on the street and sing 'peaceful lyrics,' drawing the characters mentioned in the song with white sand released from their fist, writing them in real time in the dirt. People would see the characters and know to not walk over them, and also gather into a ring to look at them. This circle established a stage to perform, and an audience.

"In this piece, the drawn character starts as '人'—*person*. Then, by adding strokes, it becomes '火,' (*fire*), '灾' (*disaster*), and finally '容' (*tolerance*).

"The story has a positive meaning to it, which is good, but the main thing it did was draw attention. In less than a minute, the xiangsheng performer would have cleared a stage and drawn in passersby who were wondering, 'Who is singing? What is he talking about?' To get the story takes the sort of focused attention from the audience that the performer needs to make jokes."

It seemed so different from the other parts of xiangsheng I'd learned.

"I've been studying xiangsheng for months now. How have I never heard of this?" I asked.

"Nobody really does it anymore. It was meant for street performance, and xiangsheng quickly moved from the street to the teahouse, then to the radio, TV, and now internet. The Pacific Lyrics are passed down, but rarely performed. It's too slow for TV."

"Internet audiences might like it," I suggested.

"Audiences might like it, but only at very refined venues. Perhaps you have refined internet channels?"

Whether it counted as singing or not, when I got up onstage at the Fengtai Cultural Arts Center, blasted out my Beijing opera, and got a round of applause from the locals, I didn't care that I wasn't singing. I just enjoyed it.

> JESSE (*singing*): 啊！三将军进了宝帐为着谁来？ (*Ah! The general has entered my command tent, in search of whom?*)
> DING: 老张就是为着你来！(*The general seeks you!*)
> JESSE: 您找我吗？ (*You have come for me?*)
> DING: 真是！(*Yes!*)

The climax was here. Master Ding, playing General Zhang Fei, approached me, scowling enormously and growling like a lion. As he advanced, he swung his arms in circles to accentuate his movements and made wild noises before arriving at my "throne," which was a folding chair we had brought onstage.

Looming over me as I sat, he finally locked me in a death stare, and shouted a war cry one foot from my face.

> DING: *ZHA ZHA ZHA ZHA ZHA . . . WAAAAAAAAYAAAAA!!!*

The showdown was here. How would I, as Zhuge Liang, respond?

> JESSE: 你别生气哦，税都给你免了，宝贝！(*Don't be angry! I'll exempt you from the tariffs, baby!*)
> DING: 宝贝？(*Baby???*)

At the end of my line, I reached out and grabbed his face by both cheeks and rubbed his face like a baby's.

The audience roared, first with shock, then with laughter.

Got 'em.

Master Ding laughed, and I laughed, and we stood together and bowed to the audience, whose sustained applause washed over me.

I could speak, imitate, joke, and, to my American standards, sing. I could do it in Chinese, and make the guys in polo shirts with bad teeth and foghorn laughs lose it.

During the hour-long subway ride back to my apartment, I felt like I must be radiating some sort of electric glow of pride. Part of my pride came from the effort I had put in. For moving myself and my life to Beijing. For spending countless hours in the Happy Classroom, or rehearsals, or spinning around in my bathroom.

But another part of it came from somewhere deeper. It came from sense memories from an hour ago: The feel of the folded cloth of my robe against my wrists; a louder-than-normal laugh from a single man somewhere halfway up the left side of the theater; a dull pulse from bruises on my palm and the outside of my left knee, earned by going all out on a pratfall.

Comedy is a live art form. It lives in our bodies. We love it so much, and need laughter so badly, that we try and bottle it up. We turn it into internet shorts, movies, and memes, with the desire that we can have it when and where we need it, because our bodies crave it.

But those media are just shadows of the real thing: being in a room and laughing with other people.

As a comedian, no amount of preparation guarantees you those laughs. No skill or technique guarantees you those laughs. The only thing that live audiences care about is seeing a true performance, one where the comedian is out on a ledge, one leg on solid ground, the other flailing over a chasm.

For comedy to mean anything, there needs to be a real chance they could fall.

I had spent months preparing, and tonight, I had dangled my leg over the chasm. I had opened up myself to the audience, to their culture, to their beloved art form.

I could have fallen. They would have understood.

But I did not fall.

The subway sped along underground, and I glowed, silently.

A Fifth of One Lung

One week, Master Ding canceled our Happy Classroom meeting.

I didn't think much of it at the time. I actually silently rejoiced, since I had another show I wanted to do and now didn't have to feel like I was playing hooky.

But the next week it was canceled as well. And the next.

I called up some of the other disciples. Was there something wrong?

The word came back, in slow, low whispers: "Master Ding has lung cancer."

I had missed Master Ding's smoking days. According to the older disciples who'd toured the country with him for weeks on end during the heyday of foreigners-doing-xiangsheng mania, he had for as long as they could remember dragged through pack after pack of cigarettes. Beijing smog and a decade performing for coal miners probably didn't help his diagnosis. Though he'd quit cigarettes for a decade by the time I arrived, it appeared the habit had caught up to him.

For a few weeks, we didn't know much about his condition, other than that he would respond, "I'm doing fine!" to anyone who messaged. If we pushed, he gave us more routines to study to occupy our time, since clearly we had too much of that on our hands if we kept trying to WeChat him all day.

Master Ding was the type of person who could walk into a room of strangers and in five minutes be at the center of the room, without being braggadocious or untoward. But when it came to some things—his health, especially—he could clam up so completely that none of his disciples could get an idea of what was happening. Later, I would realize it was precisely because he was so talented at connecting with people that he was also so good at stonewalling them. Some people are extroverted because they need the attention and crave it so much that they will connect with anyone. But that doesn't work for comedians. If the audience feels you *need* their attention, they smell desperation—and nothing's worse than a desperate comedian. Master Ding could command attention, but didn't *need* it. This meant that, just as he could command attention, he could also refuse it.

After a few months, the Happy Classroom was back—though, for the first week, we met at his apartment. I scooted into his apartment complex, which was across the street from the North Korean embassy, near the Temple of the Sun. I walked by the doorman and into the elevator.

When I was in middle school, I visited Myrtle and Margaret—a pair of elderly twins who looked after me as godparents—in their hospital beds. Both lived to over ninety, walking down the stairs from their second-story home every single day to go to Dunkin' Donuts or Star Market. They were vibrant and vital one day, shrunken and skeletal the next. I remembered how their skin had drawn tight over their bones. I feared I might not even recognize the person who had now spent months sequestered in this apartment, even as it was festooned with awards bearing his name.

I suppose my deepest fear was to see Master Ding alive but humorless . . . that would be worse than death.

But on the couch, the Master still looked like the man I'd known—albeit perhaps a bit thinner, and with an IV pouch attached to his arm.

"You're here! Fantastic!"

When I heard his voice—that voice that filled the whole room, stage speech brought into the real world—I knew he was the same.

"We were all very worried about you," I said. "Are you OK?"

"I'll be fine. They cut out a fifth of my lung."

I knew Master Ding had been sick; I knew he had cancer, I knew that surgeries like this happened. But for some reason, hearing such a specific amount of lung chopped away like offal at a marketplace shocked me. It felt like a sick reminder that, though we spoke every day together of humor, history, and wit, all these things seemed weak and invisible when considering we were both ultimately bags of meat.

"Will you—are you OK?" I stammered, not sure what to say when someone tells you their organs are being cut away piece by piece.

Master Ding laughed out loud, a bomb of a noise. "I said a fifth! I've still got 80 percent left!"

And he laughed so loud I started laughing, too.

Success Is Just Showing Up, Part One: Comas and Mud

During my tenure in the Happy Classroom, Master Ding cast out one of his students.

I wasn't there when it happened, and so exactly what transpired was never really clear to me, but according to other disciples, the expelled in question was a Romanian woman who had been doing xiangsheng with Master Ding for the better part of a decade and had missed a show that she had confirmed she would perform.

The punishment seemed a bit extreme, but it also reminded me of one of the few times I had ever seen Master Ding lose his temper.

I can only remember him yelling—true, angry yelling—twice.

The first time had nothing to do with missing shows. He blew up at a TV booker who said in front of all of us that his disciples (ostensibly because we were foreign) weren't doing "real xiangsheng."

Master Ding, who knew we weren't, by pure comedy standards, the greatest xiangsheng performers in the world, nevertheless took our teaching very seriously and tried to hold us to the same standards as his Chinese disciples. For the booker to invite us on the show and then say we weren't doing "real xiangsheng" was an affront against the dignity of his life's work, and he lost it.

Master Ding got right up in the booker's face. His eyes bulged and his face turned red. Veins stood out on his neck as he pointed his finger and laid into him with harsh language. The booker stared vacantly into space like a kindergartener who was asked to read in front of the class, knew he couldn't, and now wished he'd faked being sick and stayed home.

To hear that voice used in fury was shocking and terrifying. This was the voice that ballooned alongside the laughter it inspired; now it was a vehicle for pain. I felt like a tourist who'd spent the afternoon with a tame lion that suddenly mauled a safari guide. I knew he was my father, but it still took a while to feel safe sitting next to him after that.

As my adrenaline wore off, I looked at Master Ding and saw for a moment not just my teacher, but an old man who had spent his life doing one thing and one thing only, and set a great store by its value. A bad show, even incompetence, could be forgiven. But reducing the value of his life's work, his disciples, and his cherished art form to a dog-and-pony show was treacherous.

The only other time I'd seen him yell was over another case of a disciple who canceled on the day of our show. He had missed our bus heading into the countryside because the TV show he'd been shooting the night before in another part of the country had gone long. He'd rushed back to Beijing the next morning, but we had already started off without him.

I heard about this through the very loud phone conversation Master Ding was having in the front seat of the van. "You said you would be here, so you need to be here," he shouted. The van, usually humming with conversation, jokes, and snippets of opera, was deathly quiet. "Get to the show, or don't bother coming to the Happy Classroom again."

The student took a cab four hours into the countryside. He arrived half an hour before we were to go onstage. We threw together a brief rehearsal and got through the show; afterward, the disciple apologized to Master Ding profusely.

"Don't apologize to me," he said. "Apologize to Jesse. He had to learn all your lines in the car, in case you didn't make it."

The ride home was chilly and quiet, but the next week, when the disciple showed up at the Happy Classroom, Master Ding met him with his usual mirth.

Not showing up was the worst thing you could do, because Master Ding showed up. He was famous for it. We never learned about his early shows from him; instead, tales of his past exploits abounded amongst the disciples, traded around like collectible coins. "Master Ding makes the show" stories were a staple of our idle chat, like ghost stories around a bonfire.

My favorite of these stories always came from Lao Cui, a sixty-year old disciple from Beijing who looked like a Chinese version of Casey Stengel. Lao Cui knew more Master Ding stories than anyone. Though by xiangsheng genealogy standards he was technically only my "older brother," since we had the same master, he was still a xiangsheng performer with over forty years' experience, and so in many ways was a teacher to me just as Master Ding was.

While Master Ding ran the Happy Classroom, Lao Cui was there every meeting, and I soon found myself spending time with him outside the Happy Classroom as often as I could. I would scoot my e-bike fifteen kilometers out to the apartment he lived in near the airport with his son and granddaughter.

"A performer is a professional not because his best show is good, but because no matter what will happen, he gets onstage anyway." Lao Cui told me. "You can have a bad show, and sometimes the audience won't like it. But if you don't show up, then there's no chance. The show bookers will never have you back. It doesn't matter how good your best show is if your word as a performer—'I'll be there on this date at this time'—isn't trustworthy."

To Master Ding, this meant the worst thing one could do is commit to a show and not show up. Lao Cui told me he'd had this mentality since way back when.

"Back in the Cultural Revolution, Master Ding and I were performers in the Shanxi Coal Miner's Cultural Work Unit. Every year, we could write one routine, and we'd do it for the authorities to get it approved. They'd show up, and we'd do the whole thing with no audience, so nothing was funny. But they'd still tell us to change this, change that . . . Two weeks later they would come back and we'd do it again. Usually, we didn't actually change anything, but this time they would clap and tell us we'd done a great job. So that would be our xiangsheng routine for that year.

"We performed all around Shanxi Province for the coal miners. Every day, a different mine. We'd set up a stage and a thousand miners would crowd around, surrounding us. Then we'd do xiangsheng, and sometimes we'd stay and chat afterward. They were so happy to have us there.

"Well, one show, we were on our way to one of the mines and the rain had turned the road to mud. This was before they had paved roads in Shanxi. Our car got bogged down. Someone came by and told us they were going for trucks to get us out, but Master Ding was fretful. He didn't think they'd make it in time to get the car out and get to the show. So he took off his shoes and started wading through the mud, heading toward the mine.

"We shouted and shouted and he wouldn't turn around. He was going to get there for the show. But if he got there alone . . . what, a single xiangsheng performer? We'd be too ashamed to get there late if Master Ding had managed to make the show. So, me and all the other performers took off our shoes and we waded through the mud, too! We got there just at showtime, with muddy feet and all our equipment miles away . . . and the audience loved it."

These were the stories that percolated within our circle. Master Ding never had to give a list of rules; we knew the rules because you heard the stories. Your ride could break down. You could be sick. You could be far from prepared. It didn't matter. To Master Ding, you just showed up, and that's all that there was to it.

Once in 2007, Master Ding felt weak and light-headed before going onstage. He powered through, took his bows, came offstage, and immediately collapsed.

The sirens wailed as the ambulance shuttled him through the city to the nearest hospital. His disciples surrounded his bed, a ring of people from the four corners of the world. Was it dehydration? Was it the flu?

It turns out it was none of these things. Master Ding was in a coma.

The doctors made a diagnosis: Legionnaire's disease, a rare viral infection that normally knocked people out so quickly there was little time to do anything other than take them to the hospital. Master Ding had performed under bright lights, joking and singing, as the virus ate him away.

A day went by, then two, then three. Master Ding did not move.

He remained in the coma for three months.

"I wasn't there when he woke up," Lao Cui told me, "but apparently he sat straight up like he'd had a bad dream and asked, 'Did they pay us for the show?'"

When I go home to America, people always ask me how I started doing Chinese comedy. I definitely took a lot of proactive steps, but there definitely feels like an element of fate was involved. When I give the general "LinkedIn answer," I am actually thinking not of my years of learning Chinese, or stage experience, but of Master Ding in a hospital bed, in a coma, when I was in high school.

What if he had never woken up?

If xiangsheng was my introduction to Chinese comedy, and only one master took foreign students . . . it seems certain that nothing I've done in my entire career would have happened.

I don't know if working oneself into a coma is something worthy of praise. But after seeing what Master Ding put into his craft, his intense reaction to not showing up made sense to me. Bad shows could be fixed. But someone who canceled and left the show in a lurch—that person could not be tolerated.

This is what I remember thinking when we'd heard that our Romanian disciple was gone and would not be returning. Her name became anathema in the Happy Classroom, an environment that was probably one of the purest and most accepting that I'd ever known.

From that day forward, I realigned my priorities. First thing first: Make it to every show. Get on the stage. Soak up the stage time. All other things—personal improvement, show quality—came afterward. It was not my job to wait until I felt completely prepared, like I would definitely pay off the show. No—get all the stage time, at any level of preparation, possible.

At first glance, interpreting "Just Show Up" to mean "be OK not being fully ready" might seem to be an unprofessional mentality. After all, if you're a professional, you're being paid for your art! What kind of self-respecting artist sets the bar so low? At first, I chafed against going into shows unless I felt fully prepared for just this reason.

But after a few months with this mentality, I found that Just Show Up actually had a liberating effect on my comedy. Not only did I worry less, but my shows got better. Much better.

Before Just Show Up, I would worry about shows, sometimes for months beforehand. Would I be prepared? Would the jokes work? Would there be travel issues? I lost sleep, felt sick, and would have random spasms of panic throughout the day. *DON'T YOU KNOW YOU NEED TO DO TEN MINUTES IN CHENGDU IN THREE WEEKS?* I would think to myself, usually when trying to relax or have fun with friends.

I would go to parties in Beijing, drinking beers in the cool fall evenings on the rooftops of the *hutongs*. Chinese and expats alike chatted while overlooking the dragon-scaled tile roofs, and my Chinese comedy stories were often the center of attention. Outside, I was all smiles: Look at how much fun I'm having! I'm my own boss! I do comedy for a living! I can sleep till eleven if I want, any day of the week! Inside, I would be a sour mess. *YOU HAVE A SHOW COMING UP AND YOU'RE NOT WORKING ON IT EVERY SINGLE SECOND!*

Just Show Up gave me a way of placating my inner turmoil. It gave me a way to be professional without masochistically hating myself for every moment of idleness.

It worked for me because it made me realize that, ironically, my own neuroses would protect me against a lot of these worst-case scenarios. I enjoyed doing comedy and willingly spent seven nights a week rehearsing or performing. My jokes would be ready because I practiced, went to the Happy Classroom and open mics, did improv rehearsals. And when I bombed—which happened often—it was rarely because of something another hour or two of practice could fix. I was doing the work I needed to be doing to get good. The worry just made my life worse.

I wouldn't disrespect the audience or let my act fall into disrepair, because I'd go crazy if I did. Which meant what I had to do was . . .

Just Show Up.

When I started doing stand-up in Chinese, every single show sucked. I was writing my own material in my second language and going in front of crowds at bars and restaurants that had never seen or heard of stand-up. People would eat loudly and chat and otherwise disrupt my already belabored flow. My material was composed of middling ideas, all poorly executed.

I reminded myself that I was doing what I needed to do, bombing or not, just by getting onstage.

Just Show Up.

Once, I was asked to perform Chinese stand-up at a birthday party. I was told the birthday girl was a big fan of stand-up. I was not told the birthday girl was seven, had never heard stand-up, did not know what stand-up was, and had only asked for stand-up because she thought *stand-up* meant "children's radio shows."

I was also not told the party was in a restaurant. Not even in a private room—just at a restaurant.

So, in the middle of the restaurant, I did jokes for a seven-year old girl, her friends, parents, grandparents, aunts, and uncles—and, by proxy, all the other patrons within a thirty-foot radius. I didn't freak out; I did what I could, got some chuckles, collected my seven hundred kuai* for the gig, and left to enjoy the rest of a smogless Sunday.

Just Show Up.

I've Just Shown Up to perform xiangsheng, stand-up, and improv in English, Chinese, and both languages. I've Just Shown Up to shows in the countryside of Mainland China, Hong Kong, Taiwan, Macau, America, and Canada. I've Just Shown Up to corporate parties, underground clubs, fancy TV studios, and man-on-the-street video blogs.

---

* About $100! Better rates than in LA, for sure.

As I write this, I estimate I'm probably pushing past the thousand-show mark. I couldn't have gotten better if I'd been existentially worried before every show about anything else except for showing up and letting my comedy habits make the show good.

Then there was the cruise ship incident, where Just Show Up was put to the ultimate test.

Success and Showing Up, Part Two: High-Speed Boat Chases on the East China Sea

I'll include a more detailed section about life performing on the East China Sea for Chinese cruise ship tourists in a bit. For now, suffice it to say that it is every bit as surreal and outrageous as you imagine it to be.

For this story, however, know two things. The first seems obvious: If you miss the ship, you miss the ship. You can't swim and catch up with it. It's just gone.

Which leads to the second point: The cruise ships also run on the Just Show Up principle. On the ships, the main stage shows are performed for 1,400 paying customers each night, and the Chinese cruise customers never miss the main stage shows. Either I do my one-man stand-up show and perform fifty minutes, twice a night, for 1,400 tourists, or the stage is literally empty.

If I show up and people leave happy, I've done my job very well—and spared the ships the expense of bringing in a whole band or multiple entertainers.

But if I don't show up, I never get to do a cruise show for that company ever again. There are no excuses. It's the classic "you had one job" situation.

Once you're on the ship, the pressure is a bit abated. You don't need to bring "Live at the Apollo" energy to the theater. Indeed, many in the audience might be younger than ten or older than sixty and first-generation middle class, so it might literally be the first theater show they've ever been to. It's a space where professionalism is paramount and groundbreaking artistry is appreciated but not required.

What *is* required is getting on the ship.

This is why the cruise lines insist you travel to the port one day before the ship arrives. I've performed on ships that left from China but sailed everywhere from Korea to New Caledonia. This meant I sometimes had to fly to a second country, stay overnight to await the ship, and board the next day.

One fateful show, I was supposed to fly to Nagasaki, boarding a Shanghai-bound cruise liner. Unfortunately, there were no direct flights from Beijing to Nagasaki, which meant that I needed to transfer at the airport in Shanghai.

Problem 1: Beijing-to-Shanghai flight is delayed.

Problem 2: I miss my connecting flight.

Problem 3: There is only one flight a day to Nagasaki, and my replacement flight the next day leaves too late to board the ship.

Problem 4: The cruise line is based in the United States and nobody will pick up the phone because they are asleep.

I knew what I had to do: just show up.

The next morning, I took the first flight to anywhere in Japan. I landed in Kyoto around 11 a.m. I had to get to the ship by 4 p.m. The next five hours were so stressful, I sort of mentally blacked out, almost in the way one goes into shock when you break a bone.

Traveling across a whole country with no time to spare is hard anywhere, but after landing, I realized I was illiterate again. Being a white dude who could speak, read, and generally keep my shit together while living in Asia had become so much a part of my identity that it was shocking and embarrassing to land in Japan and turn instantly back into the stereotype know-nothing, bumbling, culturally illiterate *gaijin*.

Here's the plan: high-speed rail, transfer, high-speed rail, transfer, light rail, cab. I needed to cross virtually the entire width of Japan in one afternoon with no cell phone data and the three hundred Japanese words I'd learned watching *Naruto* in middle school. If I pulled it off perfectly, I'd arrive one hour before the ship left.

Once on board the high-speed train, in an attempt to relax, I bought a bag of peanuts and a big can of what I thought was fruit juice. After the first sip, I found out the drink was a grapefruit-flavored alcoholic cocktail. But I was stressed, so I just kept drinking, munching peanuts, and getting sloshed as the Japanese countryside flew by the window.

Transfer. Onto and off the light rail. Hail a cab. Show the port info in Japanese. *Fune! Fune!* I said, using one of my three hundred words. Ship! Ship!

It turned out most of the Japanese words I knew were about ninjas and were less useful in everyday situations than I'd hoped. I relied mostly on miming and cringed internally. *I am a linguistic performance artist in Asia! I am better than this!*

But I ate my pride and spread my arms wide. "Big ship! Big ship!"

Japanese cabs are embodiments of stately service; the drivers wear little caps like police officers and spotless white linen gloves. My driver was a consummate professional; I was a little drunk at three in the afternoon, wide-eyed and manic, making a beeline for the ocean. I can only imagine what this serene and sanguine fifty-year-old Japanese man thought of me.

Probably something like: "These foreigners are fortunate we are so accepting of their barbarian nature."

We reached the port and I saw the ship—sixteen stories of gleaming glass windows protruding magnificently from the pale concrete dock. But the car stopped. There was a fence; the guard said we couldn't drive past it.

I got out, paid, slung my luggage over my shoulder, and ran. The ship was still there. I'd made it!

But I ran and ran and the ship didn't get any bigger. It turns out the ship was so massive and the dock so bare that I'd misjudged the distance between myself and the dock. I thought it was a few hundred yards. Later, I looked on Google maps and found it was more than a mile. I tried to keep my backpack and duffel bag lashed to my back, put my head down, and pumped my legs.

And I made it.

I put my hand out and touched the cold steel shell of the outer hull. The ship towered above me, bowing outward slightly and higher than a skyscraper.

And then, the moment I touched the ship, like out of a bad comedy—

WRURRRRRRRRRRRR!!!!!!!!!!!!

The horn.

The ship started floating away—very, very slowly.

WRURRRRRRRRRRRRR!!!!

I kept my hand on the ship for ten seconds, and then there was a yard of water between me and the ship. Then two yards. Then ten.

WRURRRRRRRRRRRRR!!!!

I thought I had an extra hour. In fact, I'd lost that hour traveling east to Japan and entering a new time zone. Since my phone had no data, it had never adjusted my clock. My trip had been doomed from the start to—in the best-case scenario—get me to the ship the moment it left.

I watched the enormous vessel float off into the Pacific. Like an ant beneath an elephant, I waved my hands frantically. Twelve stories above, in a glass bubble protruding from the side of the ship, I saw a half dozen human-shaped specks staring down at me.

It was over. I'd missed the ship. Unless I had a helicopter, or . . .

BURRRRRRRRRRRR . . .

Just as all seemed lost, a tiny motorboat, no bigger than a fish compared to the whale that was the ocean liner, puttered out from around the stern.

It was the Japanese coast guard. They were very confused.

"I'm the comedian! I'm the comedian!" I shouted in English, as the two men on the ship passed each other a fantastic look whose meaning in Japanese I can only guess. One of them beckoned me onto their boat. I hopped onto the boat and underneath a small canopy roof.

Then we started the chase.

The ocean liner wasn't going to stop, and the tugboat was not built for speed. The captain of the tiny ship gunned the motor, and dark smog billowed out of an upright exhaust pipe, swept away immediately in the rushing wind. I stuck my head out the window and felt eight hours of nervous sweat on my forehead as the wind whipped my hair around. Tourists leaned over railings, floor after floor of colorfully clothed specks, standing a hundred feet above, watching the spectacle from the main decks and private verandas.

We were a ways out into the ocean by the time we managed to get parallel to the ship. We matched its speed, thirty meters or so of ocean between the vehicles. By this time, a portal had opened about two stories above the waterline, where a slew of ship officials stood in their gleaming white uniforms.

"WHO ARE YOU?" an Indian man holding a clipboard shouted across the water, his voice barely audible above the waves and wind.

"I'M THE COMEDIAN!" I shouted. I mimed putting a microphone to my mouth, which, I realized later, probably looked more obscene than anything else.

He ducked his head and conferred with his cohorts, then his papers. I felt like I was on trial. Much would be decided soon.

"HOW DO YOU SPELL YOUR LAST NAME?" he shouted.

"A-P-P-E-L-L."

He looked at the paper.

"TWO P's, TWO L's?"

"YES!"

Another short conference.

"WHAT IS YOUR PASSPORT NUMBER?"

It was like someone had tried to make a version of *Mission: Impossible* where all of Hollywood's production values were being spent getting through a TSA check.

Another conference. My fate hung in the balance.

"GET HIM UP HERE!"

The tugboat lurched underneath me; the back of the boat swung out as the ship maneuvered itself to be perpendicular to the cruise liner. Its nose got closer and closer to the ship, eventually ramming its point, which was covered with a massive rubber tire, right up against the porthole into the ship, two stories above the waterline.

"STEP BACK!" came the shout from above. The Indian man threw down a pile of chains. When it reached the tugboat, I saw that these chains unfurled into a ladder.

I didn't hesitate. I swung my backpack and duffel bag over my shoulder and started climbing. As it turns out, when you're hurtling into the Pacific Ocean at thirty miles a hour, trapped between bewildered Japanese coast guardsmen and confused Indian shipmasters and someone throws you a ladder, you climb it, because it seems the only polite thing to do.

I've heard when climbing ladders, the best advice is to not look down. So of course I looked down and I saw the waves crashing over the bow of the ship, and the faces of the coast guardsmen, and thought to myself that this was madness, utter madness.

Then I had a hand on the lip of the ship and the cruise ship agents dragged me on board.

One person whisked my bags away and put them through a metal detector; another came at me with a blocky, silver, 2004-era point-and-shoot digital camera.

"Smile! We need a picture for your ship ID!"

I smiled. *Flash!* He nodded. The porthole to the outside ocean closed and the room got much darker in an instant.

The Indian man with the clipboard came up to me, smooth as could be. "Welcome on board," he said. "The buffet opens at six."

International Waters

I actually thought I was getting scammed when I got my first invitation to perform Chinese stand-up on a cruise ship.

I got a private message on Weibo (Chinese Twitter) from an account with a woman's picture and a Chinese name. The message told me the writer was David—he claimed to be the American husband of the Chinese woman—and he said he was a cruise ship booking agent looking for a last-minute replacement for a ship gig.

"My wife saw your videos on here and thinks you're funny. I can't understand any of it, but we're in a crisis here. Do you have twenty-five minutes of clean stand-up in Chinese?"

"Of course," I said confidently, surprised to hear myself sound confident.

"Can you get to the ship in Fukuoka four days from now?"

At that point, I was actually in Hawaii, where I had been teaching American middle schoolers Chinese-language improv comedy for a summer language camp. The camp was over and I was looking out over the Pacific Ocean on what I thought would be the beginning of a vacation.

I still didn't think this whole thing was real, but I couldn't see where the scam was. So, I cut to the chase, told him, truthfully, that I could do it but I was on vacation, and I'd only cut my vacation short if it was worth it, and I didn't want to do any lengthy negotiations.

He told me I could make three thousand US dollars for the show.* I said that sounded great. The negotiations took about twelve seconds.

It wasn't until I got an email with my plane tickets that I actually believed any of it was real. I cut my vacation short, and in what seemed like no time, I was somewhere on the East China Sea, backstage at a packed theater of 1,400 seats, wearing a borrowed suit and frantically reviewing my set list.

This was about two years into my comedy journey in China, and I had twenty-five minutes of clean material—barely. I would need to scrape up some jokes I'd only ever done at a few open mics, but I had the material. But I had no idea if my Beijing club jokes would work for an audience of Chinese third-tier-city vacationers who had never seen stand-up comedy in their lives.

Backstage, I quickly realized the true audience was not in the seats at all. The true audience was the cruise director, the person in charge of all the entertainment on the ship. Every ship had one cruise director, each with their own unique taste and all the power of a petty dictator. If they liked your show, it meant as many bookings on their ship as you wanted—which, at that point in my career, meant about a hundred times the paycheck I'd receive doing a Beijing bar show. If they didn't like you . . . well, every ten or fifteen years they switched people and you could audition again. Maybe.

By the time just before the coronavirus, when I performed my last shows on the ships, these cruise directors were mostly Chinese people.

---

* This meant the same income as if I did a little girl's birthday party show every day for a month!

But in 2014, the cruise companies were rushing to fill the demand from the Chinese market and had simply sent their existing ships over to China—cruise directors and all. This meant my fate would be decided by a British man in his mid-forties who couldn't understand any of my jokes.

The cruise director did have a Chinese "assistant"—in this case, a twenty-five-year-old Chinese woman from Shanghai with impeccable English. She shadowed him from morning till night to translate and assist him on a ship that every month had more and more Chinese employees, and fewer English-speaking ones.

From what I could tell, the true job of the assistant was to do all her boss's work while weaving an elaborate illusion that allowed him to plausibly believe he was doing it himself. Here, I saw, was the real power on the ship. If the assistant liked me, I was good to go.

When I came onstage, I was met by a great noise—not just applause, but also screams, mostly from children, who were crawling everywhere. They slithered around on laps, in the aisles, over the backs of the seats, on the ground on the second-floor balcony. They would line up on the mezzanine, sticking their small heads through the balustrades, their bright eyes looking down at me from the roof like a flock of bats. It was unlike any audience I'd performed for before.

I did all my cleanest jokes, mostly about learning Chinese, living in Beijing, and trying to make friends in China. I got some laughs, but the noise of the children never stopped. It threw off my timing completely. If comedy lives in the silence between the joke and laugh, what did it mean that my audience was constantly screaming?

I started to sweat. A lot. Enough that I had to constantly wipe my brow with my floppy, ill-fitting borrowed suit jacket.

This is a bad look for a comedian. A little sweat is OK. A lot of sweat is called "flop sweat." When the flop sweat comes out, you lose the crowd, no matter what. Whether you are comfortable onstage or not, the audience sees the sweat and thinks you've completely lost control.

I tried to remember what Master Ding had done in cases like this. We had done some bad rooms together—mostly banquets, where the clatter of forks and knives mixed with dim conversation from people who cared enough to keep their voices down a bit but not enough to stay quiet entirely. One or two of these people are OK, but at a banquet, every single person more than two tables away from the stage is having a full-on conversation during every performance.

A few hours before one of those banquet shows, Master Ding had brought me along to walk the stage and get used to the angles of the room.

"If people are talking and distracted, look them in the eyes. Don't say anything, don't attack them; just look. Sometimes they stop. Usually they don't. But when you look at the first few rows in the eyes, you will see that a lot of the audience are still with you. They want the show to be good. They want you to succeed. They know it's hard."

That show went exactly as Master Ding said. Under the bright, flat overhead lights of a hotel ballroom—the staff had forgotten to dim the lights for the show to create more of a "comedy" vibe—the low chatter of six hundred guests was so loud I could barely hear Master Ding speaking right next to me.

After the show, I was fuming. Weeks of study of these complicated xiangsheng jokes felt like wasted time if the audience wouldn't shut up. "In America, you could deal with this almost like they were hecklers. Shout for silence, call them out, something . . . anything!"

Master Ding shook his head. He told me that in the xiangsheng world, it was taboo to blame the audience. "The audience is our *yi shi fu mu. Yi* means 'clothing.' *Shi* means 'food.' *Fu mu* means 'parents.' They are our parents, who feed us and put clothes on our back. A performer who blames the audience is blaming their parents for taking care of them."

Then he laughed and said, "But it is annoying, isn't it?"

Backstage after that bad show, I didn't really buy this argument. But the longer I performed comedy, the more I saw something happen to comedians who had been doing comedy for decades and decades. They lost their love for the audience.

When comedians do their first open mics, they always want laughs. They know that they are there to tell jokes, make people happy, and relieve their own stress along with the audience's. They hang out afterward, chat with random friends of friends, and bathe in the energy of people enjoying their show. They might be at the bottom of their comedic trajectory, but they're having fun.

But after five years, then ten, then twenty, comedians tend to get jaded. They treat comedy as a job, and one where they get paid by people they might not even like to spend time with. They show up later and leave earlier. They begin performing jokes more for the comedians in the back, or for other comedians in the scene at large, than for the audience in front of them. They care more about the recording of the show than the show itself. They pick esoteric joke topics just for the sake of it, or even do bits about how bad other audiences were.

Comedy is always a balance-beam act, but they choose to walk a tightrope, making the show harder more for their own amusement than for that of the audience, and they care less if they fall, since they can then blame the audience.

Some comedians drop out of live performing altogether and become writers for TV shows or movies, separating themselves so much from the audience that comedy becomes a more intellectual exercise—granted, one that sometimes involves a lot of fart jokes.

But Master Ding and the whole of xiangsheng tradition came from street performance. If you didn't get laughs, you didn't eat. You could even be attacked by rowdy crowds who thought you were wasting their time or getting in their way. Treating the audience with respect and yourself with humility was crucial.

And since the gigs with the worst conditions for comedy—like a dinner gala in a brightly lit ballroom—tend to be the best-paying ones, I came to see that this excessive humility toward oneself, almost to the point of becoming a supplicant to the audience, had its benefits. It provides a worldview where dealing with bad gigs and disrespectful audiences was part of an honorable burden, part of making an honest living, and not a sign that you've picked the wrong career.

This humility in relation to the audience was even more powerful considering the path a normal Chinese audience member had taken to get there. Instead of making me angry, it made me ask *why*. Why were they like this? Why wouldn't they control their kids, or stop talking to each other during the show? Didn't they know how to act?

My dad had taken me to the theater when I was young, and I performed high school drama to an audience of my classmates' parents. When I performed in *One Flew Over the Cuckoo's Nest* in freshman year of high school in Newton, Massachusetts, the average audience member probably had a master's degree and decades of exposure to live performance.

But in China, almost nobody's dad had taken them to a Western-style theater. Many had never gone to college. Some might have grown up in poverty. What performances people saw might have been on the street or in teahouses. There simply was a different attitude as to how appropriate it was to talk in the middle of a show.

And yet, these are the people who feed and clothe me. That is our relationship.

So, as the children shrieked from overhead, I tried to redefine my purpose for the show. I did what Master Ding suggested. I looked at the eyes of the audience in the first few rows, and I saw them laughing. There were lots of middle-aged couples, exhausted but content, flanked by their kids on one side and parents on the other. They were enjoying the show, and that was what I was here for.

Though it wound up feeling more like a scripted one-man show than a comedy routine, I got through it and earned some applause at the end. I went backstage, unsure if I would be docked points for failing to keep the crowd in check. I had no idea if I had bombed or not.

The cruise director and his assistant were waiting for me. "He's funny!" she said immediately.

"I believe you!" he said, and laughed, shaking my hand. "We'll bring you back next summer."

From then on, the ships served as a stabilizing point for my career.

On a very practical level, it was good for other people to pay for me to leave China. As an artist, there was never any hope of me having a good Chinese visa. Of the nine years I lived in China full time, for seven of them my visa required me to exit China after a maximum stay of sixty days.

In my early days, this meant a quick hop over to Hong Kong or Taiwan—which apparently counted as "leaving the borders," but these forced "vacations" were expensive and usually didn't come at convenient times for me. I always made sure to save enough money to avoid the cheapest "visa run" route—the twelve-hour train ride to Mongolia, which cost only sixty dollars round trip.*

But every time I performed on the ships, I went through immigration, my passport would get a stamp on it, and my clock would be reset until I came back to China. I found that as long as I took a few gigs during the cruise season—late spring to early fall—I could combine that with a trip home to the US during Chinese New Year and virtually never need to flee the country for visa reasons.

This also meant I got to visit many new places—wherever the ship docked. Places like Vietnam, Korea, and Japan. This was fun, though I rarely had more than a few hours to explore, as I either had to make a flight home or get back on the ship. I visited Fukuoka so often that I think I have been to every museum and park within transit range of the port.

The ship also brought me good income without needing to do any extra work, since I was always working on material, and I had to do virtually no prep to do the shows, even when they expanded my act to forty and then fifty minutes. The hardest part was getting to and from the ship, which always meant a full travel day of trains, flights, and cabs.

At first, I wondered at the expense of flying me all around Asia and paying so well for the shows. How much money do these cruise companies make? But it turns out cruise ships love stand-up comedians, since stand-ups can hold down the entire mainstage by themselves for a headline show but only need one plane ticket, one cabin, and one per diem.

---

* I met some people who had done the Mongolia visa-run trip. Apparently, the way to do it is to cross the border, buy a bottle of Genghis Khan vodka, and immediately head back on the next train, for a twenty-four-hour round trip.

By contrast, the ship also had a full cast of two dozen actors and singers, half as many stage crew, and a full eight-piece orchestra. Recruited by a long, involved, and costly process from all around the English-speaking world, these players put on two full musicals each four-day cruise. Backstage, the whole area was choked with elaborate costumes, giant papier-mâché set pieces in the shapes of buildings and trees—everything needed to do a Broadway-style song-and-dance show.

Compared to this setup, paying me to let them take a night off was the best deal the cruise companies could get. One cruise director told me later, "I don't know what your set is about, and I don't care. If people are laughing and we don't get thrown out of China for the jokes, you can be here as long as you want."

While my first few times on the ship were spent mainly on the guest side, reading books and drinking tea while soaking in the hot tub and eating food from the buffet, I found that with each trip I spent more and more time in the crew quarters, until I basically didn't leave them at all.

I had always known that the crew of a cruise ship must live *somewhere* on board, but I had no idea of the enormity of the quarters and the operations it took to keep the boat moving. A ship of three thousand guests might have 1,500 crew on board, and whole areas of the ship were exclusively for their use.

This meant not only living quarters, but loading docks, health clinics, and even a morgue. All this was packed into decks with low-hanging ceilings and pipes and wires everywhere, snaking along any flat surface but the floor. The pipes and wires, color-coded by use, evoked veins running along and throughout the gray bones of the ship, as if the whole ocean liner was a mythical living Titan, and the people were its cells.

The guest sections on the ship featured beautiful rugs, elaborate art decorations, and nonstop music and entertainment. By contrast, the crew quarters were gray and boring. Instead of paintings, there were time sheets, safety regulations, and sign-up forms for pickup basketball leagues.

As a "guest performer," I was neither truly a crew member nor truly a guest. The cruise ship companies made it clear that I was *not* an employee, but since the guests would think I was one, this meant I still had to abide by their employee code of conduct. The contracts included clauses on how to dress in guest areas, how to act if guests thought I was a crew member and needed something done for them, and even a clause stating that I could not sleep with any guests. Whether I could sleep with the crew was left—perhaps deliberately—unclear.

I nodded while signing the contract as if this all made deep, intuitive sense and wasn't simply a blatant way to avoid legal and tax obligations.

The cookie-cutter glamour of the ship was almost completely inverse to the no-nonsense world of the crew area. Each ship had unlabeled doors that shuttled people between the two realms. Every time I performed on a new ship, I would need to learn which doors were not doors at all, but portals to cross between worlds. The suddenness of the transition made them feel like dimensional rifts.

On one side of the portal, you would hear Chinese families talking about their day—Should we go to the pool? Watch a movie? Play Ping-Pong? On the other, crew from three dozen nations interacted in various pidgin languages, visiting the commissary, eating in the mess hall, living in plain clothes like soldiers given a break from the front lines. I would often meet people here in a more relaxed setting and completely fail to recognize them even two hours later, when I saw them in full dress in the guest area, their body language now in customer-service mode.

I first discovered the crew area because I had forgotten to bring shaving cream, and the cruise director's assistant told me I could buy some at the small shop in the crew quarters. There, I found a mini convenience store with surprisingly reasonably priced everyday items, everything from candies to Bluetooth speakers.

I also discovered that while the chefs on board were very skilled and made excellent food for the guests, they clearly enjoyed cooking for the crew more. While the ship's menu had a very "Western fine dining" aesthetic, the chefs would cook foods from their own home countries for service in the mess hall. This meant mountains of Filipino, Indian, and Chinese homestyle food served with giant trays of white rice.

And compared to the food served to the guests, the crew food was *spicy*. I loved it.

In the evenings, I would hang out all night at the crew bar, which was always rowdy, loud, bumping whatever club music was popular in Southeast Asia at any given time.

Most importantly, the bar had subsidized alcohol. I had thought the ship might be dry for the crew, almost like in the navy. But this was not the case at all. All sorts of bottled beers and hard liquor were available at truly impressive prices. A bottle of beer could be had for $1.50, which was cheap even for a bar in China.

Gone were my days of paying the guest prices at the bars on board the ship! I quickly found out a few dollars' worth of beer was all I needed to worm my way into any circle of friends relaxing at the bar.

The crew were fascinating. They signed up for contracts of at least ten months, and did not see home at all during this time. People were open and welcoming in a way only confined people can be—bad blood on a ship has nowhere to go, so why not play nice with everyone? It almost reminded me of summer camp: Unless you were an absolute menace, everyone was willing to quickly become close friends, for a day, for a week, for ten months . . . for ten years.

At the bar, there seemed to be a few established cliques. One was made up of the service workers—and was actually two cliques—one of Chinese workers and one of English-speaking ones.

The Chinese crew were very glad to finally have a white person on board they could speak to in Chinese. They always had tons of questions about the way they were supposed to be doing their jobs. One man, with the intensity of someone who has been wondering about a small thing for months with no resolution, asked, "When I ask if you want more water, and you say, 'I am fine,' then that means no? But if you say just 'Fine,' then that means yes?"

They clearly took a lot of pride in being part of a "Western" service crew. One of the Chinese workers on a ship told me he was leaving after his next contract to run a training department for a Chinese hotel chain in Western service technique and culture.

"My cousin in Shanghai went to college and works at a bank. But I will be making more than him," he said, beaming.

The non-Chinese crew were mostly from the Philippines, but included a lot of Indians and, surprisingly, Burmese. Sitting with this crew meant leaving the evening very drunk and with ringing ears. They would drink whole beers in one go, slam the bottle down, make a joke, laugh whether or not anyone else did, and then run up to the area in front of the DJ and start singing karaoke sans microphone, blasting their voice at full power to try and carry the song over the chaos of the bar.

Hanging out with these people made me feel awesome, like I was some sort of pirate, and by the time I hung up my sword and peg leg I would have friends in every port. They all had WeChat, and I kept in touch with some of them after I got off the ship.

But the truth was that I was very different from most of these people, who could earn more in one contract on the ship than anyone in their village back home could make in a decade.

The clique that I fit best into, and was actually the most a part of, was the performers' clique. This included all the cast and crew of the mainstage musical shows, who I learned doubled as the peppy "everyone dance now!"–type hype squad for all the manufactured fun aboard the ship.

The performers tended to be American, Canadian, British, Australian, and New Zealanders. Hanging out with them felt like being back in the theater department at Newton North High School, hanging out in the hallways, sitting on that ratty couch, discussing which musicals were good and which were shit, sharing gossip on who was sleeping with who.

One night, I had a long conversation with a girl who had been a dancer, hoping to make it on Broadway.

"I did small shows in smaller cities. Eventually, I made the leap and did auditions for Broadway. Singing, dancing, I tried anything I could to get a role. It was impossible. Everyone was so good. So, when I auditioned for the ship, I figured I would make some money and use that to live when I went back, but I loved it here. Good treatment, professional crew, awesome people. Ten months went by fast. I saved everything. I decided, 'Why not do another contract?'

"But every year, it gets harder to go back. The stage here is great, the crew is great, the quality of the shows are . . . good. But it's not Broadway. And though I make a lot more money than my friends who are sticking it out in New York, I feel like they are living my dream."

These artists really made me pause and reflect on my life as a performer who was part of a global community of artists. Up until now, I had been completely focused on making it in the "niche" world of Chinese comedy—if you could consider an audience of 1.4 billion people "niche."

But this pull between good gigs that make money and the struggle gigs that feed the soul isn't just found on cruise ships. Growing up with no artists in my family, I realized I had the naive idea that as you get better and more famous, the gigs get better and pay more money. But the reality is that gigs pay what they pay, and gigs that are prestigious or challenging rarely pay more than performing for, say, a bunch of Chinese tourists on a cruise ship.

Some of the artists on their first few contracts were torn, wondering when it made sense to reenter the harsh reality of being a singer, or a dancer, or even a lighting technician. The ones who had been on the ship for decades had no such issues. They had made the full commitment to the sea. They had few friends on land, and their "family" lived on the ship.

On my first cruise, I met one man who was on his last contract. He was the head of theater entertainment, and held court as everyone else on the ship cheered him and brought him far too many beers, many of which he passed straight to me.

"I'm fifty. I've spent my whole life performing, doing what I love, and I don't regret a thing," he said. "I never had to pay for rent, or food. When we land, I'm going to get off the boat, fly to Spain, buy a house with cash, get a dog, and drink beer in the afternoon."

"Will you miss the ships?" I asked.

He looked around the bar area, through all the colored lights and the DJ who was blasting Filipino club music, people and noise everywhere. "I think I will," he told me.

Seeing the extremes—from people who felt they had sold out on their dream for cash, all the way to people who thought anyone still struggling to make a living on land was a fool—taught me that every artist has to make their own sense of the world and the market for our services. If you don't, you will literally drive yourself insane. There was no inherent way to know who was right, what to chase, how long to chase, and when to not overthink and just take the money and run.

These were my first interactions with professional performers. I found that, to my own surprise and deep satisfaction, I was already one of them. They treated me like I was an artist and performer, and my impostor syndrome quickly faded. I had won my way onto the ship through talent, just as they had. I was fascinated with their lives on the ship; they were amazed I could be doing Chinese stand-up.

It was a moment when I realized I had indeed made it. I might have started as a researcher and academic, but I could cut it amongst the other artists, too. It gave me a confidence that has not left me to this day.

Back on land, it turns out everybody has very strong opinions on cruise ships, and they are always just waiting for you to ask.

When I mentioned I performed on the ships, some of my friends would talk about the good times they had had on cruises with their families. The rest wondered what kind of person would pay money to purposely live on a floating petri dish as far as could be from the aid of civilization. This was usually followed by them adding, almost as an aside intended to soothe me, "Of course, if they're paying you, that's a different thing."

For me, the ships were about none of those things. The ship was a retreat from reality, a chance to join the circus and sail with a crew. It meant hours and hours to drink tea and read books. It meant good meals at new ports.

Eventually, as my career took off, I found I didn't really even need the money like before. Still, I kept taking the gigs during the peak season, at least a few a year.*

In the end, the cruise ships weren't about the money. They were a step I needed to take to become a professional performer. And in a country where the comedy industry was so new and unstable, there came a time when my perspective on the rowdy theaters full of children and grandparents began to switch.

I began to look forward to the challenges of those big rooms, with their distracted and inexperienced audiences. I began to experiment. How much English can they understand? How much politics can they take before they get nervous? Can I prepare at least one joke about each province, so I can do crowd work and have something ready when I ask where they are from?

And as the years went by, and I got better, the rooms started to quiet down. I could speak more steadily, calm my movements, take deeper breaths between bits.

For their part, the audience began to change as well. Stand-up

---

* The cruise ship money eventually became the money I used to start a comedy club in Beijing. I had to give the landlady three months' rent and two more for a deposit when I started the club. I withdrew it all in cash, since it was above the limit for the bank transfer, and delivered a backpack full of Red Maos to the landlady, and felt like a boss.

The ships even helped calm my anxiety about being twenty-five years old and paying for a comedy club's rent and payroll out of my checking account. I told myself, "If the club bombs, just do a few more weeks on the ships."

started to become a real thing in China. There were stand-up shows on TV. A few of these shows were getting big enough that their stars began to rival xiangsheng performers in fame. The younger people in the audience were especially thrilled to attend a real stand-up show in the flesh, and laughed heartily.

Slowly, more and more, they wanted to watch.

Transition, No Transition

Somewhere around this time, a little over a year after my Fulbright grant ended, I went from making that developing-country comedy researcher money to making that developing-country comedian money.

I moved into a cheaper apartment, a tiny box of a room in a small flat I shared with two roommates. My personal space had been cut by a quarter, but the apartment had one major benefit: It happened to face east with a direct view into the Confucius Temple. I could wake up every day, look out at the golden-glazed roof tiles, and think that all the court officials since the Yuan dynasty had taken their imperial examinations on the street where I now lived.

To pay the rent, I did more shows, including bad shows—I needed the money. But day to day, there was very little change. I kept learning from Master Ding. I kept doing Chinese improv. I kept going to open mics.

When I came home to the US for vacation, a lot of people told me this was the bravest decision I'd made—that after Fulbright and its halo of legitimacy was gone, I continued to pursue Chinese comedy.

To me, it wasn't a hard decision at all.

Things clarified for me during a conversation with one of my fellow Fulbright scholars. Toward the end of our fellowship, the cohort assembled in Beijing for a party, journeying from the far-flung reaches of the country where we had done our research. We all mingled outside in a *hutong* courtyard drinking beer, basking in the last idyllic days of the Beijing autumn.

Our conversation, however, was less tranquil. We were all sucked toward the question of "what next" like we were being pulled inexorably into a black hole.

"What will you do?" I asked one of the other scholars who, like me, had gotten the fellowship straight out of undergrad.

"Consulting. I set it up six months ago. I'm going to do it for two years, or as long as I can take it, then quit, since I'm sure I'm going to hate it. From there, I'll use the savings to do something else."

"What else?"

"I don't know, something else. Something that's not consulting," he said, and we laughed.

I wondered whether I, too, should try to make some money early in my career and set myself up to do what I wanted later. But when I thought about this, it occurred to me: What would I want to do later?

What did I want to do any more than what I was doing now? Running my own schedule, doing my own shows, working with Master Ding? I couldn't think of anything—certainly nothing you could "apply" to.

Maybe it made sense to make more money before chasing what I wanted to do, but . . . how much money did I need to do Chinese comedy? Not much, really. Beijing wasn't cheap, but it was cheaper than any major American city. Just the cost of American health care, auto insurance, car repairs, and gas money would be more per month than all of what I spent in China. I could live in China for less than it cost not to die in America.

In the end, it was perhaps a throwaway detail of his that hit me the hardest: "I set it up six months ago."

I had been savoring my Fulbright year so much that I didn't want it to end. If I had a job set up six months before the finish . . . I wouldn't have worked as hard as I did on my xiangsheng. I would have accomplished so much less.

I had both curiosity and ambition, but I was chasing my curiosity, not my ambition. I wanted to continue doing Chinese comedy. I could afford to try—and not knowing what was coming wasn't a bug, it was a feature.

Something about living on a short time horizon, gazing forward only enough to know how to reach the goals my curiosity valued today, made me work hard and enjoy doing it. Of all the things I had learned—Chinese tongue twisters, Beijing opera, stage demeanor—none of these skills in and of themselves were that useful. And yet, when I turned around, I had grown so much in so many ways in just one year out of college.

I had six months' worth of rent and food money saved. I knew that if I applied for a job, got a boss, went to work every day, and accepted the vapidity of capitalistic servitude, something fabulous I had learned about myself would die.

Most importantly, I just didn't want to stop. And until I ran out of money, I didn't intend to.*

---

* If you pirated this book, this is your chance to go buy a copy—I need that monaaaaayyyyy.

Chinese New Year in Trench Bottom Village

If any of my Chinese comedian friends ever read this book, the funniest part about it to them will be that there's a whole chapter about Song Qiyu.

Even amongst the characters in the early days of the Chinese stand-up comedy world, Qiyu stood out for being nothing like the other comedians. He was short, with thick glasses, small eyes, and well-cut short hair. He had a collection of sweater vests and always seemed to be just a little overdressed for any room he was in. He spoke rapidly, in short bursts, with a small stutter. This would have attracted attention if it hadn't been overwhelmed by a thick, rural Shaanxi accent, which betrayed his coal-country roots.

Perhaps because of his stutter and accent, his act consisted of a lot of Rodney Dangerfield–esque one-liners.

"Raising kids is easier than raising pets. Kids don't shed."

Any time we were on a show together, without fail, he would do this joke, in a thick Shaanxi accent:

"My Mandarin is not so standard. I have been studying. Thank you, Teacher Jesse."

Some of his jokes hit. A lot didn't. It was a sign of either great confidence or great apathy that he almost never changed his act to take out the ones that didn't work.

Instead, he would follow up jokes that bombed by saying, "*Bu hao xiao,*" over and over again: "That wasn't funny. That wasn't funny. That wasn't funny," as if chastising himself.

Sometimes, this was funny, and the audience laughed. Other times, they didn't. He did it after every bombed joke anyway, regardless of the reaction. Eventually, many comedians in the scene would start saying, "*Bu hao xiao, bu hao xiao,*" after their jokes, more for the sake of breaking out a deep-cut reference for other comedians in the back than for the audience.

Song Qiyu was a polarizing figure in our tiny comedy scene. Other Chinese comedians couldn't seem to make up their minds about whether he was good for the scene or not.

At a time when the whole scene was a dozen stand-ups doing one regular open mic in a small *hutong* bar for sixty people, Song Qiyu applied for and actually got on a TV show, not telling any of us until it was about to air. This meant that the short, stuttering guy from the country was the Chinese nation's first introduction to Western stand-up comedy on state media.

Qiyu did two minutes in front of a panel of celebrities, including the greatest xiangsheng performer of modern times, the inimitable Master Guo Degang. He bombed every joke.

He bombed so hard that Master Guo made some remarks about how xiangsheng was still safe for a while yet from this new, upstart Western comedy style. These jokey but arrogant comments from a megastar, directed at an unfunny but earnest bumpkin just trying to get a break, were so pointed that they backfired and caused a viral sensation. Thanks to this, Song Qiyu has a claim—however weak—to being the first homegrown viral Chinese stand-up comedian.

Emotions in the scene were split between frustration (of all of us, how did this guy get on TV first?), jealousy that he had the chance to meet Guo Degang, anger that he had debased stand-up and possibly soured the whole of state media on the art form forever, and grudging admission that this was indeed the best promotion stand-up had had on social media in the history of the country.

One comedian friend of mine told me a story of how Song Qiyu invited him to a thousand-person theater, only to find out everyone in the audience was over sixty-five years old. Qiyu had partnered with the local retirement homes to pack the theater.

My friend bombed, forced to ad-lib lots of material since he didn't normally play the geriatric crowd, and was initially pissed off at being paid only forty-five dollars before Song Qiyu told him every single ticket had been given away for free, and he was taking a big loss on the show.

"I tried to get a big theater. Give away a lot of tickets. Pack the house. Get sponsors. But no sponsors. No money," Qiyu said. "Stand-up is hard. Stand-up is hard."*

Another friend of mine—a female comedian—said she had been invited to a show produced by Song Qiyu called "*Mei Nü Tuokouxiu*"—"Beautiful Women Stand-up."

The poster was a giant closeup of ruby-red lips licking a microphone like a lollipop. Song Qiyu was here to sell tickets, not be subtle.

"I never knew Song Qiyu was such a devoted feminist," I remarked.

"I got paid and he gave me thirty minutes of stage time, which is something none of the other clubs gave me, so I don't care what the poster looks like," she told me.

---

* Repeatedly saying "脱口秀很难的。我也是男的。" was another of his classic responses to bombing a joke.

If you asked me whether Qiyu truly cared about female voices in comedy, or simply couldn't find enough female comedians to fill out the card and gave them all lots of stage time, my answer would be yes.

He did more shows and sold more tickets than anyone in the scene at the time, and would produce shows anywhere, for anyone, at any time, for any reason. Some of them were good. Many were not. Some of them made money. Many did not.

One time, Song Qiyu asked me if he could meet Master Ding, and I invited him to our Happy Classroom one Saturday to observe. After the rehearsal, I introduced them, and Song Qiyu immediately launched into a pitch for some sort of wacko foreigners/xiangsheng/stand-up mega-show idea he wanted to tour around the country. Master Ding said he would think about it.

After Qiyu left, I asked Master Ding, "Are you really going to think about it?"

"I'm thinking about it. And now I'm done." he said, and laughed.

Some people liked him. Some did not. He did not care. He just kept producing shows with the inertia of a cannonball blasting its way through anything in its path.

In a word, Song Qiyu was a hustler, with all the glory and baggage that comes with that designation. And as our scene grew from small coffee shops to thousand-seat theaters, so did Song Qiyu, and his legend—completely unknown to the outside world and contained entirely within our nascent comedy scene—swelled and ebbed erratically.

Everybody has a Song Qiyu story, and mine is about the time I spent Chinese New Year with him and his family in Trench Bottom, the coal-mining village of three hundred people where he grew up.

I was legitimately thrilled to be heading to the village for Chinese New Year. I was eager for something different than the last Chinese New Year, which I had spent in Beijing.

Festivities in Beijing began with light and noise. Starting at sundown with a few isolated booms, the whole of Beijing lit up with fireworks. Things reached a fever crescendo as the hour approached midnight.

The salvo reminded me of the Fourth of July. As a kid, I had always drunk in the light and noise; in Beijing it was the same, though a hundred times more disorganized.

I grew up in the suburbs. I was used to watching a bucolic, carefully curated fireworks display in the park behind my elementary school that would last a tasteful twenty minutes. Buying and setting off your own fireworks struck me as a sort of back-country, semi-legal, devil-may-care activity for people who simply didn't care how many fingers they had.

In China, however, fireworks were completely and thoroughly democratized. Everyone bought their own from shambly pop-up huts, temporary shops where even the best-made fireworks looked nothing like the shiny, slickly branded rockets I saw for sale across the border in New Hampshire.

The cheapest of them cost one kuai, about fifteen cents. As I saw children scrabbling to cut each other in line and get theirs first, it occurred to me that explosives were one of those things that could, in fact, be too cheap.

There seemed to be an unspoken social contract that, at least for the holiday, all previous notions of personal safety no longer applied. Men and women of all ages would pop a squat, take a regular butane lighter, light a fuse, and amble away from the impending explosion with no sense of urgency at all. Grandmothers who doted over the health of their grandchildren and would start boiling water at any sign of an oncoming cold would hand lighters to those same four-year-olds and let them spark the ordnance.

The result was one of great madness and beauty that continued on and off for two weeks. One night, I went on the roof of my friend's *hutong* apartment, where we had a bird's-eye view of the fireworks emerging from the gridded city. The traditional tiled roofs of the old town reflected the light of the pyrotechnics, bursting forth like rainbow dandelions spreading their seeds in magnificent bursts. I looked down at the streets laid by Kublai Khan, my head swimming under the influence of Yanjing Beer, wondering how I had been brought to this moment of great contentment and wonder.

Every Chinese New Year, Beijing transformed overnight. With the out-of-towners all gone home for the holidays, the real Old Beijingers emerged from their cover like a guerilla army, reclaiming the streets with speed and confidence. You never knew when you would turn a corner and be greeted with the noise of a war zone courtesy of one of the locals lighting some fireworks—or firecrackers.

Fireworks I liked, but firecrackers drove me crazy. These were really little more than bombs, and they could go off at any time, in any place.

The tradition of lighting firecrackers on Chinese New Year goes back to folk wisdom which says that loud noises scare away demons and bad luck. In ancient times, this meant placing bamboo stalks into bonfires and waiting for them to crack and explode. With the advent of gunpowder in the ninth century, bamboo gave way to paper packed full of the "fire drug" whose sole purpose was to make as much noise as possible, as suddenly as possible.

I hated all the firecrackers, including the long, red, snake-like ribbons that seemed to explode for seven minutes before quieting down. But my least favorite by far were these one-kuai tubes of rough cardboard packed with explosive that made no light or color when detonated, but simply blew up with a noise so great, it was impossible to sleep or work.

These bombs were the size and shape of my pointer finger and had a comically short fuse. My first thought when I saw one was, *I would have paid two kuai for this with a longer fuse.*

To set one off, you needed to light the fuse and then very carefully set down the tube, pointing it into the air. This was sort of like balancing a pencil on its eraser, except that if you took more than two seconds to do it, you'd erase half your hand. Sometimes, the tube would tip over, and everyone in a clear line of sight was suddenly a participant in a high-stakes game of spin the bottle.

But if everything went "right," sparks fizzed out the bottom, a high-pitched whine cut through the air for what felt like a mile, and the whole tube shot itself into the sky, where it exploded with a giant bang.

My hatred for these tubes came from the fact that at the time, I lived on the fifth floor of an apartment complex with a large window overlooking a parking lot. It turns out that five floors is exactly the height that the tubes ascended to before annihilating themselves—and my eardrums along with them.

When the first one went off about five feet away from me, separated by that one pane of glass, I thought my ears were ringing in the aftermath—until I realized the noise was actually every car alarm in the parking lot. These alarms went off incessantly. Every hour. Every day. For almost two weeks.

During Chinese New Year, my apartment's giant window became a canvas for all sorts of fireworks. The colorful ones exploded and splattered stars against the glass, with a sort of gritty pinging noise like someone had thrown a shovelful of sand laced with pebbles. The loud ones just blew up.

I wanted to get outside and do things, but many of my friends were gone from Beijing—the Chinese back to their homes, and the *laowai* to Bali, Phuket, or Palawan. In my excitement and ignorance, I had been looking forward to being in Beijing. But outside of the occasional temple fair, there was nothing to do. No shows to perform, no restaurants open.

The no-restaurants thing was a real problem, since I was used to almost unlimited cheap and tasty Chinese food, and had no idea how to cook for myself. I instantly devolved back into a college student, eating only what was available at convenience stores. Two weeks of ramen noodles, Oreos, and Diet Coke later, I was thoroughly done with Chinese New Year.

After my Chinese friends returned, they all let me in on the secret. "The real Chinese New Year is in the countryside. That's the place to be."

"How do I go there?"

"You have to get invited!"

So when, a year later, I ran into Song Qiyu backstage at a show just two days before Chinese New Year, I might have been a bit eager when he asked me if I had any plans for the holiday.

"No, I've heard the real Chinese New Year is in the countryside!"

"You should come to Shaanxi. You should come to Shaanxi. Welcome, welcome!"

I agreed to come immediately with no other information. I did not stop to consider that most people made their New Year's travel plans weeks in advance, or that traveling the day before Chinese New Year meant fighting through literally five hundred million people on the roads at once. Every year, the rush of travel before Chinese New Year is the greatest human migration in history, and every year it gets bigger.

The journey very nearly killed me.

In 1980, about 80 percent of Chinese lived in the countryside, a total of 789 million people. Forty-three years later, when I went to the Shaanxi countryside, only 47 percent lived in the country. This means that hundreds of millions of people had left their homes to seek their fortunes in the burgeoning new market economy, but still had family back in the country. They all go home exactly once a year: for Chinese New Year. Think Thanksgiving or Christmas traffic, times ten.

Those who had hit it big flew back home. Others, who did well enough, took the train. The next rung down on the ladder took sleeper buses, where at least you could lie down no matter how long the journey was. The last resort was long-haul buses. No bathroom, no nothing, for twelve hours.

By the time Song Qiyu invited me, all of those tickets—even for the long-haul buses—were gone. Every ticket to Jiexiu, the closest city, was sold out.

I called Song Qiyu, dismayed.

"I really want to go. But I just can't get there."

"You can. You can. There is a bus. It passes my town."

"I don't see it on the system."

"It passes by my town, I know it. When you get close, tell the driver you want to get off the bus. Tell him all the tickets are gone and this is the only way. He will stop and let you off. Then I will pick you up."

I hung up the phone, grabbed the duffel bag containing my stuff, and took a cab to the Beijing South bus station, where I boarded the bus and began the twelve-hour trip.

"When we pass by Jiexiu, can I get off the bus?"

"No," he said.

"What? My friend said you pass by Jiexiu, and I could get off the bus."

"We do pass by Jiexiu. On the highway. There's no exit. No stops. I can set you on the side of the highway around midnight."

I frantically called Song Qiyu. Beijing was fading into the background. Time was of the essence.

"He said the bus passes Jiexiu on the highway at midnight, and he can only let me off there."

"Perfect! I told you it would work! My village is called Gou Di Cun (Trench Bottom Village). When you get close, look on the side of the road. I will be waiting for you. Then, you tell the driver, and get off."

I hung up the phone, looked up at the tiny television playing old reruns of New Year's Gala xiangsheng shows, and waited.

At about 11 p.m., I started looking on the map for Trench Bottom Village. I couldn't find it. It seemed to be so small it wasn't on Baidu maps, Gaode maps, or even Google maps.

I pinched and pinched my smartphone screen, searching for the village with no luck. I knew roughly how far it was from Jiexiu, and imagined an expanding circle that started at the center of Jiexiu and intersected the highway at around the right distance. This would allow me to triangulate the position of the village from the data points I knew: the highway and Jiexiu.

That might sound smart, but actually makes no sense at all and I knew that even as I tried it.

As midnight approached, I started to get closer and closer to panicking. I prided myself on making my way around China using my Chinese and not needing any help. But as the dark miles flew by, it occurred to me that this time I had put myself into a position where it wasn't a matter of my pride in not asking for help.

There was no help, and the only person I knew for a thousand miles was Song Qiyu.

I texted him.

> Where are you?

> Under the bridge.

> Which bridge?

> This bridge.

He sent me a picture of a bridge that looked like every other bridge that crossed the highway.

We couldn't pin down his exact location, and the miles continued to fly by. Then— suddenly—headlights on the side of a road, by a bridge.

A wave of adrenaline shot through me.

"*Xia che! Xia che!* Let me off!!!"

The driver said nothing at all, and for a moment I thought he was going to ignore me. But he slowed the bus to a stop. The other passengers perked up in various states of sleep and confusion; not wanting to hold anyone up, I hurriedly shrugged on my coat, grabbed my duffel bag, and stepped into the cold January air.

The bus sped off immediately. I waved to the car under the bridge and started walking toward it, and it drove away.

It wasn't his car.

I was alone on the side of the highway deep in rural Shaanxi, at midnight, in the cold.

I took out my phone. It was out of battery.

I threw down my bag and fumbled to find my computer, took it out, and with freezing hands tried to connect my charger cable to my computer USB port and the end of my iPhone. It was too dark—until suddenly it wasn't dark at all, and light blazed all around me as a car whipped by at eighty miles per hour, barely a foot away from me.

I hugged the side rail, completely blind, my retinas contracted to pinholes in the wake of the headlights, thinking that nobody hurrying home for New Year's would think that there might be a lost American comedian rubbernecking on the highway, holding an open laptop connected to a phone.

Eventually, my sight returned. The phone turned on. I called Song Qiyu, manic, and eventually, based on a sign on the side of the highway, we determined that by sheer luck I had gotten off the bus only two kilometers from where he was waiting.

"But we are in front. I can't drive backward. Not on the highway. It would be dangerous."

No driving against traffic on the highway. I had finally found what Song Qiyu thought was a bad plan.

From there, it was just a simple matter of lugging my luggage up the road for twenty minutes in the cold.

Song Qiyu had told me he would pick me up. At the time, I took this to mean that he had a car. Song Qiyu did not have a car. He was riding his elementary school best friend's motorcycle. I knew it was his elementary school best friend's motorcycle because his elementary school best friend was also on the motorcycle.

At this point, I was tired, exhausted, both too hot and too cold, and just glad to be alive. Sitting in the middle of a three-person piggyback on a motorcycle on the highway with a duffel bag slung over my shoulder and no helmet felt very safe.

One good thing about being a comedian is that when bad stuff is happening to you, while you still feel scared and cold and worried, the part of you that is a smart-ass is taking notes. General suffering is usually not funny, but detailed, unusual suffering often is.

Trench Bottom was a place like no other I have been to before or since.

The motorcycle rolled by a massive concrete wall that enclosed a huge courtyard. Flanking a tidy swath of grass, which may have been nice in the summer but was dead and covered in dust in the winter, two high-rise buildings shot out of the nondescript flat soil at a seemingly random point in the road.

As we rolled through a gate in the wall, I saw written on the outside of the wall a massive slogan in giant red characters: 建设美好沟底. *BUILD A BEAUTIFUL TRENCH BOTTOM.*

We entered the apartment block on the right, went up an elevator, and emerged into a beautifully clean and warm three-bedroom apartment. Even well past midnight, Song Qiyu's family were hustling around the house, hanging bright red auspicious New Year slogans and cute pictures of rats dressed up in Chinese robes. An auntie sat in the corner, half-watching a big-screen TV, half-watching me as I entered the room and introduced myself to a wave of welcoming family members.

"This is Trench Bottom Village?" I asked Song Qiyu. "An apartment building?"

"New Trench Bottom. New."

The next day was the day before Chinese New Year, and we hopped on a local bus to take the road fifteen minutes from the two high-rise complexes to Old Trench Bottom. The road snaked through a valley created between rows of brown cliffs and hills, some thirty feet high.

Song Qiyu and I disembarked at the bottom of a large hill, with a dirt road that continued to wind its way upward to the top of a plateau. Around us, aunties and uncles shuffled off the bus.

"Here we are. Here we are."

I saw a few isolated buildings, but most of the paths seemed to just lead to roads that hugged the hills. On the side of the hills, built directly into the cliffs, were . . .

"Are those doors?"

"Doors. Yes. Cave doors."

It turns out the brownish-yellowish hills were not made of rock. They were compacted loess soil, deposits of dry earth many yards deep. The top of the hills formed a plateau from which untold years of erosion had created huge trenches, and at the bottom of one of the trenches, villagers had excavated caves.

Trench Bottom Village was a collection of cave homes.

As the uncles and aunties passed us by, heading resolutely but slowly up the main hill, Song Qiyu told me how the village had changed since he was a kid. He grew up in one of the caves, with no running water and no electricity. Only public buildings, like the school, had anything like modern amenities.

We passed a part of the hill with a sturdy concrete platform that had been constructed to hold a three-story building with a brand-new, shining blue glass facade, which stood out from the brownish hillside like an oasis pool in the desert.

"What is that building?"

"School. It's the school."

"You went to school there?"

"No, no. That's the new school. I went to the old school. Smaller. At that time, the village was very poor. Very poor. But now things are different."

Song Qiyu told me the caves were called "窑洞"—*yao dong*. The combination of the character *dong* (洞), for cave, with the character *yao* (窑) was one I had previously only heard used to describe the sort of place one would age large earthenware pots of *baijiu* or other liquor, or a massive pottery kiln. This was different from a *shan dong* (山洞), or "mountain cave," which brought to mind hermits and bears instead of homes.

This distinction seemed important to him. Yes, they were dark and had no modern amenities—but they were built residences, not improvised shelters for destitute people.

Some doors were well maintained, and in the winter wind, I could see how the inside was a refuge, though clearly not as nice as an apartment building. Some cave homes, though, seemed completely deserted. I peeked into one. Old newspapers and some dusty toys were clustered around a big, heavy iron stove. A shrine still stood against a wall in the nearly empty room. A black-and-white photograph of a man rested on the ground.

"When I was a kid, we all lived in the caves," he told me.

"Was it fun?"

"Fun? Fun . . . hmm . . . Not fun, but not *not* fun. It was hard. No electricity. No water. To get water, you need to walk ten minutes down the hill. Then the government built the big new buildings. Everyone kept their cave, and also got the chance to buy a new apartment. Only villagers could buy. Everyone moved into the new buildings. It is better now."

"Do people like it better now?" I asked.

"Yes! Much better. Warmer in the winter. Hot water twenty-four hours a day. Also, our building is well made. Every village in this area, they all did the same thing. Every village, an apartment building. But our building is the best one. So, all the women from nearby villages want to marry into our village. Hahaha! Good for the men. Yes, they don't make a lot of money. But they get good wives."

I now realized what was bizarre about the old village. Until our morning bus arrived, the whole place had been a ghost town. Every day, the residents of the old village emptied from the apartment building and into the bus. Every day, the aunties and uncles returned to their old haunts. During the school year, the few students and teachers did so as well. Thus, the village revived during the day, neighbors talking to each other, interacting, continuing to live as they had lived when in the caves. Then, every night, they would take the return trip back, settle into the warmth, and wait for the sunrise. At night the village was like a heart between beats.

"People like it more. But around Chinese New Year it is a bit sad."

"Why?"

"Chinese New Year, you go to see your neighbors. You visit this friend, that friend. When I was young, this took all day. You go up the hill, then down the hill. We had to go ten minutes for water. It was hard. But you would see everyone on the way there and back. It was fun.

"Now, we all live in the same building. You go to visit Auntie Wang, second floor. Uncle Liu, fifth floor. Half a day, you have seen everyone. Most days, this is good. Chinese New Year, not so good. Chinese New Year, you miss things being a little harder."

We kept walking up the slope.

"Who owns these homes now?" I asked.

"The families still own them. Every family has one cave, one apartment. Why? You want to buy a cave?"

"You can buy a cave? How much?"

"Fifty dollars. A hundred dollars. Some people never come back. They stay at the high-rise all day, they don't need a cave. They will sell. I can get you a good price."

"We could start an Airbnb."

"Yes! *Laowai* pay lots of money for these things. We are close to Pingyao. Tourist spot. *Laowai* pay eighty dollars a night, *laowai* think it is cool. You get one *laowai* here one night, you pay for everything. Yes, yes, let's do it! Make some money!"

"*Laowai* would want electricity and heat, though."

"Ah, yes. Hmm. Renovations. Maybe too expensive. Hmm. We can think about it."

We reached the top of the hill. From here there was a magnificent vista, snaking rivers of chasms and valleys gouged deep into the loess plateau. It looked like a prehistoric land. Smog gathered in low clouds around the horizon, but atop the plateau, we were above some of it, and it was clear that the sky above was blue.

I looked down at the village that had produced one of the stranger comedians of the Chinese scene, and at that moment, it truly struck me that Song Qiyu was actually a badass. To come from a cave in a village that barely taught Mandarin, with no electricity and water, to get the top test scores needed to get to undergrad in Datong, then a master's degree in Beijing, and now perform comedy on TV?

Thinking of the people I had met in Beijing, I saw that it wasn't just him. Beijing and Shanghai weren't the only nexuses of talent. Look at a map and see where the roads meet: Datong, Nanning, Shijiazhuang, Dalian, Tianjin, Jinan, Hangzhou, Suzhou, Chengdu, Changshu, and Chongqing. These cities were filled with hustlers, restaurant owners, white-collar workers—every one of whom is the pride of some local village or town.

Five dozen cities of a million people or more—and none of them had comedy clubs yet. The scale of the possibility was unreal. If you toured doing a weekend of shows in every city in China with a million people or more, you wouldn't have enough Friday and Saturday nights in a year to fit them all in.

"You should do some bits about this place," I suggested, gazing over the village. "This is fascinating."

"No, no. *Bu hao xiao.* Not funny. Not funny. *Laowai* think this is interesting. Beijing people, they don't think this is interesting."

Since the Wi-Fi was bad and I only had a cheap data plan, I effectively had no internet and lots and lots of time on my hands, which was filled by a rotating cast of people asking if I was hungry every five minutes and feeding me regardless of my answer. I soon had no idea what was happening on the news, what day, or even what time it was.

The village men were almost all coal miners, used to rigid schedules and hard work, and they reveled in their vacation with a fullheartedness that was infectious. There were no mealtimes since everyone was always eating. Multiple times I was offered *baijiu*, a rice liquor that was over 50 percent alcohol, at 9 a.m. with my breakfast. I found I had to strategically manage the amount of *baijiu* in my glass—too much and they would force me to drink, not enough and they would top me off.

The women talked and watched TV and played mah-jongg; the men talked and watched TV and played card games. Any time of day was a good time to start a game of *Dou Di Zhu* or "Kill the Landlord," a card game played with a standard deck of poker cards.

I asked how to play, and four men immediately clamored at full volume to explain how the game worked. Communication was difficult, but not impossible—I didn't speak any of the local dialect, and this meant that while they could understand me (they kept commenting on how "standard" my Mandarin was), I really needed Song Qiyu to translate.

After three attempts at explanation in their thick Jiexiu dialect and Shaanxi accents, we mutually agreed to treat me as a lost cause and I just tried to keep up with the shouting of the men and slamming of the cards on the table.

Between heaping plates of dumplings, fish, and a special type of chewy, cone-shaped oat noodle called *you mian* that I had never had before in Beijing, I was brought along with Song Qiyu and half his family as they made the rounds visiting his neighbors, each of their apartments decorated with auspicious wall hangings and traditional paper-cut arts.

I quickly gathered that Song Qiyu was proud to bring me around since I was able to corroborate stories about the Beijing comedy scene. In a place where people might make only two hundred dollars a month, many thought Song Qiyu was exaggerating when he claimed to be selling hundreds of tickets at fifteen dollars apiece. I told them—entirely truthfully—that nobody was more creative at filling seats than Song Qiyu.

The comedy shows we held in *hutong* bars had seemed to me to be a world of underground artists and cheap drinks. In the early days of my comedy career, I made so little money compared to my college friends back home that I thought of myself as way out on the edge. I never needed to pay any taxes in America since I didn't make it up to the poverty line.

To the Trench Bottomites, however, our ticket sales must have looked like Hollywood box office reports. Song Qiyu's "college friends" were laborers, many of whom had not graduated high school. Selling out a theater could mean tens of thousands of renminbi in one night. That Song Qiyu could make such massive astronomical sums just from telling jokes seemed very impressive.

There was no jealousy that I could detect. Yes, people may have thought that comedy was a strange career choice for the one person out of three hundred who had made it all the way from the village to the capital. But the moment Song Qiyu told them that Beijing people would pay a hundred kuai just to hear you talk, and TV shows would pay even more, the villagers seemed completely convinced that Chinese stand-up comedy was a dream lifestyle and a clear gold mine.

The fact I was there confirmed it. There is a running joke throughout China that life is like a video game, and being born in China means being born on hard mode. Foreigners, of course, played life on easy mode, and so naturally my trek down the path that led me to Trench Bottom must have been effortless.

Compared to their journeys, I can't say they were wrong. If everyone has challenges in life, perhaps luxury is getting to pick the ones you take on.

On my final evening in the village, I was struck by a sense of realization and horror.

We had spent the day out in a nearby village, where I had learned how to play mah-jongg with some of Song Qiyu's relatives. The experience left me a few dollars poorer and with a raging headache from breathing in fumes from the giant cast-iron stove in the middle of the room. As the only source of heat, it was fed with occasional shovelfuls of coal, and my decision to favor warmth over air quality meant my head was throbbing painfully.

As we drove back, I wasn't sure whether to keep the windows up or down. Song Qiyu, myself, and a friend of his were crammed in the back of the car, and the driver up front was smoking. Opening the window, however, would let in cold air, and the smog outside was so thick it didn't seem like much an improvement.

I wondered which was less offensive: opening the window or asking the driver to stop smoking. While contemplating the window, I noticed massive structures by the side of the road: smokestacks, cargo bays, piles of steel, all eerily quiet.

"What are those buildings? Factories?"

"Steel factories," the driver said. "They run all day every day. Except for Chinese New Year."

Song Qiyu's friend chimed in. "Shaanxi is known for coal and steel. We mine the coal, and then use it for steel. But nowadays, we don't even use our own coal."

"Are they changing things for environmental reasons?" I asked.

He laughed. "No! Our coal is bad. Back at the village, you know that shack behind the high-rise? It's full of coal from Thailand. Their coal is cheaper and better. We don't even buy our own coal."

"You use Thai coal? So why are you all working to mine your own coal, then?"

He shrugged. "Someone buys it. The boss wants it. The boss sells it. And for Shaanxi, these are the jobs we have. Yes, the coal is bad, the steel factories are old and inefficient. But if they turn them off . . . jobs, you know? Good for the nation. Good for society. Otherwise . . . what will we do all day?"

I hoped getting out of the car would help my headache, but the two-minute walk between the car and the high-rise only made things worse.

We went upstairs to find some of Song Qiyu's school friends playing Kill the Landlord and tossing a television remote control to each other animatedly, seemingly all tied in a deep discussion about the remote. The tone sounded somewhere between being very important and a running joke.

"No, no, the women don't know how to do that. They don't have any training."

"What training do you need? Take the buttons, put them in the right place."

"OK, sure, and who makes the buttons?"

"They have machines for that!"

I asked Song Qiyu to help translate the discussion for me, since I wasn't able to pick up so much rapid-fire Jiexiu-dialect speech.

"They're debating if they could turn the village into a remote control factory. Each family could learn a different part of building remote controls."

"That's crazy!" I said, laughing. "Isn't it?"

Song Qiyu didn't say anything at first, then said, "Most of the women here don't have any work. If they could make something during the day . . . that's a bit more money."

"Jesse, what do you think?" one of the friends asked me, seeing I was now in on the conversation. "Could we pull it off?"

"I . . . I think it would not be easy," I replied.

"Jesse will help us get investment!" Everyone laughed, then got right back on with their plans. One of them smiled and offered me a cigarette.

Just seeing the cigarette set my head to pounding. I simply couldn't take any more smoke.

"I don't smoke, thank you. Thank you. No, really, thank you, I'm going to take a walk."

I went down to the courtyard, where a few kids were playing with the one-kuai bomb-like firecrackers. I tried to distance myself as much as I could from them, while still watching so that I could prepare my nervous system for any sudden noises. The air was not much better out here than inside.

I thought about the village, about these people and their place in the world. There was so much they were a part of, and yet had no say in.

I was impressed by how admirable—how American!—their boot-strapping ethos was. They didn't complain. They didn't shy away from work. They didn't ask for handouts, they wanted to build their own factory and make money in a better, cleaner, safer, more high-tech way.

But I don't think they could conceive of Foxconn, the industrial megaplex in Shenzhen that assembles iPhones for the world. They didn't know about the enormous scale of modern manufacturing. Tens of thousands of buildings, each the size of their whole village. An incredibly complex system of international finance and investment needed to bring things to bear, the highly skilled labor needed to run the machines, the robots that would do all the work they hoped the village women could learn.

Forget all of that—these villagers could barely speak Mandarin. What internationally competitive factory is run in the Jiexiu dialect?

The market economy was the undeniable engine that had lifted these people up from caves without water and electricity and into a warm apartment building. China's economic rise meant everyone was having a happy New Year with lots of food and decorations. That they had enough to feed and host me as long as they wished.

But in my ears, I still heard Song Qiyu's friends debating preposterous hopes for the remote control industry to salvage the town; in my mind's eye I saw the hulking shells of the steel factories. They littered the side of the road like the carcasses of titans, or gods. Factories, uncompetitive in the market, kept breathing by a system that forced air into their lungs as if through a set of giant bellows. A system unwilling to let them die, unable to make them prosper.

My headache pounded. The air outside was bad. The air inside was bad.

I opted to go back inside and face the light and the cigarettes, where at least it was warm. I sat on the couch, clutching a pillow to my face in a vague attempt to filter the air coming into my lungs, trying not to give in to a panic attack that, to them, would seem completely out of nowhere.

The villagers didn't notice. They just kept playing cards, throwing down fifty-kuai bills, and laughing.

Once, during COVID, Song Qiyu gave me a call out of the blue.

"Hey Jesse, are you still doing your one-kuai *chuanr* joke?"

Song Qiyu knew about my *chuanr* routine because there was a period when we all did the same shows and I used it to end my routine every single night while I was working on it.

Chuanr—classic Beijing lamb-on-a-stick street food—was always a funny topic. It was cheap, it was everywhere, and it was covered in cumin, cayenne, and oil of questionable cleanliness. Eating *chuanr* was always a bit of a gamble as to what meat was actually being served. At the cheapest places, there was a lot of pork masquerading as "lamb."

My five-minute routine on *chuanr* started with a few jokes about the veracity of the meat:

"My dad came to Beijing and I thought, *I have to take him to eat* chuanr. We get some on the street from a guy fanning the coals of the grill with a hair dryer. My dad is like, 'Wow, this is good, is it lamb?'

"'I don't know.'

"'You can't read the characters on the menu?'

"'No, I know what they *say* it is, I just don't know what it *is*.'"

From there, I moved into a very sad and dramatic self-reflective fugue on how the times had changed. One kuai used to get you a big skewer of lamb. Now, the one-kuai *chuanr* was a victim of the same inflation that saw rent in Beijing rise ten times in one generation.

"I saw an eight-kuai *chuanr* yesterday," I would tell the audience, as if announcing the death of a family member. Every time, the audience would let out a huge collective sigh.

The grand finale of the bit was a song and accompanying music video, where I took the chords of the heartbreaking crooner song "Where Has the Time Gone" and replaced it with "Where Has the One-Kuai Chuanr Gone?"

Dressed in the kind of Chinese-style greatcoat a security guard might wear, I forlornly roamed the *hutongs*, searching vainly amongst increasingly dingy alleyways for hand-scrawled signs boasting one-kuai *chuanr. Long I have searched for you / Piece after piece of meat on a stick / Inflation is so strange / How can it be this expensive?*

The song was a tearjerker, literally. The bit worked so well that, at a corporate party, a portly man in a suit and tie rushed over from the massive round table with all the company bigwigs to meet me as I left the stage. He was crying.

"I miss the one-kuai chuanr, too," he told me, and shook my hand. I grasped his hand hard. So did I.

None of these jokes work in LA.

"Nope, haven't been doing that one," I confirmed to Song Qiyu.

"Cool, cool! Can I buy it?"

"Buy it?"

"Yeah. I'm doing online comedy shows. But nothing is funny. *Bu hao xiao, bu hao xiao.* So, I need good jokes. Can I buy the joke?"

What possible universe there is where my one-kuai *chuanr* routine works for some random Chinese comedian Song Qiyu hires to perform online over Tencent Meet, I do not know.

I asked him to give me a quote. He asked me to give him a quote. I asked him to give me a quote. He said he would, and he never followed up on it.

Somewhere out there, a tree is falling in a forest where no one hears it. The moon orbits slowly around the earth. Fish are born and die underwater in the dark, never seeing the light of day. And Song Qiyu is hustling up comedy shows, filling seats, and figuring out things as he goes along.

Play to Your Audience

The theater was a brand-new construction made of clean black lines and matte wall panels. It stood in an empty scar of flat land surrounded by wheat fields.

We were in Kenli, a suburb of Dongying city in Shangdong Province. Dongying was what might be called a fifth-tier city, one of the many Chinese urban areas where a proliferation of KFCs was the extent of internationalization. Kenli was forty-five minutes away.

This was the type of show that Master Ding had done hundreds of times with many sets of foreign disciples. He and five or six of us disciples would pack into a "bread van"* and ramble two to six hours on the road to the countryside. As the miles rolled by, the van would bubble with xiangsheng lines and unexpected bursts of opera as we would each go over our routines.

Then we would roll into the parking lot of some brand-new, state-of-the-art theater built in the middle of nowhere—like the one I saw right now. The provincial authorities had built it.

During the Maoist era, most art was co-opted for political use.

---

* This is the Chinese term for that type of nondescript white van that Americans might call, in a culturally revealing manner, either a "sniper van" or a "pedo van."

Then, China opened to the outside world, began to liberalize, and noticed that one area where the country was lagging far behind was in arts and culture. For a country with such a long and rich history in those areas, it was a shame that needed to be rectified, and so the relevant authorities started pouring money into public arts infrastructure. Nowadays, the arts are generously supported in addition to being co-opted.

A lot of these fabulous theaters are buildings as fantastic as they are unnatural. Their fantasy comes from every local town's desire to have a gorgeous architectural calling card to signify its arrival in the modern world, while the unnaturalness comes with the utter disconnect between these buildings and everything else around them. They were built with what I thought of as "airport logic," the idea that every province should have arts infrastructure, since even if there were no art classes in schools, every province had some sort of graduate school of arts.

Building theaters is easier than fostering artists, but one of these goals was achievable now and the other was a problem for the future. So, while we often performed in the sticks, we always did so on a gorgeous stage full of brand-new, top-flight lighting and equipment.

"OK, everyone," Master Ding projected. We all perked up where we sat, scattered around a changing room full of harsh white fluorescent lighting, simple folding chairs, and messy makeup desks. "This is the Shandong TV regional New Year's Gala. It will be aired to the whole province, over one hundred million people. We want to show a good performance."

We all nodded. This was a provincial New Year's gala, which meant it wasn't the important one that makes or breaks careers. Still, I thought . . . a hundred million people? Is that possible?

"Now, as you all know," Master Ding said, "we're not doing regular two-person xiangsheng today. We're doing a group xiangsheng. What's the difference?"

"Group xiangsheng isn't funny," I said seriously, and everyone broke out laughing.

"Correct!" Master Ding said, laughing himself. "I've seen a lot of bad group xiangsheng in my day . . . but it's necessary, because some of you have not been studying long, and can only do one *guankou* monologue or sing one song. But between the six of you, we can do twenty minutes, a whole routine. I will introduce you one at a time, you do your bit, and then step back and give the stage to your brothers and sisters."

We rehearsed the show once in an empty theater and then waited backstage as the audience filed in. For government gala shows, the audience is always bussed in from a combination of schools, senior centers, cultural organizations, and anyone else that will show up. The audience never paid; sometimes, if outreach wasn't effective enough, "professional audience" would be called in.

The professional audience members were usually blank-faced and uninteresting, just warm bodies happy to see a show and make fifty kuai. But the people who brought them in were the opposite. I loved the audience wranglers, who were all hustler-businessmen types who wore cheap suit jackets over T-shirts and fake leather shoes, making call after call on brick phones coated in fake gold and speaking in thick rural accents. They had discovered they could make money by bringing their cousins and cousins' cousins to random events, and they roamed the backstage amongst the glitz and glamour like scarecrows on the red carpet, completely unaware of their incongruence, getting shit done by shouting, "How many we got? Twenty-five people? I need ten more!" I saw them as people who were stuck in the minor leagues of human trafficking. They were the unsung heroes whose entrepreneurial labor made the TV images of the great socialist future happen.

I learned at these rural shows that while the audience's knowledge of the West and its relevant associations (the English language, film and TV references, placid acceptance of the neoliberal worldview) faded the further one got from major cities, there is some material that works everywhere. Namely, everyone likes hearing comedians compliment their city and their local points of pride—especially if those comedians are the first white people they've seen outside of a TV screen and they're doing it in Chinese.

And so I found myself in rural Shandong, singing a Chinese duet with our Vietnamese comedienne Thiên Tú. The tune was an Anhui opera classic; Master Ding changed the words:

> **THIÊN TÚ:** I want to be from Kenli!
>
> **ME:** I want to move my family here!
>
> **THIÊN TÚ:** The anti-Japanese War Memorial left me somber and contemplative.
>
> **ME:** The big white bridge is great and vigorous!
>
> **THIÊN TÚ:** The local culture is deep as a lake; my heart leaps and pierces the clouds.
>
> **ME:** The industrial park has gardens within gardens.
>
> **THIÊN TÚ:** The streets of Kenli are designed to ease the lives of the elderly.
>
> **ME:** The harmonious society warms the hearts of the people.
>
> **THIÊN TÚ:** Eco-friendly construction is evident everywhere you look.
>
> **ME:** A healthy lifestyle is sweeter than honey.
>
> **THIÊN TÚ:** I want to work hard here!
>
> **ME:** I want to prosper here!
>
> **BOTH:** And work together with everyone to make a better Kenli!*

---

* It appears that local officials heavy-handedly touting what they've done for their constituents is not uniquely American.

The professional audience applauded and the cameras broadcast the show live to a hundred million people in Shandong Province, where it played in the background of family dinners during Chinese New Year.

Backstage after the show, Master Ding whipped off his robe (which I folded correctly this time) and we rushed out into the frigid night air. We had four hours of van time ahead of us before getting back to Beijing, and Master Ding, who had probably done a thousand of these shows, was eager to get going.

The disciples and I shivered as we waited for the van. Master Ding's head swiveled, his eyes gleaming in the light, and when the van pulled up, he hooked his hands around the doorframes and hurled himself upward into the vehicle with such strength that I marveled at his vigor after a long day performing on the road. You could never tell he had only four-fifths of a lung.

On the way back, the van was quiet. The show was over, so there was no banter, no singing. "What did you think of the show?" Master Ding asked me. I didn't know what to say. The audience had clapped. The people who invited us were happy. But to be honest, I thought the whole thing was a pile of crap and I wished I hadn't come.

I think Master Ding guessed this from my silence, and whatever words eventually came out of my mouth, his answer was in response to that silence. "The audience was happy today. They liked you. You know that Anhui opera song now, which you can change the words however you want to for your own jokes. Start thinking about the next show and what you want to do."

He took out a brown envelope with a Shandong TV logo on it, withdrew a wad of crisp, red 100-kuai bills, and divided them into six parts, one for each of the disciples. "Here you go," he said, and he gave each of us our take—400 kuai, about sixty-five dollars. He crumpled up the empty envelope and put it in the cup holder, then curled up between his seat and the car door and fell asleep.

I stared out the window at the passing fields and yawning sepia highway lights. I wasn't sure how I felt about this whole trip. The way I'd been looking at it, the show was lousy, one step above direct propaganda, and several steps below what I'd "come to China to do." The funniest part of the whole show for me was the way people had unironically enjoyed an American singing Chinese Anhui opera about an industrial park. That was some high-quality absurdum that tickled my *Julia Raps* sensibilities. But the show itself?

It had aired to a hundred million people and I prayed nobody I knew ever saw it—a special type of bitterness I'd never felt before. But Master Ding's words—and his actions, and temperament—made me look at it another way. If you think about what we'd done, the show really was a small miracle. Master Ding had taken a group of foreigner amateur comedians from six different countries, bused them into the boondocks under bright lights for millions of people, constrained by an audience who knew nothing about the West while consoling stringent state media overseers with no sense of humor, and still made the audience laugh, clap, and walk away happy.

The American in me wanted to do a good show even if bad things would come of it.

My Chinese master had made me do a bad show in a good way.

Did that make it a good show? Would I feel happier if I'd called them out and everyone went home upset?

I felt like I was a shill for doing this show, but the truth was that with that client, and that audience, the sort of comedy I'd grown up watching—the social commentary, storytelling, culturally aggressive stuff—was never going to play. But that wasn't really about China at all. That sort of underground comedy stuff I "wanted to do" wouldn't have played well in rural America in English, even without state media getting involved.

In the end, I realized my angst came from comparing a hypothetical view of what I wanted to do in some vague future comedy career with the reality of the world that was actually in front of me. I could do the comedy I wanted—just not on the Shandong TV airwaves. Master Ding was giving me the skill set, the stage time, the ability to say I'd performed for millions. I hadn't performed the comedy I wanted to do tonight, but I would one day because I'd keep making good stuff by my own skill, finding my audience, and fighting for stage time amongst other comedians.

The van trundled into Beijing just past midnight. I cabbed home and slept till noon.

In my first year or two in China, we did many of these gala shows. One of them was in a soccer stadium and had ten thousand audience members sitting in makeshift rows of folding chairs. I learned that, with that crowd size, the people in the back hear the joke later than the people in the front, and the laughter moves backward at the speed of sound rather than the speed of human thought. I sang the same Anhui opera song, but this time we praised a new housing complex erected in a nearby suburb instead of the industrial park.

The whole time we did these government gala shows, Master Ding was teaching me lessons in being a professional comedian:

Approach every show with professionalism, even if your hosts are unprofessional.

Never think you're above a gig.

Make the audience happy, make them like you, and take it from there.

Finish each show with new skills, bits, or experience.

Keep what worked, ditch the rest, go to sleep, and don't worry so much.

Around 2014, there began an anti-corruption campaign in the highest levels of the Chinese government. Massive galas for which ten thousand people were bussed in to present a positive image of local infrastructure development was now seen as extravagant.

I should be clear: They had always been extravagant, but now they *seemed* that way, too. The problem was not necessarily the extravagance, it was the seeming.

There were rumors going around that these shows—sometimes with budgets in the millions of dollars—were merely crony-capitalist schemes meant to enrich contractors and local officials. True or false, people believed the rumors to be true, and so generally approved of these shows being canceled.

This meant the mysterious and fragile artistic unicorn that was the infrastructure-themed variety show gala disappeared virtually overnight from the cities and villages of the Middle Kingdom. No more Anhui opera about elder care and ecotourism. My muse wept.

In the beginning, many of the xiangsheng performers rejoiced. Lots of us had these shows booked eight months in advance; since the government's aim to fight corruption was simply to remove the appearance of corruption, these massive shows still paid the performers—only now we were being paid to not show up. Before, clients wanted a show. Now, they wanted a not-show, which was fine, too.

But then, as the anti-corruption campaign deepened and all levels of government including culture and arts were affected, performers began to realize that their livelihoods doing "real" comedy in clubs, teahouses, and on tour relied in large part on someone paying their bills with these well-funded, albeit vapid, gala variety shows.

For older xiangsheng performers like Master Ding and our troupe, this just meant fewer shows. I never relied on xiangsheng for my income, and after fifty years on the road, I think even Master Ding didn't mind taking fewer five-hour van rides.

But younger Chinese xiangsheng performers had to turn to other work. Some hosted weddings, some wrote on TV variety shows, some taught comedy classes.

A lot of them started doing Chinese stand-up, and our small stand-up scene began to swell with xiangsheng performers used to playing for professional audiences.

Seeing traditional artists begin to show up at our stand-up open mics was my first experience with how the macroeconomics of media shape the shows we watch. Artists are always taking part in a balancing act between the type of art they want to make and the realities of the market.

In 1861, it was the death of the Xianfeng emperor and the banning of Beijing opera during the mourning period that inadvertently gave rise to xiangsheng. Could an anti-corruption campaign a century and a half later destroy xiangsheng and give rise to stand-up comedy?

Just Words

I walk onstage.

"不行, 不行! 再来!"

No, no, no! All wrong!

It's a Saturday, and I'm in the Happy Classroom. Master Ding has assigned me a new piece to study for this week: five pages of lines, one thousand words. "Be ready to put it onstage this Saturday," he'd told me.

When I first started studying xiangsheng, this might have taken me a month, or more. Master Ding knew this, and he knew that I knew this. He was challenging me, I thought, and I was going to come through.

I'd done the crunch time. I'd put in the work. I'd memorized the piece.

So imagine my surprise when I walked onstage and Master Ding yelped before I'd even opened my mouth. He waved his arms in front of his face. "It's over, it's over, it's not funny."

I am a lifelong sufferer of diarrhea of the mouth, but I was truly speechless. What could I have possibly done wrong before I even opened my mouth?

"Look at how you walked on the stage. You had your eyes fixed on the audience the whole time. But you were walking to the left. So you were just like a crab—" He jumped up onstage, landed with a *slam!* and started scuttling exaggeratedly across the stage, nodding his neck left and right, eyes bugged out.

Everyone laughed. "Are those the laughs you want? Because that's what you'll get."

"What should I do?" I asked.

"Look at me." He took my place offstage right. I slipped down to the side and watched at an angle.

He strode forward onto the stage, natural, just looking at where he was going, the side of his head facing the audience. When he reached the right spot for the Joker, just off to the right of the low table, he pivoted.

His eyes rose and he looked at the audience. No, not looked; he saw us—really saw us—smiled, and bowed. Everyone applauded. It was just like the first show I saw in the xiangsheng teahouse.

You could see in his eyes that there was no place in the world he'd rather be than performing xiangsheng for these specific seven people who happened to be in this whitewashed classroom in Beijing University of Chemical Technology on this Saturday afternoon.

Then he cut off the smile and the air shifted instantaneously, leaving an empty, yawning space like a balloon had just popped. He looked over to me, back in teaching mode.

"See! The eye contact is a greeting. You greet the audience and say hello! You don't yell it the whole way out onto the stage."

He scanned the classroom, picking out a more experienced student. "Lao Cui, you go up. Jesse, sit back down."

"But . . . I . . . all those new jokes!"

Master Ding locked eyes with me, serious. "The comedy is not about the jokes. The comedy is the communication! The jokes are just words."

The Chapter Where I Start a Comedy Club

"The music is too loud!" I mouthed at the bartender, hoping to attract his attention over the heads of the hundred-or-so audience members who were watching the stand-up show.

The bartender saw me—he definitely saw me—but just shifted his body and kept talking to a customer at the bar.

Trying to maneuver as quickly as I could through the narrow space between the audience in their folding chairs and the brick wall of the event room, I slunk over to the bar.

"We're in the middle of a show," I told the bartender.

"So do your show," he told me.

"It's a comedy show—people need to be able to hear the jokes."

"The bar is still open. We need to play music."

"I rented the room!"

"And the music is off in the room you rented. You didn't rent out the whole bar."

I stood there, fuming. As host, I needed to get back into the event room in case the comedian onstage finished early.

I took a deep breath. "If it's not too much trouble, could you turn it down just a little?"

A pause, then: "A little."

"Thank you."

As I squeezed my way between the wall and the seats to get back to the "backstage" area—which was just a small curtain obscuring a corner of the room—I vowed to never put on a show at this place again.

Even though I was pissed, I was not surprised. This wasn't the first time it had happened. There were many bars in Beijing, but none of them were comedy clubs, and they didn't really care about the quality of the show; just how much money they could get for the use of their space.

As I sat isolated behind the black curtain, the waves of laughter rolled throughout, buoying me. I floated, trying to keep my mind on the show, but I kept coming back to two thoughts.

The first: *We have something here. These shows are not just as good as what's on TV in China—they're better.*

The second: *Nobody from the actual entertainment or media scene will understand that if we're just in the back of a bar that won't even turn the music down for us.*

The jokes were good enough to be respected. But to be respectable, we needed a comedy club.

Imagine you are a Chinese resident of Beijing. A friend tells you there is a place in the old town with a free event on Wednesday night.

"What is it?" you ask.

"I went last week. It's like performing, but you don't really need to act, just play games . . . It's hard to explain, but a lot of fun!"

So, instead of hopping on a long subway ride back home after work, you stay in the city center. You take the subway to the Drum Tower stop, walking past the colossal Drum and Bell Towers that have loomed over the neighborhood for the past six hundred years, and follow your cell phone's directions deep into the maze of winding alleyways that make up the old city.

You snake through the *hutongs*, clogged with dusty bicycles, empty old paint cans waiting for the day they will be needed again, and Audis with wooden squares of particleboard lashed to their hubcaps to prevent scrapes from the flow of people and cars. Torn fliers for underground music shows hang on the walls and lampposts. The light is dying; children ride their bicycles, shouting to each other; old men smoke cigarettes and play Kill the Landlord on a folding table beneath a streetlight.

Finally, you reach a point where the app fails. The alleys are too small now. They have no names and are not mapped. The theater should be on the right . . . but where is it?

Down that way, there is a path about thirty yards long, too narrow and uneven to be a road. The moment you think the whole thing has been a waste of time, you notice a cheap, foamcore sign duct-taped to a tripod. There is a big black logo with a microphone in the middle; on one side of the microphone is the English word *ha*, on the other, the Chinese character for *ha*, in the style of a laughing face. Underneath reads: US–CHINA COMEDY CENTER; an arrow points down the pathway.

As you pass the public toilet on the left, you start to hear surprised shrieks of laughter from ahead.

Then you reach the end of the alley and detect that the noise is coming from a courtyard inside the messy complex of seemingly randomly constructed low buildings. The doors lay open: thick wooden doors, painted bright red with handles made of heavy loops of cold bronze.

Stepping through the doors, there is a short, uncovered walkway of gray stone; the passageway ends with a large display piece of slate, on which has been written in chalk: "Beijing Improv Wednesday Night Workshop! 北京即兴周三工作坊！"

To the right is a gray, circular arch of bricks: a moon gate, leading into an open courtyard.

Beneath a deep blue summer twilight sky, thirty people are milling about in the open air, drinking beers from bottles being handed through a window from a makeshift bar set up in the kitchen. But you mostly see their backs—people are already wandering through the wooden doors to the north-facing room.

Inside, the light is dim, and as your eyes adjust, you see that the people have started to intuitively form into a standing circle. You take your place in the circle, shoulder to shoulder with the strangers next to you, and look around to see a strange and wonderful mix of people: an American study-abroad student, practicing his Chinese with two Beijing girls; a Chinese banker, still dressed in black pants and a collared shirt, practicing his English with a blonde Canadian woman; a mother with her seven-year old daughter; a small auntie in her sixties; a tall Dutch lawyer.*

The whole back wall is covered with a huge black backdrop banner, covering the wall to the ceiling, with a massive version of the *"HA HA!"* microphone logo printed in the center.

"Welcome to our Wednesday Workshop!" says a Chinese man in English.

"Huanying lai women zhousan gongzuofang!" says the American next to him, translating.

---

* Stephon Marbury showed up once to one of our open workshops, so there is a nonzero chance you'd see him there also. I was hosting and leading games when I saw some new people enter late and beckoned them over to join, but I didn't recognize him immediately. So I was surprised when within two minutes, half the workshop participants were suddenly gone; they were all taking pictures with Starbury in the courtyard.

"Let's warm up!"

"*Xian re yi xia shen!*"

"First we will shake our left arm, counting to eight."

"*Xian yao yi yao zuoshou, cong yi shu dao ba!*"

"Then the right arm, the left leg, right leg, and then, the butt!" He wiggles his butt, and everyone laughs—the kid's laugh leading the way.

Everyone looks at the American for the translation, but he simply says, "Butt!"

Aaaand . . .

ONE TWO THREE FOUR FIVE SIX SEVEN EIGHT!

YI ER SAN SI WU LIU QI BA!

Suddenly, chaos. A space big enough for twenty to stand comfortably is now packed full of failing, laughing, shouting people, trying to keep up with the count, shaking their arms, now their legs, now their butt.

You've been here two and a half minutes. This is great—and it is free.[*]

Within a week of opening, the normally sleepy courtyard was packed virtually every night.

Master Ding came to our opening night. We performed "Singing the Three Kingdoms" to great applause; afterward, I dragged him onstage to try out improv games. I beamed with pride as he improvised marvelously, winning the audience over with his effortless stage pres-

---

[*] In working with Beijing Improv, we held free workshops every Wednesday for years and years. The free workshops helped build the club's audience for shows and, eventually, for the comedy school I opened in the courtyard.

ence. The joy I felt in inviting him onstage instead of the other way around, in a theater I had built, and sharing a small bit of my American comedy inheritance with him was the best part of the entire evening.

The free workshops, which we continued to hold every Wednesday, built us an audience base. The comedy communities I had been a part of over the years instantly coalesced into a rotating calendar of performances.

Friday and Saturday were our big show nights. Friday night was the showcase for my Chinese improv and sketch comedy troupe, Ao Ye Comedy. *Ao ye* technically means "all-nighter," but I picked the name because I thought *ao ye* sounded a lot like "oh yeah," so one name worked for both English and Chinese.

When I started the comedy club, it was a perfect excuse to call up the people I believed to be the best in Beijing and see if we could get a regular Friday night show together. Some of these people, like my friend A Qiu, were professional actors signed to major companies who had performed on many comedy shows before. Tang Long was a screenwriter. Zhi Zhi led corporate improv workshops and taught improv in elementary schools. Xiu Yu was on the forefront of the Chinese mime scene. Du Kang was a talented writer determined to make comedy his career.

To round our group out, we had Com, my Uighur comedian friend who boasted both enormous energy and physical comedy talent. And finally, there was Tom Xia, a calm and collected Chinese-American from LA who had gone to film school at USC and who also had experience in Western-style sketch writing in Chinese.

When I finalized the plans to rent the theater, we made a pact to try and do what no other Chinese improv group had been able to do: perform every single Friday night as a regular group. Some nights, some people couldn't make it and we performed shorthanded, but I am proud to say we succeeded in our goal. Ao Ye improv performed a show every Friday night in that theater for over four years, ending the run only because of the outbreak of COVID.

Every Friday night, we would muscle the six-foot-tall "Wheel of Improv" out of its storage space in the courtyard bathroom and lift it onstage, an old-school spin-and-win wheel on a giant tripod. The wheel's face was separated into many small slices, each with the name of an improv game on it—"Ding Ding Ding," "Death by Improv," "English-Chinese-Gibberish." We invited audience members onstage to spin the wheel, and we played whatever game it landed on.

For the second half of the show, we would do long-form improv: forty-five-minute-long comedy plays created fully on the spot. The laughter was the highlight of my week, though keeping track of the many characters and story lines, as well as joining in with my own characters exactly when was needed, all with no script and in Mandarin, was probably as difficult as doing xiangsheng.

Saturday nights, we rotated between four shows: English stand-up, English improv, Chinese stand-up, and our student graduation show for my Chinese improv school, which I established to help grow the scene and pay the rent. Hundreds of Chinese students, along with the occasional brave foreigner, progressed and graduated from our comedy school. Each level, from A to D, meant doing an intensive twenty-hour weekend workshop, culminating in the class show. Some of our graduates went on to found their own troupes, or become actors and drama teachers.

Before the shows, people would mull about in the open-air section of the courtyard—Americans, Chinese, Europeans, and the rest of the melting pot of the Beijing underground arts scene. When the show began, the crowd would pile unceremoniously into the north-facing room. On show nights, the open area where we held the workshops would be stuffed full of eight rows of seven folding chairs each: exactly fifty-six seats, maximum.*

A member of my staff scanned their tickets—seven dollars apiece—and a volunteer† ushered everyone to the front row. This was necessary because the audience members, especially the Chinese ones, were terrified—and excited—that they might be dragged into some crowd work. As such, they clogged the back rows and late arrivals would sometimes rather stand outside, poking their heads through the open windows, than disturb the show and go to the front.

I loved the show nights with all my heart. There was no better feeling in the world than running in through the side door that led from the courtyard directly to the stage, flanked by my comedy troupe friends, hearing the wall of sound as the audience greeted us. I had begun my journey as a Fulbright scholar hoping to find ways to use comedy to bring people together. Peering through the glare of our jerry-rigged spotlights to see such a unique audience, it occurred to me that an upside of not having enough space was that it forced everyone to sit shoulder to shoulder. The venue was, indeed, intimate.

Weeknights, the courtyard was filled with rehearsals for the various

---

* We tried all sorts of configurations but just couldn't fit a single chair more than fifty-six into that room. Eventually we found we could disassemble half the stage for standup shows—because the performers didn't have to move much—and get another six seats on the side of the stage. The shows were generally sold out, and occasionally we emptied out the last two or three rows of seats and replaced them with standing room tickets. You might think people would not want to stand to watch an hour-and-a-half comedy show, but we got clear feedback that being packed like sardines in an underground bilingual comedy club was cool enough to be worth the discomfort.

† We had about a dozen volunteers, many of them local high schoolers. I am very proud that one of these high schoolers wrote her college admission essay about her time at the comedy club and was accepted into Brown University.

groups who made the club their home. Mime groups, xiangsheng pairs, and screenwriting clubs would clear out the folding chairs and use the audience area as their meeting place.

The club was a home for lost *laowai* looking for a way to interact with local Chinese without fear of making language mistakes. It was a home for Chinese comedians who wanted to experience Western-style comedy in an environment that felt authentic and unfabricated. It was a place where everyone was welcome, as long as they were willing to laugh at themselves.

The courtyard quickly became my home base. I turned a glorified closet behind the theater room into a tiny office for myself. I bought a large stone tea table and a new tea set made of glass, so that I could see the color of the tea as I brewed it. I would show up to "work" in my "office," look out the window into the courtyard, drink tea, listen to the magpies caw overhead, and wonder that this glorious reality could be held together by nothing but laughter.

Running a comedy club was not all fun and games.

One night, in the middle of a summer heat wave, the air conditioner broke half an hour before a show. There was no way that sixty people could survive being stuffed in that tiny room for two hours with no AC and the hot stage lights glaring down from above.

I had to jump on my scooter—by this time I had upgraded to an electric motorcycle—and burn rubber down the Second Ring Road to the nearest appliance store.

I tore into the store and maniacally swiveled my head around, looking for the air conditioner section, where the lone sales associate was closing up for the evening.

"I will buy an AC unit immediately if you can deliver it right now and install it."

The guy didn't even blink. "Let's go," he said.

Thanks to the most ride-or-die appliance salesman I've ever met in my life, we managed to get a van with the AC unit to the mouth of the *hutong* entrance, and I and a crew of six employees, volunteers, and customers picked up the seven-foot-tall tower of plastic and metal and carried it through the maze of *hutongs* like pallbearers. Customers milled in the courtyard, drinking cold beer as the appliance salesman broke out a toolbox covered with pictures of Sailor Moon and installed the machine and foil-wrapped outflow pipes. We started the show only thirty minutes late.

The air conditioner was a relatively easily solved problem compared to some. My friends in America kept asking me if I was worried about the club being raided by the police. Small shows were a gray area: In theory, all comedy shows needed approval from the cultural bureau; in practice, small shows were allowed to go on unmolested as long as they didn't post ticket links on major platforms.

Our private WeChat groups, filled up by hundreds and later thousands of workshop attendees and returning customers, allowed us to fill the fifty-six seats, though sometimes it did smart to see worse comedy shows outsell us because they could access ticketing platforms.

I told my friends the truth, that I was far more worried about the neighbors filing a noise complaint than having police descend on the club. If worse comes to worst, I knew Master Ding would corroborate my story at any hour of the day: We were here to make people laugh, not cause problems.

Besides, what could I do? I didn't have the connections to formally submit our scripts to the local cultural department, and improv shows didn't have a script. I had to hope that the purity of the mission and the penumbra of Master Ding's aura would protect us if there were issues.

The club's biggest threat was actually the market. Fifty-six seats, even with every show packed, wasn't enough to pay the rent and my employees' salaries.

Further, I found our competition was not only for real estate. Other comedy companies started copying our business model, using a live house to soak up the collected talent of the underground comedy scene. A friend of mine, Shi Laoban, started the Dan Li Ren comedy company and performed his first show in our courtyard. A few months later, he had investment from some big tech/media companies and set up a second courtyard theater only two minutes away.

I actually had no problem with this whatsoever, since the whole point of the club was to help build the comedy scene, and I loved that my friends were the ones in charge of the money and clubs. I would sometimes do a set at my own club, twist through the *hutongs*, and head right onstage at his. I took great joy in watching his rise; I took less joy in the actions of some of our other competitors, who used their venture capital money to pay comedians to sign noncompete clauses, blocking them from performing at other venues.*

But it was soon clear that while my club might be able to survive, my competitors would thrive, and the investment that made the difference was something I couldn't get as a foreigner.†

---

* I actually sat across the table from the VC types who founded this company as they told me they were planning on spending three million US dollars to lock up the best improv talent in China. They eventually went bankrupt, and to this day I'm not sure where the money went because I talked to the improvisers they hired afterward and they certainly weren't rolling in it.

† I actually did take meetings with potential investors, but they kept asking me when I intended to return to America, and nothing I said or did convinced them I would be sticking around. While legally I may have been allowed to get an investor, in practice, it was impossible.

The biggest blow came after the first* trade war began in 2017. Leadership on both sides of the Pacific had decided conflict was preferable to coexistence, and funding for Project Pengyou's bridge-building programs was cut.

Alyssa, the director of Project Pengyou, told me the blunt truth.

"No more renting the courtyard nights and weekends. We're losing our lease in two weeks. Either rent the whole thing, or close the club."

I probably should have closed the club. But I loved the club. I didn't want it to die, at a time when US–China relations were at their worst.† It felt like we were being given a choice: watch the bridges burn, and pick a side to stay on when they were gone, or try and fight to keep them open.

My courtyard comedy club was one of those bridges.

I decided to fight.

At twenty-six years old, I dug into my checking account and withdrew $22,000 in cash—three months' rent and two months' security deposit. With no salary or stable income, I handed these bricks of cash to the landlady of the courtyard, an eighty-year-old Beijing woman. The pain of each stack of 100-kuai notes leaving my hands felt even worse knowing how many Chinese comedy shows I'd had to do to save that kind of money.‡ I was committed. This *had* to work.

I expanded the improv school by inviting improv teachers from the Upright Citizens Brigade in Hollywood to do high-priced master

---

* I had to add "first" here since we've had at least one more in the time between when I first wrote this chapter and when I sent it to the publisher.

† Spoiler: Things got worse.

‡ As I stated before, though, I did feel like a baller doing it. For me, being a baller is always enmeshed with pain and anxiety.

classes; I started leading corporate improv workshops for companies like Volkswagen and China Telecom. I stopped taking money in salary; I funneled income from my cruise ship shows into the courtyard. It seemed to me a strange reality, that my comedy club had become an alchemical black box that converted Royal Caribbean's money into a lot of laughter and my eighty-year-old Beijing landlady's retirement income, and somehow always left me back at zero by the end of it.

We needed a breakthrough. The courtyard theater was a beautiful place, but it couldn't survive as a theater. Its uniqueness, however, didn't lie in selling tickets. The theater was unique because of the people who performed the shows, as well as the people who watched them. Its specialty was the merging of Western and Chinese comic styles and sensibilities, and its role as an experimental stage.

What we needed was the exact thing I had wanted when I decided to open the club. We needed a major TV show, or a streaming station, to see the potential in the comedy we were doing, and pay us real money to get the comedy out on the national stage. We needed a shot.

As it turns out, we got one.

Diss Family

Remember the beginning of this book?

Me, wearing my ridiculous Italian explorer/Japanese game show suit jacket, at a table with Chinese comedians, one of whom had a fake bird with glass eyes on his shoulder?

Studio audience? Seven cameras? Chinese *SNL*?

That's where we're going now.

Live, from Shanghai, it's Saturday Night!

It was always a dream of mine to appear on *Saturday Night Live*. Though I never really said so out loud—and I did a lot of talking about comedy, so I think it means something that I never said it out loud—my heart always wanted what my head knew was madness.

To perform live comedy, written that week, performed in front of an audience alongside celebrity guests, and aired to the whole country? *SNL* is a beautiful anachronism, the last remaining show whose format harkens all the way back to the early days of television, radio, and even vaudeville.

Making a single episode of a live-recorded comedy sketch show is a logistical and creative feat of ludicrous proportions. Add in "China issues"—there are too many to list here—and it seems almost impossible. It is almost like baking a cake, if you didn't start with the ingredients at hand, but needed to instead source wild seeds and invent agriculture before you could even start the stand mixer. Also, if you needed to invent the stand mixer, too.

As a recipe, it might read:

Assemble a cast of varied acting, writing, and directing talent, all of whom must be arrogant enough to be willing to fight to outcompete each other for stage time, yet cohesive enough to work together;

Concentrate these people in a small space for hours and hours every day, six days a week, for months on end;

Find a company willing to shoulder the financial—and political—risk of attempting a new comedy show format based on speed and satire in a country where every script and broadcast must be approved by the Department of Culture;

Detail a process to write, rehearse, perform, edit, rewrite, re-rehearse, and re-perform dozens of comedy routines in a seventy-two-hour period;

Construct new sets, find props, sew costumes, and get ready to put on a show with no more than two days' prep and often no live rehearsal; and

Account for the possibility that your celebrity guests might be late, incompetent, unfunny, or all three at once.

If you do all that, and the lights go up—then the comedians had better not mess it up. They have to kill it. They have to kill it, live.

You can see why, nowadays, nobody makes shows like this anymore. It's too expensive, too all-consuming, too prone to disaster.

And yet, that's what comedians love: having one foot out over the precipice, twisting around for strangers. The brutality of the fall is yin to the yang of the glory of pulling it off.

And if you can do all these things, and pull it off live, the adrenaline is so great it makes you forget the exhaustion and the stress, the challenges and the trials.

If you fail . . . well, you get a day off after each episode.

It seems impossible. But I felt like I had a real shot at making it through the crucible. After years of work with Master Ding, I had learned traditional Chinese comedy. In America, and now in China, I had done years of stand-up, improv, and sketch. I had my own comedy club to serve as an incubator, and knew all the comedians in the scene who were really good at Western-style comedy in Mandarin.

My dream could become reality—maybe not in America, but possibly in China.

Assemble

In America, there are places where comedy shows scout talent. For hungry, ambitious comedians, these clubs become so iconic they almost seem otherworldly: the Laugh Factory, the Improv, the Upright Citizens Brigade Theatre.

By "getting passed" at one of these clubs—becoming a regular performer on the roster—you have a real shot of rising to the top of a messy but still ultimately meritocratic system of comedy shows. If you can make people laugh, eventually you get auditions. If you get auditions, eventually you get work. If you get work, the work gets bigger and better.

In China, none of this was true. There were no agents watching improv, sketch, and stand-up in Chinese bars and small clubs at this time. And yet, I and all the Chinese comedians in the scene resolutely believed that even here, even in a media market such as China's, there was still hope of being scouted. We knew that the most popular comedy shows in the country were not as good as the ones we were doing in small clubs. But in order to get scouted, we needed clubs—places with consistent shows that could get buzz.

My US–China Comedy Center was not famous, nor even that impressive compared to some of the flashier theater spaces that were sponsored by big entertainment companies to incubate their signed talent. But we had two advantages over others: we had people who had actually written and performed sketch comedy in the States, and we had an unusually diverse cast. Nobody else had the mix of people we had: Americans, Chinese Americans, Chinese actors, writers, and even Uighurs.

Even though there were absolutely zero people at the time hiring writers and cast members for *SNL*-style live sketch comedy in China, we all took to the project with a great thirst. We wanted to make sketches, good sketches, different ones from the glacially paced fifteen-to-twenty-minute Chinese-style sketches that were aired on the New Year's Gala. We wanted to hit audiences fast and hard, cut the lights, and start again without warning.

At our weekly rehearsals, we would brainstorm combinations of characters, locations, and social hot topics, pick permutations of them, and use improv to find the funny, doing run-throughs of each sketch with no script or outline.

"A self-help group, but entirely of clean freaks who love mopping and just can't give it up. Go!"

"A doctor who is scared of delivering bad news and finds that rapping the diagnosis calms him down. Go!"

Each week, we ground our way through the dark. Friday afternoon meant rehearsal, which meant rapid iteration of ridiculous scenes. The best ones we saved and wrote outlines for—opening, beat 1, beat 2, beat 3, blackout. Then we would grab dinner on at a Xinjiang restaurant on Gulou East Street—a big plate of chicken, *nang* bread, and eight-kuai lamb *chuanr*—and head back to the theater, where the audience would already be filing in.

Fifty kuai—around eight dollars—paid for a ticket to our show. Each week, anywhere between twenty and sixty audience members would sit in rows of folding chairs set up in front of the comedy center's stage. We played short- and long-form improv games and formats. Finally, I would officially "end the show."

"But!" I told the audience each week. "Before you go, we have some sketches that are really, really rough. But if you want to stay and see them, we'll do them for you!"

Not a single audience member left, ever. Their confidence in us was only somewhat misplaced—we mixed hits and flops together so briskly, it was sometimes hard for even them to keep up.

"Mops Anonymous" was a flop. "Rapping Doctor" was a clear success. Most were some sort of messy in-between. Our method was wild, and sometimes we chased the jokes that were working at expense of the structure we'd written, so the live audience reaction didn't tell us much about whether our original idea had legs. But we had a compass that pointed toward the funny, and we were willing to try anything.

While we didn't have a dozen winning sketches, even our bad ones were structured well, packing into three to four minutes the number of jokes that a Chinese-style sketch might stretch out across ten or fifteen minutes. It really felt like Western-style sketch comedy, done in Chinese, for a Chinese audience, and not an imitation of Western sketch done by people who hadn't ever seen it before.

And so, when our preparation collided with opportunity, we were ready. The zeitgeist slowly shifted. Over the period of a year or so, word began to go around the comedy scene: Someone was going to buy the rights to *SNL* China. Sketch was going to be the next big thing that major media companies were going to invest in. Through the grapevine, we heard that not one, but two Chinese shows were looking to do Western-style sketch comedy for the first time on Chinese TV.

Two days later, I got two requests—one from each show—to see Ao Ye Comedy perform live. I gave them both tickets to the US–China Comedy Center's Friday night improv and sketch show.

We broke out the rapping doctor, as well as the best of the rest, and got a good reaction from the crowd. After the show, I had a series of awkward meetings where I had to negotiate with representatives from each show separately, even though we were all in the one-room theater together. By the end of the evening, I had gotten assurances for paid train tickets and hotel rooms for my troupe to go to the final auditions in Shanghai.

As they left, I sat in my silent theater. I sat on the cool stone floor, surrounded by our cheap folding chairs, looking out into the courtyard through the windows, their small panes of glass set beautifully inside intricate tessellations of woodwork.

A few months ago, there had been no map of comedy clubs to scout for talent. Now, the map was being drawn, my club was on it, and my troupe was going to get a shot at the big time.

"We meet Wednesday at Beijing South Station. Don't be late. And also . . . there are some things I want to discuss."

The whole troupe was packed into my tiny office in the room behind the theater. Propped against the wall was our massive collapsible stage, which we hauled out for each show; the remaining space was taken up by a giant tea table, where I sat pouring tea for the troupe members, who sat around in a loose ring.

"What is it?" Zhi Zhi asked.

"If we do a good job at this audition, they are going to try and destroy Ao Ye."

Chinese entertainment is a very rough industry. Because all shows need to have their scripts and final versions approved before they go to air, individual comedians, even major comedy companies, have no hope of hitting it big without support from a very small group of people who have connections with the approval agencies.

This meant that comedy in China effectively ran on a K-pop model. The few individuals with the connections and money to even have a shot of getting on air didn't invest in scripts, they invested in people and contracts. By starting talent agencies, and funneling access to the few approved shows through them, comedians, actors, and writers would throw their own best friends overboard for just a chance to play.

The contracts these agencies offered were ludicrous and abusive. I looked at some of them under nondisclosure agreements, but not all of the agencies required silence to look at the papers: Ten years with no salary was not unheard of, with a "profit split" of future gains being the only promised payment. The result? Companies who had these connections knew they just had to dangle the carrot, a shot at the big time, and then say, "There's more for you if we don't also bring them." They would causally tear apart comedy troupes and friendships to lock down talent under a better contract.

Even before our audition, this process had already begun to erode our troupe. Com, our Uighur comedian, got a shot at being a contestant on a separate comedy show run by one of the two companies inviting us. It was too good a chance to lose, and nobody begrudged him leaving. He would go on to have great success at the show, which made us all happy . . . but while we still got to see each other in Shanghai and remained friends, I never performed with him again.

So, my main worry was not that we would fail to get on the show. I believed that if this show didn't work out, others would start circling. My worry was that my troupe, composed entirely of my personal friends who were trying to do something new together, would be picked apart.

"They will take their favorites and offer us separate contracts. I would be shocked if they didn't. But I feel like we earned the auditions as a group. So I want to make sure that if we go, we all agree that nobody goes off on their own, and we negotiate as a team, to get the best deal for all of us."

I didn't even share my deepest fear: If huge TV companies had no respect for the troupes, they would have even less respect for the one troupe represented by an American. I worried that they would not see me as a true leader, merely a foreigner who obligingly scouted and trained their new employees for free and could be discarded at the first excusable moment—and that moment would come as soon as I asked for a reasonable contract for me and my team. I wanted a shot at the shows, but I had no intention of signing ten years of my career away for it, or asking my friends to do the same.

We talked in circles, but in the end, we made a pact. We would go together, and only break off from the group if the group agreed it was best.

"I'm sorry, sir," Tom said solemnly. "I have the diagnosis right here, but . . . could you drop a beat?"

"A what?"

"A beat. You know."

Tom started to beatbox. I, playing the patient, stared at him blankly with a weak, sickly demeanor.

Our first audition was for Eastern Television, a major TV station based in Shanghai. They were looking for talent to fill out their roster for season two of the hit variety sketch show *Jin Ye Bai Le Men*.

When I saw the towering TV station building, a mountain of blue glass and steel, I felt very glad indeed for my training with Master Ding. We'd been in and out of so many TV stations over the years that I did not feel overawed at seeing the huge stages full of equipment and half-built sets.

"What do you think?" I asked the casting director afterward.

"Don't finalize anything with Xiaoguo until after talking with us," she told me.

Xiaoguo Wenhua—also known as Fun Factory—was the second company who was casting at the same time. Their headquarters were in a nondescript office building, and we performed the sketches in a cramped meeting room, cluttered with scripts and whiteboards packed with jokes.

Compared to the lights-camera-action drama of the TV studio, you might assume that this audition would be less stressful, but I found it was the opposite. Chinese TV companies look grand, but are part of the old world of Chinese entertainment, where what the boss says goes regardless of audience reaction, and talent has a hard time rising through the politics.

Xiaoguo, however, was a comedy-focused company that held lots of open mics and shows, and while they still subscribed to the K-pop model, their signed comedians performed real comedy in front of real audiences. They were almost single-handedly responsible for bringing Chinese stand-up to China with their hit show *Tuokouxiu Da Hui*. Who knows what kind of talent had been in this meeting room?

In the end, we had tentative offers from both shows. The money was close. The question was whether it was a better idea to go with the old world—Eastern TV, a huge famous TV station—or Xiaoguo, who were with a major internet streamer but not on legacy TV.

Du Kang wanted Xiaoguo. Zhi Zhi wanted Eastern TV.

"Eastern TV is a provincial-level TV station," Zhi Zhi said. "That's brand power. That goes on the résumé forever."

"But we don't know them, and we know half the people at Xiaoguo. Xiaoguo is made of real comedians, and Xiaoguo made *Tuokouxiu Da Hui*, which is the best comedy show in the country. The people at Eastern TV took one trip to New York and watched one sketch show, and now they think they know what sketch is," Du Kang countered.

"But season one of *Bai Le Men* was a hit! Season two will be a hit, and if they really don't know anything about sketch, then we'll be the only troupe there making good stuff, and we'll get on the show every episode!" Zhi Zhi insisted.

"If they can recognize good stuff," Du Kang said in a low voice.

I interjected with some new information: "I talked to Suolan, from the People's Society of Improv, who works at Xiaoguo now and is going to be on the show. She says that Xiaoguo has poached a lot of the directors from Eastern TV's last season. So if season one of that show was good, maybe season one of Xiaoguo's show will be good."

The conversation went on without resolution. Tensions rose. I was numb and exhausted, slumped in my chair, unable to even turn my body to look at my friends as we argued. There was no clear choice to be made. I just wanted my troupe to stick together. I didn't want to be the deciding factor—even if it meant refusing both shows.

In the end, both companies threw a last-minute wrench in the gears and independently lowered their offers. At the rate we had negotiated, there was only money for three people to join.

For some reason, this bad news clarified my thinking. I didn't know which opportunity was better. I just didn't want my troupe to consume itself trying to make an impossible decision: who gets on and who goes home with nothing.

"OK, they have a budget for three people. I say this: We should pool the money and split it amongst all of us, and still all go on the show. They can't complain if they get more people for the same money, and that keeps us together. And . . . if we're going to not get paid as much, I would rather work with real comedians. I suggest Xiaoguo."

The energy shifted. Nobody in the troupe liked the idea of being paid less, but it did make clear that working with better comedians seemed to be the deciding factor. It looked like we had made our decision.

An hour later, Zhi Zhi approached me and told me she had called the Eastern TV team, and was going to their show.

"This is the right move for me," she said.

"We went into this together," I said.

"I want to get on a real TV show, and this is my chance. I've been doing comedy for a long time, not just with Ao Ye."

"You auditioned with us."

It didn't matter. Zhi Zhi would only go with the group if we all went to Eastern TV, and everyone else had decided Xiaoguo was the best option.

I felt a strange combination of frustrated rage and calm resignation. The anger came from the fact that we had written and auditioned as a troupe. In my mind, after the introductions were made to the show teams as a group, nobody could claim to be here simply representing themselves. The resignation came from the fact that if people wanted to defect, there was nothing I could do, and once they didn't want to be part of the troupe, I felt no reason to fight to make them stay. I felt sick at the result and relieved of a burden.

Meanwhile, Tang Long finally had enough details to call his boss at the screenwriting company and check to see if he could get leave to come to Shanghai. He learned that moving to Shanghai would conflict with his screenwriting obligations. He, also, was out.

That left four of us. In the end, Tom Xia and I agreed that we would both move to Shanghai and work at Xiaoguo. Du Kang and Xiu Yu, both of whom had day jobs, couldn't quit their jobs for a partial payment to go on a show with no guarantee of success. So, we decided we would split the third payment between the two of them, and they would work as writers from Beijing, pitching ideas and working on our scripts. Zhi Zhi left the troupe. I signed the contracts.

As I scrawled my Chinese name on the bottom line of the contract, I felt a mix of pride and sadness.

The pride, of course, came with signing my Chinese name to make real money writing comedy for TV. Seven years after arriving in Beijing for study abroad, barely able to speak and knowing only a few hundred Chinese characters, I had earned my way onto the show team, not as a foreigner to plug into one sketch, but as a true cast member and writer on a major show. It wasn't Hollywood money, but we had guaranteed contracts with bonuses for getting sketches on the air. I had also brought along some—if not all—of the people who helped get me there, even negotiating that Ao Ye Comedy be listed on promotional materials as a producer.

The sadness, of course, came from Tang Long missing out on the show, and Du Kang and Xiu Yu not being able to join us in person. And, of course, Zhi Zhi. We had worked together for five years, had many common friends, and I didn't know if we would ever speak again.

As I sat on the high-speed train back to Beijing, watching the countryside whiz by at 150 miles an hour, it felt impossible that all of that had happened in less than twenty-four hours.

Perhaps I seemed despondent. Perhaps I *was* despondent. Tom Xia noticed, and in his regulating, resonant, film director voice, consoled me.

"She's her own person. She has to do what is best for her. It always comes down to that. But you got us on the show. You did a really good job with this."

I hadn't realized the pressure I had been putting on myself until I considered releasing it. I choked back tears. He was right. I had tried my best, and I had done a good job. I had won a victory, even if that victory didn't look like what I had thought it would in my dreams.

The audition drama taught me many things, and chief amongst them was that to speak for others, you must first become strong yourself. Master Ding had spent decades cultivating an aura so persuasive that it could help me secure a Fulbright fellowship from half a world away. I simply wasn't at that point myself.

I called him on the phone.

"Hello?"

"*Shifu*, it's me."

"Jie Xi! How are you?"

"Good. Actually, very good. I and my comedy troupe from the club have been hired to write on a show in Shanghai. It all happened very fast. I'm actually heading to the airport right now."

"Excellent! Congratulations. You are a good performer. You will do well there."

"I will be back right before Chinese New Year. I'll tell you all the stories then."

"Go, go! Good luck!"

I hung up the phone. Now I was on my own.

Concentrate

"Do you hear that?" I asked, running my hands through my hair, exhausted. It was eleven at night and the scripts were far from done.

Tom Xia looked up, his head cocked at an angle. Joey and Suolan, two Chinese improv comedy friends from the old days in Beijing who now worked at Xiaoguo as writers on this same show, looked up from their computers and shot each other a look I couldn't quite read.

"What?" I asked. "What am I missing? Listen, there it is again!"

Soft, punctuated moaning. Rhythmic creaks. It was faint, but undeniable.

"Jie Xi, you know where we are, right?" Joey asked.

"At the hotel?"

"It's a love hotel."

"What???"

"Come on. The first table read is in fourteen hours, and we don't know how to end the beer bottle factory sketch."

Comedians from the top comedy groups all around China had relocated to the neighborhood of Xiaoguo's headquarters to write and act on their as-yet-unnamed sketch show. Shanghai, a megacity the size of Los Angeles with the density of midtown Manhattan, was flashy, expensive, and somehow always short of places to rent.

Where could all these comedians live together, close enough to be able to work on sketches deep into the night? The production team researched every option in the area. When we signed the contract, we were told we would be able to get some sort of Airbnb-type situation. I had begun to imagine my lifestyle, living with Tom and other writers in some sort of multi-bedroom high-rise apartment.

But in the end, there was only one place within a short distance of Xiaoguo headquarters with the space to host a score of comedy writers: the Blue Orchid Concept Hotel, a three-story building with inexplicably solar-system-themed carpets that made most of its money renting out rooms by the hour to people who might not know each other well but loved each other very much.

My room was a small living room with a hot plate to make food, a couch and a table, and a loft space above with a bed. There was only one light switch in the whole room, with three settings: on, off, and purple. The first time I discovered the "mood lighting" setting and the whole room flooded with purple light, I thought I had just suffered an aneurysm.

Most but not all of the second and third floors had been rented out by Xiaoguo for the writers and cast for the duration of the show. As such, we were always running up and down the hallways, popping into each other's rooms at any hour of the day, yelling, laughing, and making noise. Meanwhile, couples power-walked through the corridors and disappeared into their own rooms to make noises of their own. We were always louder.

Each room had a completely different layout and theme, and I got to see a bunch of them while visiting other writers. I think these were the "concepts" referenced in the hotel's name. One comedian's bed was in the shape of a heart, with a red velvet blanket. Another comedian's bed had metal hooks on the bedposts.

"For ropes," I said, nodding.

"*Wo kao!*" he swore. "That's what those are for?"

"What did you think they were for? You've lived in this room for two months!"

"I never really thought about it."

Outside the hotel, there were only two parking spots, one of which was often occupied by the owner's car: a BMW with a full, custom, bright-orange wrap of a giant image of every Dragonball Z character. In a city awash in garish wealth, I greatly respected its absurdity.

To live in the Blue Orchid Concept Hotel was to be constantly confronted with new concepts. One of these came in the form of business card–sized advertisements that were slipped under my door. My first day on the job, I came back from headquarters, opened the door, and almost slipped on four of these cards, which were scattered at my feet. Both sides had the same full-color picture of a Chinese girl with massive boobs in a tiny string bikini. Her face had been photoshopped so pale and small, it looked like she was doing a sexy Voldemort cosplay.

The text read, "Lonely college sisters are waiting for you!" and had three WeChat numbers underneath.

Perhaps due to their continued loneliness, the cards continued to be slid under my door every day for the five months I lived at the Blue Orchid Concept Hotel, without fail. I kept them all in a stack in the corner of my room, and eventually I had hundreds of them, thinking I would use them for a bit at some point when I would first show one, then another, then suddenly hundreds.

It turns out they were too lewd to even work into a bit, but I did have a fabulous moment when I told the story of the cards to my family at Thanksgiving the following year.

"No! I don't believe you!" Tom, my mom's fiancé, was incredulous.

"Wait here," I said, and retrieved the giant stack of cards from my room and placed them in his hand.

My whole family erupted into chaos. Three solid minutes of noise and shrieking ensued. The cards were like a magnet rapidly flipping poles: they would repel everyone, then attract them to take another look, then repel them again.

Another concept the hotel explored was the elements. As the seasons changed in Shanghai, my room was always freezing cold. The Shanghai winters are not too bad—the temperature hovers in the forties and fifties—but they were wet and rainy, and none of the buildings had any heat. The Communist Party heavily subsidized heating in cities in the north, but their definition of "north" included anywhere north of the Huangpu River, which happened to flow right through the city of Shanghai. We were only half a mile from the river on the "southern" side—which was actually to the west of the river, at the same latitude as those on the other side that had heat, though that apparently didn't matter—and as such, none of the buildings in our district had any heat at all.

I bought three space heaters and left them on all the time, willing to take on the risk of accidentally burning the whole hotel, and every single one of its concepts, to ashes. The heat, however, simply floated to the loft area above. This meant I wore three layers at all times downstairs and stripped immediately to my underwear the moment I went upstairs. By the time I woke up every morning, my sleeping area was thirty degrees hotter than my living room downstairs, and every morning I had to summon my willpower to go downstairs and shower.

Also, the shower was enclosed in clear glass doors and was in the middle of the living room. This may have been another concept.

Whatever concepts were at play at the hotel, security was not one of them. I found this out one day when I pitched the show team an idea for a video sketch. A news story had come out about how younger people were moving away from cheap, unhealthy ramen noodles, and sales were down 25 percent.

"Can we make a 'Save the Noodles' PSA short video, with Sarah McLachlan's 'In the Arms of the Angel' in the background? Lots of slow-motion shots of ramen noodle bowls with googly eyes, looking forlorn and abandoned, covered in dirt and stuff?"

Pan Jie, the showrunner, stared at me blankly. Of course. I was parodying something they had no idea existed. But I still thought it would work, so without the team's preapproval, I roped Tom in to help me find dirty, sad-looking places nearby to shoot a rough mockup of the sketch. The plan was that I could edit the footage myself and win over the directors with a fully formed product, so they could get an idea of what I wanted to do.

"The fire escape stairwell in the hotel is pretty sketchy," Tom said.

We went from our rooms on the third floor, down the emergency stairs to the first-floor landing, which was covered in dust and detritus. It was perfect. We got our shots, and then before leaving, I checked the street-level door, which looked busted. It swung open with no resistance.

"There's no lock?"

There wasn't a lock on any of the other floors, either. Anyone could just walk in through the fire escape and enter the hotel at any time, bypassing the front desk.

I went immediately to the concierge. "Did you know the fire exit door is unlocked, and leads directly into the building?" I asked.

"Yes," she told me. "It's like that so people can get out if there's a fire."

"But if there's not a fire, then anyone can get in!"

She frowned, clearly annoyed. "It's our responsibility to look out for the safety of our guests," she told me without a hint of irony.

My exposure to so many new concepts made up a fair chunk of the stand-up routines I did in Shanghai. Hitting two to three open mics a night was crucial to my being able to work out bits for the show. I was supposed to be focusing on hot topics, character bits, and stuff that might actually be useful for the program. But in my first week in the stand-up clubs in Shanghai, I found my favorite topic to be the Blue Orchid Concept Hotel. It turns out the Shanghai audience also thought the idea of an American unknowingly moving into a love hotel for months was hilarious.

"The Blue Orchid Concept Hotel," I would repeat again and again into the mic. "What are these concepts? Why can't I understand these concepts?" No good answers ever came, but I did get some laughs.

The truth was, as much as I loved making fun of the concepts, I absolutely loved living at the hotel. It was basically like a college dorm, but full of comedy-writing friends. I could go to any of the comedians' rooms at any time, ask them if they thought my ideas were funny, and help punch up their scripts. Also like a college dorm, you learned to move quickly through the hallways and ignore occasional hookups happening behind closed doors.

The hotel turned out to be a sanctuary. We worked all day, almost every day, from the morning until evening. Compared to the headquarters, where we did our table reads and sat for hours on end awaiting the verdict of the show's directors about whether we would get on the show that week or all our work had been for nothing, the hotel was relaxing, fun, and social.

One night, I joined Suolan in her room, where, along with Tom and Joey, we made dinner and watched imperial palace dramas. Suolan, who was from nearby Hangzhou, was familiar with Jiangnan-style cooking and had bought hairy crabs online. These were delivered to our door in a Styrofoam box the size of an ottoman, packed with dry ice to keep the living crabs cool.

"You can buy live crabs online?" I asked.

"In China, you can buy anything online, and with two-hour delivery!" she said.

We steamed the crabs in bamboo steamers set atop an electric hot plate. Suolan taught me how to crack open the carapace and find the good, yellow bits of the crab while avoiding the tough gills.

We drank beers and joked while the TV played in the background, the drama playing beneath a wave of rolling netizen comments that whizzed across the top of the screen, so many comments that it blocked the faces of the actors and made the show impossible to follow. We drank, and ate, and laughed, and ordered boba online, and laughed, and ate, and drank.

Hours later, I wandered back down the hallway to my room, shoes in hand, socks sliding across the planets and stars printed in the carpet below. Vague grunting noises came from a nearby room.

I stumbled past, entered my room, hit the purple lights, and lay down on my bed, completely content.

This was a concept I could understand.

Account

"I tell you, Herr Wu, the bottle is of top quality," I said, offering a beer bottle for inspection.

Fifty people sat and stood in a semicircle, watching my every move, as I tried to perform a German accent in Mandarin. It was the first table read of the show, and everyone was trying to write sketches that would allow the first celebrity guest, Wu Zhenyu, to act alongside the cast.

Wu was a C-list actor known for his roles in beat-'em-up Hong Kong gang films, and in this sketch we had placed him alongside my character, a German quality assurance manager at the Tsingtao beer bottle factory.

Joey, my writing partner on this sketch, was standing in for Wu. He took the bottle I offered, looked at it for a moment, and viciously smashed it over my head. Shards flew everywhere. All the cast, crew, and writers screamed.

"Not good enough!" Joey yelled, and all the other side characters in the sketch rushed to agree, bobbing their heads sycophantically.

One of the writers picked up a broken piece of glass and ran it over in their hands. After the table read, he told me, "Everyone, I mean *everyone*, thought it was real!"

The bottles were made of sugar—those fake bottles meant for stage fights and movie props. The moment I saw it, I was giddily eager to get this bottle smashed over my head in front of the show team. I felt like a kid who had just discovered some crazy skill, like I had double-jointed elbows, and couldn't wait to show it off at recess.

In the coming five months, these table reads would come to be the times I most looked forward to—and also most dreaded. While they were called "table reads," in reality we needed to stand up on a "stage" created in the empty space of a semicircle of all the cast, crew, writers, and directors. This was our test audience. We acted out the sketches with scripts in hand.

Xiaoguo placed a huge amount of emphasis on audience reaction, which in my opinion was one of the best parts of the company's culture. Chinese state media channels tended to be very hierarchical, and the director had total say. Xiaoguo, however, did not have the luxury of state support for their shows, and if the shows weren't funny, they would go off the air.

The focus on results from the table read meant, however, that if you had a good sketch but just didn't have it "together" in time for the table read—blocking down, jokes practiced, etc.—your sketch would die on the vine.

The bottle idea had come in a roundabout way. When the show had told us the first guest would be Wu Zhenyu, I had no idea who that was, but my fellow writers brought me up to speed.

"He gets into a lot of fights," Joey had told me while we were brainstorming. "Hits people, roughs them up, breaks bottles over their head . . ."

"Breaks bottles?" I asked. The idea was born.

The show had told us not to write anything too difficult for the celebrity guest, since Wu was from Hong Kong and apparently did not speak Mandarin very well. I thought it was strange to kick off the show with a guest like that, but I soon discovered the logic behind the plan.

"Xiaoguo has the rights to the actual *Saturday Night Live*," Joey reminded me one day at dinner. "But they bought them along with Youku, who is the streaming partner. Youku has their own signed talent, and they will want their people on *SNL*, not Xiaoguo's. So, Xiaoguo is making this whole show as a way of training their signed people to be able to outcompete Youku's people—but their big budget will be spent on *SNL*, not here."

I had also underestimated how much of the celebrity buy-in on *SNL* came down to having fifty seasons of examples to show that it was, in fact, a good move for your career to make fun of yourself on TV. Many Chinese celebrities had no interest in getting anywhere close to a joke of any sort, not to mention one about themselves. This thinned the pool of possible guests, despite nonstop recruitment efforts by Xiaoguo's production team. The result was that we got mostly C-tier celebrities to work with. Sometimes those celebrities were from Hong Kong and barely spoke Mandarin. Sometimes they didn't look at our work until the day of the show. Sometimes they canceled at the last minute and we had to throw out all our sketches.

Those decisions, however, were above my pay grade. Either way, I figured writing a sketch heavy on physicality would play well, and so when I found out we had a guest known for breaking bottles, the only question in my mind was: "How do I get this guy to break as many bottles on my head as possible?"

The idea of hiring a gangster to be a quality control expert at a bottle factory definitely fit my sense of humor. The harder part was figuring out how to get myself into my own sketch. In comedy terms, every character needs to be "justified"—they have to make sense in the world of the sketch. As a white person on a Chinese sketch show, this was a bit of a challenge. Why should there be a white guy in a scene with a Hong Kong gangster? A roundabout route led to the character of a German quality control expert at the Tsingtao factory, and after only one bottle test and a few read-throughs, we had to put the sketch up in front of the whole company.

There were probably about ten to fifteen cast members and twenty or so writers on the show. I say "probably" because the number was always changing. Xiaoguo had a ton of signed talent, mostly recently graduated college students locked into long-term contracts, who were working for the company full time but had no experience doing TV. These signed writers and cast members were mixed with people like Joey and Suolan, who had done both live and TV comedy, as well as people like myself, who were professional comedians but had never done a full TV season.

This meant it was not really clear who was "on" the show at any time, what their job was, or who I should work with to put together my sketches. Writers would fight to get their scripts on, regardless of who was in the cast. Cast would fight to get into sketches, regardless of who wrote them. I was one of the few trying to do both—but I had no choice, since Chinese writers almost never thought to include foreign characters in their sketches, so I had to write my own if I wanted to act.

Each week, we had to come up with ideas to present at these table reads, which meant alliance-building amongst the cast and writers—I help with your sketch, you help with mine, and we both now get two lottery tickets in our quest to hack and smash our way to the top of the table read, and then after that, the real show.

If I had to battle my way onto the show, I wanted a secret weapon—surprise. And so when we wrote the bottle sketch, I asked Pan Jie, the showrunner, if they would buy us the bottles we needed.

"The audience reaction has to be real. If the cast and writers don't know it's going to happen, then when I get hit, that will be a true stand-in for the audience reaction at home."

"OK. One bottle."

"Can we have two? One to practice first?"

In the end, we got two bottles delivered by rush mail an hour before the table read. Joey and I ran out into an alleyway to rehearse. He smashed the bottle over my head, and we heard a yelp. An old lady walking her bicycle down the alleyway had been watching.

"It's fake! It's fake!" we yelled down the alleyway, doubled over laughing. She shot us a look like she didn't believe us.

That first week of the show was probably the most fun I had in the entire process. The show hadn't aired yet, so the directors truly didn't know what the audience would like, and they were open to some crazier ideas. Having grown up watching American-style sketch, I had a bit more of an eclectic taste than the other writers.

One sketch we pitched was a scene between three iPhones in a bathroom. iPhone X had just been launched, and the question went viral on the internet: We went from iPhone 8 to X—so what happened to iPhone 9?

I hit Joey and Suolan with the pitch: "I play iPhone 9. Cut to: Tom, dressed as iPhone X, pushing my face into a toilet, insisting we allow him to cut the line and launch early, while iPhone 8 tries to get him to stop torturing me."

Joey and Suolan stared at me blankly. Then Tom walked into the room, four pillows strapped to his body with clear packing tape to turn him into a rectangle, with color-printed app icons taped to the pillows. He looked truly stupid.

"Yeah, the table read will love that!"

After the first table read, in which the bottle sketch and the iPhone sketch had both gotten a positive reception, I went with Tom, Suolan, and Joey to eat Japanese barbecue and go over the sketches. Suolan and Joey were less excited, since their sketches had not done as well in the first round of notes.

Tom and I consoled them as we ate our food. It was just about the last time that this happened, since for the next five months the process was almost always done the other way—them consoling us.

Shoulder

While I had quirkier, more unusual sketch ideas than any of the Chinese writers, I found myself to be far, far behind them in a second skill: dealing with notes and the second table read.

Between the first and second table read, each team got one day to adjust their scripts and performances according to notes from the directors. But I quickly discovered that a lot went into these edits that I was not aware of.

The most immediate issue was the most obvious.

"They want me to cut the German quality control character," I told Tom when I read our notes from the show team.

"What's the problem?"

"My face."

Sketch comedy is called "sketch" because unlike a drawing with lots of shading and detail, a sketch is meant to give the outline of something, fast and rough. This works well for topical comedy, since you need to come out with new episodes weekly, and keep up with current events.

The challenge is that the more "sketch" and less depth something has, the more important it is that the audience knows exactly what is happening, as soon as possible. Who, what, when, where, why, and how are essential, since the comedians need jokes to start as soon as possible, leaving the audience to fill in a lot of gaps.

The problem in the bottle sketch turned out to be the same problem I would have with every single sketch I submitted to the show: There are simply very few character archetypes that Chinese people understand for foreigners.

If I play an English teacher, and the sketch is set in an English classroom, Chinese people can get the who-what-when-where-why immediately in a way that they understand. They've been in English classes and can imagine having a foreign teacher.

But a German quality assurance inspector at a bottle factory? Speaking Chinese? The company thought this character, which I thought was funny, creative, and justified, was just unnecessarily complicated. The directors liked the idea of the sketch, they liked the bottle smash, but I was a complication. They suggested that for the second table read, we either cut the character or replace me with a Chinese actor.

The most frustrating thing is that I knew they were right. At that point, I had five years of experience performing for Chinese audiences, from xiangsheng to stand-up to improv, from comedy clubs to cruise ships. I'd performed for urban and rural audiences, Hebei migrant workers and Shanghai millionaires. The common thread between all of them? I was the first American comedian they had ever met doing Chinese comedy. I was indeed a distraction.

In stand-up, this didn't matter much, since I could make jokes about these topics directly and ease the tension in the room. In improv it also didn't matter, because everyone switched characters every five minutes. But sketch comedy is about patterns. If we did a sketch with two Chinese people and one foreigner, the audience would think we're playing a "rule of three" game where the two Chinese people are straight men and the foreigner does something silly on the third beat. What other option is there? There had never been a single comedy show in China where a foreigner was "just part of the cast."

Of course, I believed these were issues I could solve. I threw myself into the work wholeheartedly, writing deep into the night. By writing interesting characters, introducing them succinctly, and acting well, I was confident I could make the audience suspend their disbelief.

The issue was time. We were always on a clock. Making the foreign character work took more time than replacing the character with a Chinese actor, and I was the only one who had any experience working characters of different races or nationalities into their scripts.

This meant, time and time again, I had to try and solve the problem myself. I would write scripts featuring Western characters who fit into the sketch, only to have the sketches themselves move forward while my role was cut.

I tried being Sylvester Stallone in a sketch with a martial arts star; I tried playing Michael Phelps in a sketch with Olympic swimmer Sun Yang. My character was cut from both. Both sketches aired, and while I got a writer's credit and $500 bonus, inside I felt completely defeated.

As the weeks turned into months, I shot wider and wider. I asked if I could play a Mandarin-speaking Donald Trump (HARD NO!). I asked if I could play Bob Dylan ("Who?"). I asked if I could play Steve Jobs (Apple isn't a sponsor, so, no.)

The truth was that Xiaoguo was trying to accomplish an impossible balancing act. Since the show aired on state-run media, it meant the state in some way sanctioned everything that aired, so any representation of a foreigner on a nationwide show was considered to be actual foreign policy. I could control what I said, but I couldn't control how it would be interpreted, either by Chinese, or by people outside the country.

This was my particular challenge, but every sketch faced some sort of similar issue when any hot social topic was mentioned. In effect, this meant the first table read was all about being as funny as possible, but the second table read needed to showcase a sketch that was airable in China. Otherwise, all the time and money spent on costumes, set, and filming the show would be wasted if the sketch got blocked. Knowing what could and couldn't be aired was technically the job of the director, but in practice it was left to the writers. There was a significant gray area to play in, but we weren't supposed to pitch sketch ideas that had no shot at all of getting through.

That difficult balancing act was clearest in my favorite sketch I wrote for the show, which I called "World Internet Forum Elementary."

"There's a story going viral about Jack Ma, the CEO of Alibaba," I told Tom and Huanzhu Didi, one of the other writers on the show I knew from the Beijing stand-up scene. The show scraped the headlines on social media and sent us occasional dossiers with hot topics to consider for sketches. "The other major tech CEOs were meeting this week at the World Internet Forum and all had dinner together. The one person they didn't invite was Jack Ma."

Huanzhu Didi added: "I saw this. People asked Jack Ma about the snub and he said, 'Well, they didn't invite me, but I might not have had time to go, anyways.'"

"Doesn't this sound like little-kid behavior? 'Don't sit at my table!' 'Fine, I didn't want to anyway!'"

Everyone laughed and we immediately started laying out beats to the sketch. We cast all the biggest tech CEOs as elementary schoolers in the school cafeteria. Jack Ma comes over to join, but is rejected, then says he doesn't care. The other CEOs tease him with kid's rhymes and bully him. Everything looks bad for Ma—until Mark Zuckerberg shows up outside the school entrance.

"*Let me innnn!*" I whined at the table read, banging on a pretend door.

"*Nuh-uhh!!!*" Jack Ma shouted, and all the other CEOs clapped and whooped like children.

"A hundred and eighty other schools let me play, why are you the only school I can't enter?"

I tried to scale the walls but failed.

"I CAN'T GET OVER THIS WALL!!!"

We got huge laughs from the writers and show team. Eventually, Ma defeated me at range with magic kung fu, and the sketch ended as the other tech CEOs danced around in circles, chanting kid rhymes in praise of Ma.*

The sketch ended, and the big laughs calmed down to a trickle, then to complete silence.

"Well," the director said in a voice that cut cleanly across the room, "you've got your work cut out for the second table read."

I heard a whisper from one of the office workers in the test audience. "That's never going to air."

I knew we were playing on dangerous ground, but I thought I'd

---

* We sang: "马云马云真伟大,扎克伯格赶回家!" which could be translated as: "Ma Yun, Ma Yun, you're so great / You sent Zucc back to the United States!"

hit a line ball here—right on the edge. We had gotten big laughs, so I eagerly awaited the notes from the director's team with specifics of what we could do to massage the edges. But after two hours, there were still no notes from the director's team. As everyone started making adjustments to their scripts, I just sat by myself, alone, as if I had just been fired from the show but nobody wanted to tell me.

When you live in another country, you start with the humility to know you don't know what's going on. You ask friends, they tell you, and you learn. It's the only way to find out, even if it's embarrassing to ask things like "Why is that funny?" when you're a professional comedian.

I was already feeling isolated from the rest of the cast and writers because of my inability to get any non-Chinese character into a sketch. Now, I had just gotten big laughs, and nobody said a single word to me. I had missed something big. I had embarrassed myself somehow, and truly not known it, and I didn't even feel comfortable to ask what I had done wrong.

That night, back at the Blue Orchid Concept Hotel, I swallowed my pride and visited Huanzhu Didi to ask what the hell just happened.

"I didn't know you actually wanted the sketch to go on the show," he told me.

"What did you think we were doing by writing the sketch?" I asked, incredulous.

"The sketch idea was funny, and you asked for help, so I helped you. But that was never going to air. I thought you were just doing it for fun."

"We can take it back a notch—"

"No, you can't," Huanzhu Didi told me. He rubbed his eyes—he was always running on no sleep—and sighed. "Look, Jack Ma runs Alibaba. The company can't make fun of Jack Ma, or Alibaba might never work with Xiaoguo again."

"We made fun of all the CEOs—"

"Exactly! Why would the company make enemies of the most powerful people in the country?"

"They're not the most powerful—"

"In China, it's dangerous to make fun of *any* powerful people. Not just tech people. You understand? The people who make decisions here don't have a sense of humor about this. They will hold it in their hearts and never let you know. That is, until you need them, and then they will punish you by doing nothing, so they can't be called out. It's just not worth it. Make fun of celebrities, that's fine. Make fun of regular people, that's fine."

"Or Mark Zuckerberg?"

"Also fine. Oh, and that wall joke? That's not happening."

The "proper" thing to do probably would have been to not even put the sketch up for a second review. It would have shown I had been properly chastened for overreaching, and that I now understood the right way to go about things.

But I refused to withdraw the sketch. The show's leadership had told us again and again—it was our job to write the best sketches we could, and their job to get them on air. I was angry. I wanted to hold them to their word. So I dulled the edges, changing the names of the CEOs from their real names to similar-sounding names by changing a tone here or there to give the show some deniability. I cut Mark Zuckerberg entirely. I also added Sun Yang, the Olympic swimmer, into the sketch in the third beat as a physical education teacher, hoping that slipping him in would make the directors want to support the sketch since it was always hard to shove the non-actor celebrities into anything.

The new version of the sketch sucked. It got almost no laughs, and by the time it had ended, I felt physically sick. Coming up with ideas was one thing, but getting them through the gauntlet to air was proving to be too much.

It's hard to blame Xiaoguo. During the show's run, they would time and time again put their money where their mouth was, spending precious shoot time to record sketches they had been told could not air, in hopes that a final edit could convince the powers that be that the jokes were OK.

But they, and all of us, were practicing comedy on a sort of Schrödinger's tightrope—there was no way to know if you were safe until you checked, and checking risked finding out the whole tightrope never existed in the first place. Years later, one single bad joke about the military would effectively put Xiaoguo into hibernation for six months, wipe out tens of millions of dollars of stock value, and send the director of our show to jail.

But that's not my story, and it's not the story of Chinese comedy, either. It's easy to say that these restrictions define Chinese comedy. It's easy to say that because it's not true. To think so simplistically would invalidate all the work of the comedians, writers, and actors who worked on our show. It would invalidate Master Ding and his life's work, which was done in a time far more restrictive than the one we live in, and which brought real laughter and joy to so many people.

Chinese comedy is much bigger than these issues, and so are the people who make it.

Kill

I was at one of my lowest points of all my time in China. The *SNL*-style dream of doing wacko sketches and Chinese Donald Trump impressions had faded away. What's more, the Chinese writers had begun to learn and then copy my Western-style sketch-writing techniques.

They had begun the season pitching rambling ten-to-fifteen-minute sketches, but now their sketches had clean and clear beats. Combined with their better ability to adapt to notes in the second table read, I felt each week was bringing me further and further from where I wanted to be.

It took just a few weeks for me to drop from high excitement to rock bottom. I felt almost like a pariah, or a ghost. Other writers avoided working with me on my sketches, knowing that I hadn't gotten anything through in a while. Nobody interacted with me unless I first interacted with them.

I wandered backstage on shoot days amongst my friends dressed up in ludicrous outfits—one day a Qing dynasty empress, one day a glass of red wine—wishing I were in that week's show. It was a special kind of torture to spend sixteen hours a day watching all my friends have fun and not take part. I fell into a depression, unable to sleep, every night watching YouTube videos of an Australian man fabricating a pocket watch, hand-filing each brass gear tooth with a rasp, until 4 a.m.

I even considered resigning from the show. I wouldn't have been the first to do so—many of the college students, and even some of the professional comedians, had quietly slipped away after the first couple weeks. While Ao Ye had negotiated salaries, many of the other writers apparently were working on spec, with no money unless they got scripts on the show. With no experience in sketch writing or acting, and no ability to break through, the show's team got smaller each week.

Suolan, who was a true friend through this period, offered some of her time each week to help me figure out the foreign-character problem. In the end, we—mostly she—managed to write a sketch with a foreign character that finally got through: a boss who ran "The Most Chinese Foreign Business in China."

In the sketch, I played the boss of a foreign company in China who had gone native. While my staff wore suits to work, I wore *hanfu*, and spoke in a combination of *chengyu* and old-time Communist slogans.

"We must address the failings of the capitalist system!" I insisted, and berated my Chinese employees for their lack of traditional Chinese dress. Eventually, I embraced a merging of the cultures—allowing my team to wear suits, but only if they were sewn from *mian ao* fabric—a style of garish colorful flower pattern popular in northeastern China.

It was actually a clever sketch that looked on the surface to be patriotic, but actually made fun of people who insert nationalism into every detail of life. For the first time in weeks, I got to stand onstage in the darkness, feel the lights turn on, and face the hundreds of cheering audience members and feel like myself again.

"Thanks for writing me in. This was so much fun," I told Suolan after I came offstage. The rush of finally getting to perform in front of the live audience for the first time in weeks was intoxicating.

"It was a challenge, but the writing wasn't the main issue. There was . . . a rumor I heard. Some people on the show team think you are going to forget your lines. That might be why you aren't getting cast as much."

I was flabbergasted. I knew that being a non-native speaker might be an issue. But I spoke Chinese to everyone on the staff, all day, every single day. I delivered my scripts in Chinese characters. There was no reason to think my language would be an issue. I had always trusted that Xiaoguo's reliance on live shows would mean that it didn't matter—if it's funny, it's funny, and if I got the laughs, I would get on the show.

"I don't forget my lines!" I shouted, incensed. "I do cruise ship shows for forty-five minutes and don't forget my lines!"

"I know, I know!" Suolan said. "But you should make sure when you go to the table read you have the whole thing memorized. Otherwise, they'll think you can't do it."

There is a term used to refer to foreign performers in Asia: "performing monkey."

I'm sure there's already an image in your head: overacting, clownish, vapid. A tool in the hands of another people, a hammer used to smash the perceived privilege of the West for the simple satisfaction of the masses.

Being called a performing monkey is a singular sort of disrespect. For the reward of some scraps—a life that looks like fame—you would be willing to lose face for yourself, your country, your people, your culture, your race . . . *

A lot of Westerners see conspiracy in these awkward performances, but the truth is many of these oafish roles for Westerners just look stupid because professional Chinese writers just assume they will never find talented, bilingual *laowai* that can pull off anything more difficult.

I learned early on in my career that speaking Chinese fluently and being able to do comedy onscreen was not useful in a market where foreigners were expected to be blond, blue-eyed backdrops to the main drama unfolding between the Chinese characters.

And so, I passed up the boring gigs and easy money, spending the entirety of my Chinese comedy journey in the actual Chinese comedy scene: apprenticing with a master to learn xiangsheng, doing stand-up in the Chinese clubs with no other foreigners around.

Now it had led me to where I wanted to be: writing on actual Chinese comedy shows, with Chinese writers. And here, at the level I

---

* The modern version of this is the idea of the "shill influencer," who will take money from anyone who needs good things said about them, and doesn't know or care who exactly is paying them.

wanted to live in, I felt I was being told that none of my comedic sensibilities mattered, and they didn't even trust me to remember my lines.

This is why I was so focused on not just playing a "foreigner" in a sketch. I worried that if I didn't find a way to convey some true, real, individually human identity across to the audience, then my stage persona would just be a gimmick.

A monkey, worthy of that ignominious disrespect and dismissal.

I feared that if I could not get on this show by being myself—if I couldn't justify my character onstage in this country, in this language— then perhaps they were right. Perhaps all of it, everything I've learned, was a big nothingburger, just a thinly veiled willingness for the Chinese audience to laugh at a foreign face.

In ways both big and small, I had allowed this prejudice to dominate my thinking. I worried that if I read as fake to the audience, either the Chinese or Western audience, then that "fakeness" would not be read as a natural part of every artist's journey of self-discovery.

It would read as a sort of cultural treason.

The price of living in multiple cultures is being the smallest planet in a sort of cultural three-body problem. I found myself somewhere in the space between America and China, the gravitational pull of these two massive, incongruent realities tugging and stretching me as they both continued on their own heedless, momentous paths.

Was there a stable orbit? A path through the dark space where I could live this life between the worlds, without being ripped apart?

And if there was a space, had I arrived at the right time?

The closest I ever got to getting an answer to that was from a Chinese-American friend of mine, over drinks at a bar in the *hutongs*.

"Hearing you talk like this . . . it was like this for Asians in Hollywood. Fifty years ago, no screen time. Then, a trickle. Now, a bit more. Maybe you can pull it off, and maybe you're fifty years too early."

The injustice of this rumor—which, to be fair to Xiaoguo, I never managed to confirm—soured my heart. With the move to Shanghai looking like a flop, I fell back on the only thing going well for me: stand-up.

Since moving to Shanghai, I had ground the open mic scene six days a week. I would ride my electric scooter from mic to mic, hitting up Storm Xu's Comedy UN shows, then going to Andy Curtain's Kung Fu Comedy, before finally hopping on one of the Xiaoguo-led mics to get as much stage time as I could. Afterward, I would bask in the glow of the adrenaline and eat *mao cai*, a kind of everything-soup dish, and drink watery beers. Full and tipsy, I would slowly make my way home, sated until the effects of the food and alcohol wore off, and I started getting anxious again about being so stuck.

Possibly just to prove to myself I was, in fact, still funny, I decided to pool all the stand-up jokes I had written over the last five years together for the first time in my career and try to do an hour-long special. I hit up Andy, booked Kung Fu Comedy's room, and started hustling up ticket sales.

The show wasn't a huge hit—I only sold about forty tickets. But every joke worked, some a little, some a lot. I got laugh after laugh after laugh.

Onstage in that small dark room, drunk in the flow state of going from polished bit to polished bit (and never forgetting my lines), I realized just how far I had strayed from what I knew made me funny.

My stand-up jokes were about my life, my perspective, and my journey in finding my way in this new home country of mine. I didn't talk much about hot topics, or glass bottles, or internet CEOs. I talked about things in my daily life, and I didn't take myself too seriously.

After the show, I got to smile and chat with the audience. I felt enormously fulfilled and relieved despite the low turnout. During the set, I had discovered a new path.

If I couldn't play a character, I would have to be myself.

The lights went up—but I wasn't onstage.

WANG JIANGUO: Hello, everyone, and welcome to *Stupid International Incidents*. I'm your host, Wang Jianguo. Our guest today has lived in China for many years. Welcome to the show, Ai Jie Xi!

I walked onstage from stage right, waving to the crowd, and sat down beside Jianguo at the "Weekend Update"–style desk.

> **JIANGUO:** How's everything, Jie Xi?
> **JIE XI:** Great! Well, except that my electric scooter got stolen.
> **JIANGUO:** *Hahaha!* I mean, I am sorry, that is very upsetting.

After my stand-up special, I spent an hour watching my own show and marking down jokes that I could convert into some sort of "sketch." I wanted to take my tight, fully memorized stand-up bits and turn them into a dialogue.

By matching with Jianguo, one of the company's signed stars for whom they were always interested in getting more stage time, I could come onstage as Jesse and do Jesse jokes, fully justified.

Kind of like xiangsheng. Kind of like "Weekend Update."

> **JIANGUO:** Well, tell people about yourself first, Jie Xi.
> **JIE XI:** Sure! I've lived here for five years, and I definitely had to make some adjustments.

JIANGUO: Like how?

JIE XI: Well, for instance, the traffic lights mean different things here. In America, red means stop and green means go. But in China, both red and green mean "Can I make it???"

JIANGUO: That's enough, that's enough. We know that's not right. Well, tell me about this bike. You have an electric scooter?

JIE XI: Yes! I love electric scooters. It really is the best way to get around Shanghai . . . until you get hit by a car.

JIANGUO: No, no, that won't happen! So, did your scooter really get stolen or not?

JIE XI (smiling, taking out a big set of keys): It really did.

It really did. I loved my electric scooter in Beijing so much that the first day I moved to Shanghai, I went to a secondhand scooter store and bought a junky scooter for $200. I enjoyed it for four days until the cheap lock I'd bought for it got snipped and the bike was, for lack of a better term, Shanghaied.

I was honestly shocked, since I had lived in China for a long time and never had a bike stolen. But after that incident, I decided to double down and buy a new scooter for $600. In addition to being less dented than the first one, it also had an additional security feature: a microchip that could be tracked by an app.

JIANGUO: Well, Jie Xi, how do you like the new bike, then?

JIE XI: Oh, it's great. But it's scary riding these bikes. I saw a delivery guy going the wrong way. He got hit. The food went flying!

JIANGUO: That's horrible!

JIE XI: I know! All that food, wasted! I'm joking, I'm joking!

JIANGUO: You better be. Life is precious.

JIE XI: You are completely right. It actually wasn't a bad collision, everyone was fine. Although, I did notice something interesting when he got hit.

JIANGUO: Oh?

JIE XI: I found out people from different countries make different noises when they get hit by cars.

JIANGUO: What?

JIE XI: Like, Americans? We go (*smashing noise*) "*Ouch!*" Japanese go (*smash*) "*Itte!*"

JIANGUO: Chinese?

JIE XI: Chinese go (*smash*) "*Compensation!!!*"

After the first table read of this script, I had gotten laughs at just about every punch line. I was confident I would, since some of these jokes I'd been doing in stand-up for over three years. Perhaps more importantly, I had the lines down so well there could be no chance the show team would think I could forget them.

"Jesse's finally admitted he's not Chinese!" Pan Jie, the showrunner, said, and the whole team laughed.

I honestly didn't like that reading of things at all—abandoning my efforts to be "one of the guys" in sketches still felt too close to selling out for me to find any humor in this. But it was true that the moment I accepted that the audience was going to see me differently, and that this show at this company was not the place where I could fight that, it became easier to carve out my own space.

The show team had been trying to push me to play more of an archetypal "foreigner" for a few weeks now. I resisted this because it made me feel like a pawn. Liaoning TV had wanted me to do stupid accent jokes, and while Xiaoguo at least knew the content had to be good, it still felt like an existential-scale bummer to make it to the big leagues and find out things were still basically the same.

Huanzhu Didi inadvertently helped me find another way to look at this. One night, as we worked late into the night, I got up to leave.

"You going to sleep?" he asked.

"No, actually. The New England Patriots play at 1 a.m. today. I'm going to watch the football game."

"Oh, the Patriots! Tom Brady!"

My mouth literally hung open. "You know Tom Brady?" I asked.

"Well," he admitted, "I really only know two things about American football. One, there's a player named Tom Brady, and two, he deflated footballs."

"OK, FIRST OF ALL THEY WON THAT GAME BY LIKE FORTY POINTS—"

I saw his expression change from shock, to horror, to amusement, and finally back to horror as I gave him the first-ever full Chinese-language breakdown of the stupidest scandal to ever hit the NFL, free of charge. He must have thought I had literally lost my whole mind.

The fact that the NFL was such a big thing in my country, with all the games and emotion of the fandom and the history of the sport . . . and the only thing he knew about it was that Tom Brady deflated footballs? I think about it a lot. I think about it probably once a week. There are so many things that mean so much to people in one country and nothing at all to people in another. Every country, every culture, every religion—every group of humans has something they care about a lot that everyone else knows nothing about. As with comedy, I try to gravitate toward and learn about those things, because I feel like anything that people care so deeply about is worth trying to understand.

That night, while watching Brady scorch the Cleveland Browns with completely legal and regulation-pressure footballs, I thought about the fact that a football team and our show team had about the same number of people. We, too, had players, coaches, ownership . . .

And, like a football team, not everybody plays quarterback. Some players play special teams, coming on for one specific task—blocking punts, kicking field goals . . . even just holding the ball so someone else can kick field goals.

Not everybody starts. Not everybody even plays every game. But for the team to win, everyone has to do their job. That's what it means to be a professional. Help the team win, even if only in a small way.

I wanted to play quarterback on this show, but that wasn't going to happen. I was clearly on the bench. But I could still play special teams. There must be something I can do to help us win that nobody else could.

Comedy-wise, I felt this meant embracing being the only American on the team, and giving up on being "one of the guys" in sketches . . . at least until I could show the coaches I deserved to start.

JIANGUO: So, your bike was stolen, did you get another one?
JIE XI: Yes, I did!
JIANGUO: So everything worked out, then.
JIE XI: No, that one got stolen, too.
JIANGUO: Really???
JIE XI: It really did.

It did really did, again. After buying the new scooter, I turned on the microchip app's alert function, which buzzed my phone as if I got a phone call whenever the bike was moved. Three minutes after setting it up, I got a buzz and rushed downstairs—only to find it was just someone moving their own bicycle, and they had bumped the scooter.

Apparently, the microchip was so sensitive it was virtually useless. Four hours and ten notifications later, I disabled the notifications, confident in my slightly better lock to dissuade thieves. Unfortunately, this meant when the bike was actually stolen a few weeks later, I didn't realize until the next morning, when I went to the bike rack outside the Blue Orchid Concept Hotel and found it was missing.

JIANGUO: So, what did you do?"

JIE XI: Well, this time I had a location-tracking microchip in there. So I looked at the app, found where the chip was, and called the police.

JIANGUO: Oh?

JIE XI: I said, "My bike was stolen, but I have it chipped, so I know where it is."

JIANGUO: What did they say?

JIE XI: "Well, if you know where it is, what do you need us for?"

JIANGUO: *Hai!*

JIE XI: They did send someone to help me, though. As we walked down the street toward the bike, he told me, "You'll never find it! These thieves, they'll have taken care of that chip for sure!"

JIANGUO: Disgusting behavior.

JIE XI: The signal was coming from an apartment building parking lot. We looked and looked—couldn't find it. But then!

JIANGUO: Then, what?

JIE XI: I saw there was a security camera! I took the policeman to the front desk, and asked if we could see the security footage.

JIANGUO: What did the front desk say?

JIE XI: She spoke directly to the policeman and said, "He thinks those cameras are real!"

JIANGUO: *Hai!*

All this was totally true. It took some convincing, but the local public security bureau did send someone to go with me to the location of the chip, which the thieves had apparently ripped out and thrown in a covered parking lot full of scooters. We never did find the bike, and the cameras were not on.

JIANGUO: Is your visa up, or are you just looking to get a free flight out? I don't believe you, Jie Xi, I want proof!

JIE XI (*Places second set of keys on the table, then a beeping noise rings out*): My bike! It must be nearby! (*Starts to leave.*)

JIANGUO (*Holds me back*): We're doing a show, Jie Xi! Think about it—which is worth more? Your crappy scooter, or your paycheck for this show?

JIE XI: (*Thinks . . . then bolts offstage.*)

I actually did get two bonuses for getting the sketch on, one as a writer, and one as an actor. The total? Eight hundred dollars—exactly what I had paid for my two scooters combined. I was back to break-even, and had never felt better about it in my life.

That night at the wrap party, for the first time since week one, I felt like my body and soul were both at the party. Joey, Suolan, Tom Xia, Huan-zhu Didi, and Bobo (who had helped me write Jianguo's dialogue) all hit the town with me. We went to an "American-themed bar" called Cages where they had fancy imported beer, cornhole, and—amazingly enough—baseball batting cages.

I showed Huanzhu Didi (who apparently had an untapped interest in American sports) how to swing a baseball bat. All of us took turns trying to smash balls from the pitching machine, whooping and letting out the stress of the week. As we got more drunk, we swung the bat more and more wildly. This irresponsible mixing of alcohol and weaponry made me homesick for America.

I don't know if I can really say I ever made the starting lineup of the show, but I did become a much better special teams player. I would pop in and out of other people's sketches, hitting a line here or there. Now that my original work was confined to trying to make another episode of *Stupid International Incidents*, other writers perhaps felt less threatened that I would take their slots, and invited me to help and then cowrite some other sketches that made the air.

I also started a free series of workshops on how to write Western-style sketch comedy. A lot of the recent college graduates who were signed to the company had been in over their heads from day one, mostly getting to act but not write. I led writing and brainstorming workshops that helped one of them get their first writing credit on a sketch that aired later in the season.

By the end of the show, I was thoroughly exhausted, but in a much better place. The gauntlet of Diss Family had been a roller coaster ride, and I made it out in one piece. It was a harsh wakeup call to the fact that even the most forward-looking comedy company in the country had no interest in figuring out the identity issues needed for me to thrive as a foreigner in Chinese comedy. Still, I had gone toe to toe with professional comedians, been a part of making the show a success, and had not given up.

The final evening, the company threw a huge party. The big boss sent thousands of renminbi in red envelopes to our show's WeChat group, and people jabbed at their phones' screen trying to grab them. Tom and I, representing Ao Ye, bought a giant stuffed teddy bear as a gift for Pan Jie, the showrunner. It was about six feet tall, but with weirdly skinny legs that made it look more like nightmare fuel than a cuddle buddy.

We dragged this bear all over town to the post-party events—karaoke with the whole crew, then a spur-of-the-moment 2 a.m. bowling session.

As I stumbled back into the Blue Orchid Concept Hotel, I thought about what sort of stories I would tell Master Ding about my experience when I returned to Beijing in two days.

I wondered what he would think about the fact that my breakthrough during my hardest time on the show essentially came from writing a xiangsheng script and hiding it in a "Weekend Update"–style sketch.

I never got to find out.

My Daughter, in America

I saw the WeChat post in the Happy Classroom group at ten in the morning on January 20.

"Oh no," I wailed out loud, to no one, to me alone. It was a sound I'd never heard myself make before. I crumpled into a lump on the couch and sobbed, first silently, then loudly and deeply.

My show in Shanghai was over. It was only two days before I was to return to Beijing. I was two days too late.

I had not even said goodbye in person before leaving Beijing. I'd gone straight to the airport.

That short phone call I'd made to him on my way to Shanghai was the last time we spoke.

I would never see him again.

I felt empty, like I was falling into a pit.

I shambled around my tiny room, smothering my face with one of the hotel towels. It was rough and my nose was raw from a cold I'd been pushing through. The towel hurt as it chafed my swollen nostrils, but for some reason that felt good. The physical pain distracted me from my anguish. I felt grief at losing the person whose life's work had brought me to this country; I felt shame at not having been there for him. Why hadn't I known his illness was this bad?

Part of me knew this was how he was—he didn't tell anyone about the return of his illness. He never had. He could avoid people with the best of them. But on that day, I didn't know what I knew. I only knew I wanted to hurt. Hurting was painful, hurting was penance, but at least hurting was feeling, and I wanted to feel and not be numb.

Why hadn't I kept in closer touch? Why had I thought this show was so important that I couldn't go back to Beijing occasionally and see the people in my life who mattered more than these directors and ad men and producers?

I cried into the towel. Then I got mad at the towel. The tears felt right. The towel felt wrong, this stupid towel from this stupid hotel in Shanghai. I shouldn't be in Shanghai now. I shouldn't be holding this stupid towel. I should be back in Beijing, in the hospital. If I were there, I wouldn't even need to do anything; I could just be there, doing nothing, waiting for . . .

Whatever came next.

What came next?

It was my first moment of internalizing what it meant that I had lost my guide. I had been allowed to let my passion drive me forward, like a bowling ball gliding heavily down a lane. With Master Ding guiding me—acting as bumpers blocking the gutters—all I needed to do was hurtle forward and be guided to the pins.

Now my safety rails were gone. I was fading toward the gutter.

I looked at the towel, at my hotel room, then out the window onto Jiangning Road. The light was flat and heavy. It was cloudy and looked like it might rain.

What came next?

In the afternoon I got a WeChat message from Dashan. The disciples were conferring. Master Ding had left a message behind to the disciples, telling us to hold no special events, not to mourn, to send no flowers. That was his job as the Master—to tell us not to worry, and to put us at ease.

But we couldn't do that. We wouldn't. For the first time, it was our job not to listen.

Dashan had reserved a room at a hot pot restaurant near Master Ding's house. The restaurant had two important qualities. First, it was tasty, and since Master Ding was himself quite a chef, he wouldn't go anywhere that couldn't make food at least as well as he could. Second, in the early days of the 1990s, he had often taken his disciples there because it served halal food and Master Ding was ethnically Hui, one of the Muslim Chinese.

The next morning, I rose in a fog, trundled down to Shanghai Hongqiao Station and took the train to Beijing. I spent the ride half asleep and half numb. I cabbed directly to the restaurant, staring out the window at the Beijing traffic and the landmarks I passed. I had been so excited to return after four months in Shanghai. Now there was a storm in my heart that had a soporific effect on my body. Internally I writhed; externally I slumped against the window of the cab and watched the world flow by.

I hopped out of the cab. Dashan had just arrived. We closed in to shake hands, which turned into a hug, which turned into both of us bawling our eyes out. When our breathing steadied and we extricated ourselves from each other, we confirmed what we both knew: Master Ding would want us to send him off with laughter.

One by one, Master Ding's disciples arrived from all around the country. Cameroonians and Canadians, Rwandans and Japanese, Iranians and Americans. They came from where they were working, living, or touring. They came in, smiled, broke down, drank as strong a drink as their religion allowed, smiled again, and laughed.

So many foreigners in one room, and their common language was Chinese. This seemed a testament of sorts to Master Ding, who made us joke our way to fluency. Even if he hadn't been teaching us to mourn, he'd given us the language to do it with.

A cynical part of my mind realized that this room was some sort of anthropologist's dream. *How do peoples of different cultures deal with loss?* It seemed like the sort of question that would be followed by a couple of trite statements about "culture" in an airline book on Doing Business in China, sandwiched between the chapter telling people to hold business cards with both hands and the chapter about "saving face."

The truth of culture, of course, is that it's made of people. We came from disparate places with different rules for nights like this. But we had built amongst ourselves a new culture, the Happy Classroom culture. Laugh together, learn together—and, apparently, cry together. No hard rights, no hard wrongs. We had to accept each other because otherwise how could we learn? How could we live? How could we grieve?

Yes, we had studied jokes. And not all the jokes were super funny. Sometimes we did shows about rural infrastructure improvement. But now, looking at everyone together, eating and laughing and consoling each other in Chinese, I recalled what Master Ding had told me.

"The jokes are just words."

This was what was important.

The empty plates accumulated, the first and second bottles of *baijiu* drunk. We stood up one by one and toasted our master.

"That first group of students, back before the whole foreigners-doing-xiangsheng was a thing, he treated us so well," Dashan said, his impeccable Chinese wavering a bit here and there under the weight of his emotion, and a slight Canadian accent slipping into his *oohs*. "He and his wife would cook for us. There weren't many Westerners in Beijing then. He took us into his family.

"It was only years later that I looked back and realized how amazing it was. Why had he taken on that load, to be a father for so many wandering foreigners? He told me it had to do with his own time in America. Master Ding lived in New York for two years in the 1980s—his daughter was studying there—and he didn't speak any English. He couldn't get through the world, and he saw how hard it was to be a foreigner. His daughter was doing better, but still had so much difficulty."

I heard the next sentence as broken and shaky, but I couldn't tell if it was because his voice was shaking or because I was crying myself.

"He said he took us all in because he hoped someone would do the same for his daughter in America, if she had been alone."

Character

"Ah, Jesse, you're here!" Master Ding said as he swung open the door to his apartment. "I have been waiting."

When I entered Master Ding's apartment for the first time many years ago, the first thing I noticed was the awards. Awards on plaques, awards on scrolls, awards on paper—recognitions, congratulations, and certifications filled Master Ding's modestly sized apartment to the brim.

Also, the swag. Small radios, tiny crystal globes, trinkets and swag of all imaginable sorts lay scattered about. Books on xiangsheng lined his walls, as did many tapes and CDs. I had the feeling that any drawer I opened would be full of more of the same.

Being a famous comedian in China meant a lot of invitations to perform, and in Chinese culture it would be unheard of to invite a master xiangsheng performer to your event and allow him to leave empty-handed. This meant swag bags—decades and decades of them.

In that instant, I understood what had seemed like strange behavior to me before. When we foreign disciples went with Master Ding to shows, we had always been greeted with gifts handed over in person by the theater owners, TV station directors, or company bosses. Master Ding would laugh, shake hands, and smile from ear to ear. He would take the gifts with great respect, holding them before his body, thanking his hosts.

Then, immediately, as soon as a door was closed or a corner was turned, he would rifle through the gift bag unceremoniously, take things out, run some sort of split-second mental analysis, and then hand it over to the one of his disciples he felt would most appreciate it. This process continued until all the swag was gone.

At the time, I thought he was merely extremely generous, but the reality was that he'd probably had enough gifts for a lifetime already. These gifts had piled up, year upon year, to the point where they took over Master Ding's apartment. The mismatched style of all these separate, uncoordinated gifts made me feel like the apartment had been furnished by an influencer agency with a taste for Soviet aesthetic.

"'National First-Level Artistic Performer,'" I read, looking at one of the more prominently displayed awards.

"Oh, yeah," Master Ding said, wandering in from the small kitchen, dressed in a simple T-shirt and gym shorts, holding a glass bottle full of tea leaves. "These awards, you feel embarrassed if you show them, embarrassed if you don't."

"How does one become a first-level performer? Be really funny?" I asked.

Master Ding laughed. "That's not really how it works. But none of these are actually that important. The next show is the most important. Did you bring your script?"

"Jesse, what is your favorite Chinese holiday?"

Master Ding stood to my left, in the position of the straight man, locking eye contact first with me, then with some invisible audience. His tea lay forgotten on the table. Even in his living room, even in rehearsal, he was fully onstage.

"Lantern Festival. For sure," I said confidently.

"The Lantern Festival? Why?"

"I love lantern riddles. Want to hear one? 'My two hands hold two bowls. I drop them both—*crash!*—but only one breaks. Why?'"

"That's easy. One was dropped on the couch."

"Nope."

"One was dropped in mud?"

"Nope."

"Well . . . what is it?"

"One was made of plastic."

"You!!!"

In preparation for the Lantern Festival, which takes place fifteen days after Chinese New Year, we were preparing another classic routine. Like many of the traditional pieces, it has its roots in traditional Chinese culture—in this case, the practice of visiting friends and neighbors at night, lanterns aloft, and confronting them with riddles.

Still, I always struggled with these bits. To put it simply, the jokes were old. Any joke that still works a hundred years after it's written will lack some zip.

As such, I struggled to find the rhythm, to make the joke feel real. What kind of exercise was this? Having an American do lantern riddles? It felt gimmicky, performing-monkeyish. But even though I trusted Master Ding, and I knew that a gimmick or novelty act wasn't his end goal, I still felt like a monkey, and that resentment was tanking the whole routine. It felt fake.

Still, I didn't want to say that so bluntly to Master Ding.

So, after one of our run-throughs of the script, I asked, "*Shifu*, when you were young, did people really still do these lantern riddles?"

"Oh, definitely. They do them now, but not as often. Before, it was a highlight of every year. Going out at night, the *hutongs* in the lantern light . . . Xiangsheng comes from life and tradition, and Beijing has a lot of life and tradition. Lantern riddles, Beijing opera . . . hawker barking."

"Hawker barking?"

"*Yao huo*—calling out items for sale on the street. When I was young, you would hear them everywhere, shouted by tinkers and salespeople. People had a way of sing-shouting the items they had for sale, so the sound reached the *hutongs* in front of them, and people would come out into the street to get what they needed." He took a breath and barked out long, controlled musical shouts, each word three seconds long and crystal clear: "CILANTROOOOO!! CARROTS, WHITE RADISH . . ."

Standing two feet away from this old man yelling vegetables into the air, I felt like I was exactly where I wanted to be on planet Earth at this moment. It felt like I was watching something that simultaneously meant a great deal and yet nothing at all.

I've always felt a great affinity for things like this, that mean nothing and everything all at once. I think that's why I like comedy.

"That's what they sounded like," Master Ding said, when he had finished his hawker barking. "You would hear them throughout the day. They come by, make a sale, then wander off into the next hutong. I miss it. These arts are disappearing. Soon, there may be a day when nobody alive has heard them for real."

I felt even worse about asking my question about the value of these old jokes now, but the show was coming up soon, and I couldn't make people laugh if I felt like a fraud.

"Don't you think for me to do these traditional jokes . . . it just comes across as fake? You saw these things, you did these things. But for me to say I love lantern riddles . . . I don't think the audience will buy it."

"Who is your character?"

"What? Me, I guess."

"Who are you?"

"Jesse."

"Who are you?"

"An American? A foreigner? A Jew?" I didn't know what answer he was looking for.

"An American who has come to China to learn xiangsheng. This stuff is fun for you, right?"

"Yeah, I love it," I said, thinking back to the hawker shout, listening to the sounds of a Beijing I now could only glimpse the edges of, yet which fought to hold its shape against the onslaught of modernity.

"These traditional routines, when Chinese do them and foreigners do them, it means a different thing to the audience. When Chinese do these routines with a master, they think, *Oh, the disciple has been forced to learn the old jokes. They probably want to do young people jokes, but they're here because they're being forced to do this show.*

"But you flew to China to learn xiangsheng. You apprenticed to a master. Your character is someone who has come here, through great challenges, to learn Chinese culture, and found an interesting piece of it: lantern riddles. And even if they're old for the audience, for you, they're new.

"And if they're new for you, they can become new for the audience, too. To see their own culture being reborn under the eyes of a foreigner, this is what the audience sees. Yes, we can add some new jokes with current topics. But that won't make the routine live or die. The thing that matters is that you breathe life into the old jokes."

"And how do I do that?"

"Didn't you just say you like this stuff? When it comes time to talk about Chinese culture in the script, show people you like it! Just be you. Here, take this."

Master Ding picked out a few xiangsheng CDs from his wall.

"What are these?"

"It's good xiangsheng! You're a xiangsheng performer, yes? Listen to more xiangsheng."

I thanked him and placed the CDs in my bag. As I heaved my electric bike's massive lead-acid battery up onto my shoulder, now fully charged, I recognized the simple truth Master Ding had been trying to teach me.

Yes, I was an American, a foreigner, a Jew . . . these identities may be hard for the Chinese audience.

In America, I might have the opposite issue. I might be too Chinese for comfort, facing an audience who had no idea what to make of my interest in things like lantern riddles . . . or anything Chinese, for that matter.

If I ask, "Who am I?" what should the answer be?

Master Ding wanted to make sure I knew.

I am a xiangsheng performer. I am an apprentice of Ding Guang-quan, an heir to the lineage of Hou-style xiangsheng, part of a greater community of comedians all trying their best to make audiences laugh.

If I came onstage as a xiangsheng performer, a true xiangsheng performer, then that identity is what the audience will connect to, and the show can go on.

Joke the moon, satirize the wind.

Backdrop

After dinner with the disciples, I wandered through Beijing in the dark.

I wandered past the Drum and Bell Towers, where my Great-Master Hou Baolin used to perform xiangsheng for passersby on the street. I wandered through the *hutongs*, into a dead-end path, past a public restroom and underneath hanging trellises of drying laundry.

I found myself, almost to my own surprise, in front of the bright red door with brass handles in the shape of lions' heads. I took a key out of my pocket; I unlocked the door and stepped through the moon gate into the courtyard of my comedy club.

Tonight's show had finished hours ago. Now there was no noise in the courtyard. Inside the theater space, the rows of folding chairs sat dormant, awaiting the next time the building stopped being a building and started being a comedy club again.

I turned on the stage lights, blasting away my night vision. Sitting down in the third row, I stretched my legs out on the seat in front of me, and stared at the massive black backdrop banner covering the whole of the back wall of the club, hanging by hooks driven into the wooden ceiling post above.

The backdrop was empty except for a giant logo in the middle: a microphone with the word *HA* on the left and the Chinese character for *ha* reimagined as a laughing face on the right. Beneath it, in Chinese and English, read: US–CHINA COMEDY CENTER 中美喜剧中心.

All of my work at the club is watched over by this black banner, our logo of laughter, a gift of—who else?—Master Ding Guangquan. In 2016, I told him I had finally found a place that I could turn into a club, to do more shows, better shows. He told me he'd be there at the opening and invite the media.

"Pick something you want for the space," he said. "Something physical. Not food."

I mentioned we needed a big banner to cover the whitewashed back wall; two days later, he had it arranged. Master Ding and his Hou-style xiangsheng were officially "intangible cultural heritage" as defined by the Chinese government. This meant he was provided a fund to continue his cultural work that he could draw upon once a year. He wrote a receipt; the banner was paid for in full. Now his banner hangs and watches over every show. His is the backdrop to all the comedy I do.

After the dinner with Master Ding's disciples, my mind and my heart felt lost. My feet took me to the comedy club, so my eyes could look at the banner and see once again the man who taught me what I needed to know to make this club, this little island of humor in a roiling sea of challenges, possible.

He was gone, but he had left me the skills to make people laugh.

Which I guess means it's my turn now.

Epilogue: Where Are We Now?

I was greeted by a thin man in his fifties, wearing a cream-colored short-sleeved button-up, whom I had never met before. The moment he saw me, his eyes lit up like stars, and he rushed over and shook my hand so vigorously I could feel my bones shake. "Welcome home, brother!" he said.

It was May 2025, almost eight years after Master Ding's passing, and Ma Zhen, one of Master Ding's disciples, was greeting me in Zibo, in Shandong Province, at an outdoor pavilion in a shopping mall. Sandwiched between a busy restaurant on one side and a raucous nightclub on the other, a bright LED sign in Chinese calligraphy shone into the fading light: "The Ding Guangquan Memorial Xiangsheng Teahouse."

Brother Ma led me through the doors into a small antechamber with a ticket booth at one end and a large glass case at the other. Inside the case are three busts: In the center, the likeness of our great-master, Hou Baolin; to his left, his disciple Ma Ji; to his right, his disciple Ding Guangquan.

"We keep them here at the entrance. His disciples, and my disciples, and their disciples, they can see him every day."

I bowed three times to the bust of my Master.

"Come," Brother Ma said, and he opened the main doors.

Inside the theater, rows of square tables await the crowd. The clean floors will soon be covered with sunflower seed shells. Above a bright stage, a wooden sign carved with painted characters proclaims the name *Guang Quan Ge*—"Broad Spring Pavilion."*

Around the three other walls are glass cases full of photos, of comedy scripts, of newspaper clippings.

"We asked all the disciples for memorabilia. Anything people had from him, we got, we collected, and we selected the most important things to exhibit."

Master Ding's place had always been full of tchotchkes; in the display cases were the best of the best of many years of gifts, special events, and Master Ding's everyday habits. They featured the scissors Master Ding used to cut hair back in the army; photographs of Master Ding and Great-Master Hou on the set of one of China's first sitcoms; a commemorative lighter from Beijing Television.

"What are these?" I asked, looking at a pair of smoked glasses.

"Those are the sunglasses *Shifu* wore to watch the first-ever Chinese atomic bomb detonation, in Xinjiang. He was in the army, and he was one of a few soldiers they sent to watch the blast—from several miles away."

"I never knew he saw an atomic explosion," I said, wondering how seeing that sort of destructive force might affect a person's way of looking at the world, at conflict, at the power of humor.

All about was Master Ding's smiling face—pictures of Master Ding laughing, reacting, performing with disciples from dozens of countries, across decades of work.

---

* Master Ding's name—广泉—directly translated, means "Broad Spring," with "spring" meaning water source, not the season.

"This place is incredible," I said. I choked up. It was hard to say any more.

Brother Ma saw this and patted me on the shoulder. "After Master Ding passed, we wanted to honor him. But we didn't know how. A memorial would be nice, but none of us had enough money to get a place permanently, and memorials don't make any money. Also, we knew he wouldn't want anything too somber anyways. But then we thought, why not do a memorial theater? And then, we can sell tickets, do shows, and continue the xiangsheng lineage."

This small theater—I guessed it would fit about a hundred people, tops—was held together by the blood, sweat, and tears of Master Ding's disciples and their families.

So many famous, beloved comedians have lived throughout history, in many countries, in many places. How many of them have a memorial theater to their name?

"This place is incredible," I said again.

I was back with my family. I was home.

My journey to the Memorial Teahouse had taken half a decade.

In January 2020, I performed on a show called *Huan Le Xiju Ren*, which was basically the Chinese version of *Last Comic Standing*. I reached the top eight, ousting several famous comedians, though my sense of triumph was dampened somewhat by the stress and burnout of competing on a major TV show. I hadn't seen my family in over a year, and wanted to take a vacation.

"We're shooting again after Chinese New Year," the showrunner told me as the crew struck the lights and camera equipment.

"Can I leave and go home?" I asked.

"You can do whatever you want, as long as you're back in nine days."

As I boarded the plane to America, I saw screenshots on my WeChat moments: pictures of blocked articles about a novel virus. I also saw many news reports reminding people not to spread rumors.

I landed to find the virus was real, China was locked down, and my flight back was canceled. A few days later, my visa was canceled. After a decade in China, my life there was over.

My nine-day vacation in America lasted three and a half years.

During COVID, I was compelled to sit indoors and watch the real-time disintegration of the relationship between my two homes. Cooperation became competition. Competition became decoupling. Even the Fulbright China program was canceled by executive order.* Both sides blamed each other for the pandemic, and with the internet between the two places severed and controlled, there remained no common reality.

I had always worried that the bridges we'd built between our countries and cultures could crumble if we did not take care of them; I never anticipated they would be proactively destroyed, with so little remorse and so much self-righteousness.

COVID, of course, dealt the killing blow to my comedy club. I laid off all my employees. I hired a locksmith over WeChat to break into my Beijing apartment so a friend could pack all my stuff into storage. My friend even made their way to the courtyard when lockdown ended to make sure that Master Ding's backdrop was safely stowed away.

---

* The program is still canceled as of publication and has not yet been reinstated.

My depression at the sudden collapse of my life manifested as mania. Upon landing, I immediately began planning a charity comedy show to raise money to buy masks and medical supplies for Wuhan University Hospital. In eight days, I found a venue, sold six hundred tickets, put on a show, and raised over $12,000, which we used to buy and ship boxes and boxes of masks and isolation gowns to the hospital.*

The most lasting impact of the show—other than any lives that might have been improved by the medical equipment—was that the videos of the show went viral in both China and America. On Douyin (Chinese TikTok), the video reached the front page and got four hundred million hits.

I do a joke about this in my set nowadays:

"Four hundred million hits! This taught me two things. One, we all just want to be healthy and live in peace. And two, Douyin's view count numbers are definitely fake."

Combined with the fact that my *Last Comic Standing* episodes were airing while the whole of China was locked down and had nothing to watch, my social following exploded.

After years of being a hustler in the underground comedy scene, I gained two million followers in a few months, mostly in China.

Two million followers that I could not perform for—perhaps not for years, perhaps not ever.

---

* The golden rule still holds true. My followers in China saw what we did during February, when the crisis was at its worst in China, and when America closed down one month later and was in desperate need of medical equipment, I got no less than one hundred private messages from Chinese fans asking where they could send things to help Americans. I managed to broker a shipment to a local Boston homeless shelter during this time.

I spent the next few years trying to figure out who I was, in America.

Even basic interactions led to existential-level reverse culture shock. For instance, how should I introduce myself?

In China, if someone asked who I was, I would tell them, "I am a disciple of Master Ding Guangquan."

"Oh! Ding Guangquan!" they might say. "You do xiangsheng?"

And then we would begin a new, happy, excited conversation.

In America, I told people I did "traditional Chinese comedy." At first, people thought this was a joke. Then they found out it was real, and had no idea what to say.

Everything I had learned, and committed so much time and energy to understanding, simply made no sense in the context of America, especially one seized by COVID. There was no use for Beijing opera in the States.

Eventually, I started meeting up with Chinese students studying in Boston. Stand-up comedy was blowing up in China since its zero-COVID policy meant shows were still a possibility. The study-abroad students in America were being inspired from China to try stand-up themselves.

With no money to rent a space or any contacts in the Boston comedy scene, we began doing shows in boba shops. We were all stuck in America, missing China, caught in the sick reality of being the people left to deal with the daily aftermath of each sides' xenophobic propaganda, and throughout it all, deeply unsure about what the future would bring. Comedy let us get it all out.

"I called the visa bureau," I said onstage, getting some laughs from the audience already—*like that would ever work!* "No, no, I did! This is a true story! I asked them, 'What kind of Americans can get back into China now?'"

"'Well,' the guy said, 'the authorities made a list of all the jobs that foreigners do in China, and have ranked them from most important, to least important. So, what do you do?'"

Big laugh. I soaked it all up, letting it go as long as the audience wished.

"'Ah, that's fine, I'll just wait till this is over,'" I said, and another wave of laughs shook the little boba shop.[*]

The satisfaction in laughing, in releasing that tension, was so heart-enriching that it didn't matter that the sound of the laughter was muffled by triple-ply surgical masks.

After months offstage, doing my club routine for free brought me more joy than performing on television, even if we had to deal with confused DoorDash employees barging into the shop in the middle of a punch line.

A year into my attempt to continue my life as a Chinese comedian in America, I hit a wall.

Every day, I would sit in the kitchen in my parents' house, drinking tea and writing jokes. But after a year of forcing myself to write, to be happy and optimistic even as I spent dozens of hours trying—and failing—to get a visa to go back to China, I soured. I couldn't find any-

---

[*]   Later, I would submit this joke to a Chinese TV show, and the showrunner told me, "We can't air this joke because it isn't true."

"It is true, though!" I said, and I sent links with evidence.

"That's even worse!" the showrunner said.

thing funny. As time went on, I wrote fewer and fewer jokes, and drank more and more tea.

As a way to break the writer's block, I started making English-language videos about Chinese tea culture, a hobby of mine from my years in China, when I would go to the tea hills anytime I performed in a tea-producing region. I had lots of Chinese tea farmers in my WeChat, and during the pandemic, I paid ridiculous COVID-era air-shipping rates to make sure I never ran out of the good stuff.

Eventually, people started following my tea videos. The following grew, I started an online tea shop, and after the vaccine came out but the visa restrictions were still not lifted, I decided to move to Los Angeles, where I could do both comedy and tea.

At first, I struggled with this strange reality of having millions of followers in a country where I couldn't perform, and the decision to instead spend my time growing a new, seemingly unrelated channel on Western social media around tea.

But I remembered Master Ding.

First, make the audience like you.

All good exchange starts with joy.

Starting in 2021, every day, for a thousand days, I made a tea video. I shared how tea was a bridge into Chinese culture, and what I had learned there. I shared how my life had been improved by learning Chinese, by meeting Chinese people, by opening my mind and my heart and my creative spirit and experiencing theirs in return.

And, occasionally, I got to make some pretty funny roast videos when haters popped up, accusing me of being a shill of the Communist Party, or assuming all Chinese food must be irrevocably tainted with lead.

By the time China opened again, I was living in Los Angeles, doing comedy shows at night and running the tea company during the day.

Every morning, I woke up and checked my WeChat messages to see what the China team had been up to while I was asleep. Then, I drank tea, shot a video, and did everything I could to help the teahouse grow. At night, if I had a show, I would be answering WeChats backstage, since our China team woke up right around when I went onstage.

Then, in the winter of 2023, all COVID restrictions in China were suddenly lifted over a period of only three days. By the time I finally got on a plane back to China, I had toured North America and Europe doing Chinese-language stand-up shows. I had a Hollywood agent. The tea channel had almost a million followers.

And I had done it all through bridges, not bombs—even though the algorithm likes the latter much better than the former.

During a time when so many were selling a story of the inevitability of conflict between America and China, our countries and our cultures, I had in many ways the most rapid and productive growth in my whole career. It turns out almost everyone would rather laugh, drink tea, and live together than fight.

In exile, I discovered that whether or not Americans knew what it meant, I was still a disciple of Ding Guangquan.

"Everyone wearing clothes?" Brother Ma asked as he barged into the backstage area of the teahouse theater.

As we turned the corner, I was greeted with a wall of sound. Within that noise, I noticed people calling out to me:

"Hello, Uncle!"

"Nice to meet you, Uncle!"

My laughter was met with Brother Ma's completely serious face. "These are my disciples. They may be your age, but since you apprenticed to Master Ding, and they apprenticed to me, you are actually above them in the family tree."

"Hello, nephews?" I said. They all laughed, and we shook hands and introduced ourselves.

"Where's his robe? You there! Come over here, help your grand-uncle."

"*Grand*-uncle???" I blurted out, laughing, smiling from ear to ear, as I turned around to see a ten-year-old hustling across the cramped space, carrying a red robe on a coat hanger.

Four people got me into my robe. I tried to do it myself, but they literally slapped my hands away from the knots, eager to help.

Just as I did for Master Ding, I thought.

"We will be opening the theater soon," Brother Ma said. "I just want to show you one more thing."

We walked through the yellow curtain printed with a giant curled dragon that separated the offstage and onstage areas. As we walked across the open space, the staff—wives and cousins of the comedians—were setting out pots of tea and dishes of sunflower seeds on the tables.

"There," he said, and pointed offstage to the left. On the wall, angled to face the performers onstage, was a picture of Master Ding—but not of his face.

"It was a candid photo," Brother Ma told me. "We were performing one of the last shows we ever did together. He was sitting right behind the curtain, just offstage, looking at the performers, watching the show. I was behind him, and snapped this photo. I put it here, just offstage, so it's as if he is still looking at us, still watching our shows, still supporting us."

I looked at the back of Master Ding's head, his attention clearly focused on the show in front of him. I wanted to thank him, to thank Brother Ma, to thank everyone backstage, and everyone who would be in the crowd that night.

But I couldn't say a word. I just stood there as I slowly became overcome with tears. I cried onstage, and Brother Ma cried with me, both our eyes locked on Master Ding, his face looking away—and looking at us.

Without speaking, we went backstage to prepare for the show. The doors were opening. It was time to make them laugh.

The End*

---

* Like and follow for more books on Chinese comedy!

Acknowledgments

This book and the stories inside would not have been possible without the help of hundreds of people, too many to name here. Still, I do want to thank a few people in particular:

My Chinese teachers, specifically Zhu Laoshi, Feng Laoshi, Lu Laoshi, and Hua Laoshi, as well as the Harvard Beijing Academy, CET Beijing language program, and IUP language program;

Cui Zengguang, for being as much of a xiangsheng mentor to me as Master Ding; you are my 师哥;

Adam Brown, director of Theatre Ink, who gave me what I did not know at the time was a world-class high school theater environment to grow in and explore;

the Fulbright Commission for giving me my start, specifically Fulbright China, which I believe is not dead, but merely hibernating;

Shi Laoban, Danliren Comedy, A Qiu, Ao Ye Comedy, and all my friends in the Chinese comedy scene who have always treated me like a brother and not *laowai*;

Beijing Improv, for being the family I chose;

my online followers, especially my Jesse's Teahouse supporters, without whose support I would almost certainly not have been able to get a book about Chinese comedy published;

Amy Guay, my editor, for being so encouraging and collaborative in working with me on my first book, and reminding me three weeks before the first draft was due that the book did not suck;

as well as my agents at UTA: Kelly, for believing we could get this book published and helping me make an amazing proposal, and Ike, for making me feel like I have a place in Hollywood, and, more broadly, in the creative scene in America;

my parents, all of them, for supporting me completely through everything, even when I said I wanted to go to China and be a comedian;

all the audience members, since if you didn't laugh at any of the jokes I would definitely have had to get a real job at some point;

and finally, my master, my mentor, my friend, Ding Guangquan.

About the Author

Jesse Appell is a comedian whose original comedy works have passed half a billion views on Chinese and international internet sites, earning Silver Play Button plaques from both YouTube and Bilibili. He has been featured on the front page of *The Boston Globe* with Tom Brady and the Pope, and has appeared on a veritable alphabet soup of news media: CBS, TEDx, BBC, PBS, and NPR in the West; CCTV, Beijing TV, Shanghai TV, and China Radio International in Asia. He is also the founder and head tea guy of Jesse's Teahouse. *This Was Funnier in China* is his first book.

Please scan here to access educator notes for
This Was Funnier in China.